Inner and Outer Worlds

SYDNEY STUDIES IN AUSTRALIAN LITERATURE

Robert Dixon, Series Editor

The Sydney Studies in Australian Literature series publishes original, peer-reviewed research in the field of Australian literary studies. It offers engagingly written evaluations of the nature and importance of Australian literature, and aims to reinvigorate its study both locally and internationally.

Alex Miller: The Ruin of Time
Robert Dixon

Australian Books and Authors in the American Marketplace 1840s–1940s
David Carter and Roger Osborne

Christina Stead and the Matter of America
Fiona Morrison

Colonial Australian Fiction: Character Types, Social Formations and the Colonial Economy
Ken Gelder and Rachael Weaver

Contemporary Australian Literature: A World Not Yet Dead
Nicholas Birns

Elizabeth Harrower: Critical Essays
Ed. Elizabeth McMahon and Brigitta Olubas

Fallen Among Reformers: Miles Franklin, Modernity, and the New Woman
Janet Lee

The Fiction of Tim Winton: Earthed and Sacred
Lyn McCredden

Gail Jones: Word, Image, Ethics
Tanya Dalziell

Gerald Murnane: Another World in This One
Ed. Anthony Uhlmann

Inner and Outer Worlds: Gail Jones' Fiction
Ed. Anthony Uhlmann

Patrick White's Theatre: Australian Modernism on Stage, 1960–2018
Denise Varney

Richard Flanagan: Critical Essays
Ed. Robert Dixon

Shirley Hazzard: New Critical Essays
Ed. Brigitta Olubas

Inner and Outer Worlds

Gail Jones' Fiction

Edited by Anthony Uhlmann

SYDNEY UNIVERSITY PRESS

First published by Sydney University Press

© Individual authors 2022
© Sydney University Press 2022

Reproduction and communication for other purposes

Except as permitted under the Act, no part of this edition may be reproduced, stored in a retrieval system, or communicated in any form or by any means without prior written permission. All requests for reproduction or communication should be made to Sydney University Press at the address below:

Sydney University Press
Fisher Library F03
University of Sydney NSW 2006
AUSTRALIA
sup.info@sydney.edu.au
sydneyuniversitypress.com.au

A catalogue record for this book is available from the National Library of Australia.

ISBN 9781743327791 paperback
ISBN 9781743327807 epub
ISBN 9781743327883 pdf

Cover image by Heike Steinweg Photography
Cover design by Miguel Yamin

We acknowledge the traditional owners of the lands on which Sydney University Press is located, the Gadigal people of the Eora Nation, and we pay our respect to the knowledge embedded forever within the Aboriginal Custodianship of Country.

Contents

Introduction   1
Anthony Uhlmann

1. Constellations of Light and Image | Contemplations on Deep Space: Apparent magnitude and scale   15
Lou Jillett

2. Bioluminescence: Materiality, Metaphor and Trace in *Sixty Lights*   29
Elizabeth McMahon

3. Gail Jones' Novel Modernism: *Sixty Lights* and Literary Tradition   43
James Gourley

4. Sleep's Sweet Relief   59
Tanya Dalziell

5. Resisting Fixation in Gail Jones' *Sorry* and *Five Bells*   75
Anthony Uhlmann

6. "Moving on Metaphorical Silk Roads of Intellectual Trade": Chinese Aesthetics in *Five Bells*   91
Valérie-Anne Belleflamme

7. Utopia and Hysteria in *A Guide to Berlin*   103
Tony Hughes-d'Aeth

8. Silent Propinquities: Literary Selfhood and Modernity in *A Guide to Berlin*   119
Brigid Rooney

9	Figures in Geometry: *The Death of Noah Glass* *Robert Dixon*	139
10	Blueness and Light in the Art of Gail Jones *Meg Samuelson*	161

Contributors   181

Index   185

Introduction

Anthony Uhlmann

While fiction in general provides a crucial means for engaging with and understanding the worlds we inhabit, individual writers develop methods and techniques that are particular to their own body of works. In a recent interview in the *Los Angeles Review of Books* marking the publication of *The Death of Noah Glass*, when asked what she hoped her work might achieve, Jones responded that she hoped her novels would matter "in ways other than entertainment – that [they] might provoke serious thinking" about what things might mean.[1]

Text, Pretext, Intertext, Context

In considering the kinds of methods and techniques Gail Jones develops, and the themes she returns to, it is possible to focus on the idea of levels of textuality. One of the first things that strikes readers of Jones' work is the richness of the language; the surface text that is almost baroque at times in its interfolding of sound and sense infused by images that fork and play off one another. The opening line of the first chapter of her first novel, *Black Mirror* (2002), which interweaves the stories of Victoria Morrell, a dying artist who is engaging with a young biographer Anna Griffin, invites us into the tunnel of Victoria's memory: "Let us say that her

---

Anthony Uhlmann, Introduction. Inner and Outer Worlds: Gail Jones' Fiction. In *Inner and Outer Worlds: Gail Jones' Fiction*, edited by Anthony Uhlmann. Sydney: Sydney University Press, 2022. DOI: 10.30722/sup.9781743327791

---

[1] Robert Wood, "The Pleasure of Language Itself: An Interview with Gail Jones", *BLARB: Blog//Los Angeles Review of Books*, https://blog.lareviewofbooks.org/interviews/pleasure-language-interview-gail-jones/

memory is like peering into a night-dark tunnel and waiting for the circle of gold up ahead".[2]

The image of the circle of gold will reappear at the end of a short opening section, but transformed into a gold coin, emblematic of her mother. Firstly, however, it leads us to the entrance of a house:

> She was born in a large house, *Kathleen*, named after somebody's mother, and it is both immemorial and vague – portals, columns, a white space hollowed out which must be, she supposes, the grand entrance hall – and she remembers sounds, ringing sounds, ricocheting in its emptiness, and a spine of thin pale light slanting on a bright chequered floor, and a pair of chairs with curly legs upon which nobody sat, and an indefinable atmosphere of cold and constraint; yet with these few details *Kathleen* remains merely an incomplete entrance, as though time has confiscated the rest of the house and left it blurred into history. (*Black Mirror*, 7)

The complex sentence that leads us into the house has, in terms of function rather than grammatical categories, three parts. The first part offers us background information to the family house of the protagonist, Victoria Morrell: "She was born in a large house, *Kathleen*, named after somebody's mother, and it is both immemorial and vague – portals, columns, a white space hollowed out which must be, she supposes, the grand entrance hall –" (7). Yet the fragment of the house is not simply described; the next part of the sentence functions to steep the memory with sensations:

> and she remembers sounds, ringing sounds, ricocheting in its emptiness, and a spine of thin pale light slanting on a bright chequered floor, and a pair of chairs with curly legs upon which nobody sat, and an indefinable atmosphere of cold and constraint. (7)

Each of the four clauses here echo the others rhythmically, and are laden with assonance and consonance: the first alliterates r, repeats "sounds" and completes itself with a half-rhyme "remembers/emptiness"; the second plays on the sibilant "s", the nasal "n", the liquid "l" and the vowel "i" in "spine/light/bright"; the third rhymes "pair/chair" and stops the fluid alliteration of "c" and "l" with the plosive "t" of "sat"; the fourth plays the assonance of "a" against the consonance of "c".

---

2   Gail Jones, *Black Mirror* (2002; Sydney: Vintage, 2009), 7. All subsequent references are to this edition and appear in parentheses in the text.

So too, the aural sensations are woven among images of a) sound, b) light, c) materiality (chairs), and d) the ethereal (atmosphere).

Finally, the sentence turns again, "yet with these few details *Kathleen* remains merely an incomplete entrance, as though time has confiscated the rest of the house and left it blurred into history" (7). This returns to the matter-of-factness of the first part, as if the middle section had been an involuntary flight of fancy. Or to put it another way, after Proust, the voluntary memory of sections one and three are at once drawn together and held apart by the shock of the involuntary memories of rich sensation.

The richness of language in her works in turn is associated with recurring images, which draw in readers in this collection, of the cosmos, the stars (see Lou Jillett's chapter), colours (see Meg Samuelson's chapter) and visual motifs from painting and film (see Robert Dixon's chapter) and the splendour of days of every kind of weather in vividly imagined places resonating with their own special energy.

If surface text is important to an understanding of her works, then so are pretext, intertextuality and context. In the interview in the *Los Angeles Review of Books*, asked about the importance of narrative to *Noah Glass* Jones replies:

> My novels tend to be braided and multilayered in their form. At the centre of this one is the mystery both of a man's death and a Sicilian art theft; but these are the pretexts, as it were, for a more dispersed and unpredictable meditation on art, families, and the mystery of time.[3]

Among the surface of her works, narrative events are folded into deeper reflections on larger themes. *Black Mirror* uses the pretext of a young woman writing a biography of an artist nearing death to explore ideas of memory and the role of art in preserving what might otherwise be lost. *Sixty Lights* (2004) offers the pretext of a young Australian photographer travelling within the nineteenth-century British Empire among tropes of Victorian fiction involving perception, phenomena, and felt understanding. Her next two novels might be more readily linked with Jones' own experience, yet these frames are by no means merely autobiographical (academic research, a childhood in rural Western Australia) as the focus is shifted to allow a means of engaging with ideas. *Dreams of Speaking* (2006) focuses again on a young writer, this time undertaking academic research in order to think through the ideas she is imagined to be researching: the modern, modernity. *Sorry* (2007) follows a child who grows up in remote Western Australia with parents steeped in colonial understandings yet among friends, a young Aboriginal woman and a deaf boy, who urge her to escape

---

3   Wood, "The Pleasure of Language Itself", n.p.

the narrow norms that seek to entrap her. In so doing it explores themes that continue to resonate with contemporary Australia and the world more generally: how does one live in the here-now? *Five Bells* (2011) is overlaid with the story of a lost child but uses this pretext to meditate on the nature of identity both at individual and collective levels. *A Guide to Berlin* (2015) too includes a drama – this time involving murder – to explore precepts of communion and group formation around ideas.

This method indicates an ambivalent attitude to surfaces. On the one hand, they cover and potentially hide or repress what is actually essential; what is genuinely at stake; what is the real site of conflict. The structure in this way echoes the structures of our lives: we project surfaces and exist among surfaces under and among which complex and at times turbulent experience unfolds. Yet the attitude to surfaces is ambivalent because while, on the one hand, they might seemingly hide, on the other hand, if one examines them intently, looking for and sensing the signs they convey, they themselves also reveal what might be at the tangled heart of experience. The motif of the visual, or looking and interpreting, then, haunts her works. The pretexts are looked at once, then examined more closely, so that the threads that are woven among them might be unravelled and re-sown so as to be understood. As with Nabokov, who insisted his texts needed to be read (for the surface), then re-read (for what was hidden and inter-involved among the surface), then re-re-read (to find fuller meanings), Jones' work requires intensive scrutiny, and it is one of the pleasures of editing this collection to be able to demonstrate how such scrutiny underlines the depth of her writing.[4]

Equally important to Gail Jones' method is mobilising the potential of intertextuality. Reviewing James Joyce's *Ulysses* soon after its publication, T.S. Eliot wrote a well-known essay concerning intertextual method called "Ulysses, Order and Myth" in which he considered how Joyce, and by implication other writers, might make use of early stories, such as myths and epics, to provide a structuring scaffolding on which other works might be built.[5] This kind of intertextual method is made use of by many writers and might involve borrowing from any kinds of writing, not just myth. Yet Gail Jones' intertextuality is not simply of this kind, even when there are direct references to other works and writers, as in *Five Bells*, which refers to Kenneth Slessor's poem of the same name, and *A Guide to Berlin*, which refers to a Vladimir Nabokov story of the same name. Rather, Jones revisits the sites of these texts – the Sydney and Sydney

---

4   On Nabokov and layers of reading, see Brian Boyd, *Nabokov: The Russian Years* (Princeton: Princeton University Press, 1990), 10–11.
5   T.S. Eliot, "Ulysses, Order and Myth", *Selected Prose of T.S. Eliot*, ed. Frank Kermode (New York: Harvest, 1975).

Introduction

Harbour of Slessor's "Five Bells", and the wounded heart of the city of Berlin of Vladimir Nabokov's "A Guide to Berlin" – entering into and reinhabiting these haunted twentieth-century spaces in the twenty-first century, feeling again the meaning that resides within them.

Yet there is also a depth of allusion and resonances with other works, lives, and texts of many kinds. Showing her deep erudition and the research that goes into her writing, Jones constantly refers to, and draws out meaning from, works of literature, visual arts, philosophy, science, biography and history. A number of chapters in this book shed light on these intertextual references and their importance to her work. Elizabeth McMahon traces references to light and bioluminescence and the weave of allusion to scientific literature; James Gourley examines not only references to the history of photography, but to classics of Victorian literature such as *Jane Eyre* and *Great Expectations*; Valérie-Anne Belleflamme uncovers Jones' deep research into Chinese aesthetics; Tony Hughes-D'Aeth examines affinities with psychoanalytic thought; Brigid Rooney as well as looking at Jones' engagement with literature, considers her interest in theorists such as Walter Benjamin and Georges Lukács.

Another crucial textual element in Jones' work involves context: that is, the importance of place, and the historical moments that interact with and shape characters' responses to place. Place for Jones is both internal and external, involving the inner lives of characters whose thoughts we visit, and the memories and experiences that form them, as well as the physical spaces in which the works take place. These physical spaces in turn are not merely elements that exist in the present, but also involve and carry with them past events and past experiences. *Black Mirror* connects Australia and the United Kingdom, the memory of an old woman and the life to come of a young woman; *Sixty Lights* takes us from Imperial London to colonial India through the eyes of a young Australian in the nineteenth century, in a world which is overlaid with various kinds of anachronisms reaching forward and back; *Dreams of Speaking* is cosmopolitan in scope, moving between worlds and focusing on ideas of time; *Sorry* takes us to an earlier period of Australian history, still steeped in colonial prejudice, trauma and violence, but brings it into stark juxtaposition with ongoing injustices; *Five Bells* takes place on one "glorious" day, but its protagonists carry with them the worlds of their memories and formations, reaching across the planet and across Australia; *A Guide to Berlin* too brings together a range of protagonists from a range of life experiences; *The Death of Noah Glass* (2018) moves between Europe and Australia and back into the complex folds of art history.

If pretext involves narrative surfaces engaging with thematic concerns, context involves the threads attached to characters and settings, being woven among narrative events, to add layers of complexity to the thinking through of these themes. These themes include the nature of time and experience, the problems of history with the traumas and injustices that lie still visible (for one who looks closely) on the surface of events, people, and are folded into complexes that determine the very nature of the places that are inhabited. Intertext in turn situates these reflections among deep cultural history, which for Jones extends into engagements with Aboriginal Australian, colonial Australian, multicultural Australian, as well as Asian and European texts.

Themes: Time and Phenomena

Many critics have noted the importance of time to Gail Jones' works, and their connections to phenomenology.[6] As Robert Dixon has pointed out, Jones' work as a critical thinker informs her work as a writer.[7] She has written a number of essays on the nature of time and the experience of modernity.[8] So too, as a teacher she taught a postgraduate unit on time and literature and philosophy for a number of years at Western Sydney University.[9] She is a novelist of ideas and one of Australia's most philosophical writers in the sense that her works engage with themes that also deeply concern philosophy and aesthetic theory.

In reading Jones' works in relation to time and experience it becomes apparent that they enter into engagement with some of the key elements of temporal understanding from twentieth-century science and philosophy, as well as, as she does in *Sixty Lights*, playfully using methods from fiction, such as anachronism, to disrupt these models. Time is always *experienced* in Jones' fiction, but it is never simply a matter of a single line of duration inhabited by an isolated character. Rather, it is more like Einstein's model of inertial frames which was borrowed from insights first developed by Galileo in the seventeenth century. Here time is particular to each inertial frame, and even if it is clear that one is demonstrably moving through space one always "feels" that the frame in which

---

6   See, for example, Norman Saadi Nikro, "Paratactic Stammers: Temporality in the Novels of Gail Jones", *JASAL: Journal of the Association for the Study of Australian Literature*, 16, no. 1 (2016): 1–16; Tanya Dalziell, "The Ethics of Mourning: Gail Jones' *Black Mirror*", *JASAL: Journal of the Association for the Study of Australian Literature*, 4, 2005.

7   Robert Dixon, "Invitation to the Voyage: Reading Gail Jones' *Five Bells*", *JASAL: Journal of the Association for the Study of Australian Literature*, 12, no. 3 (2012): 1–17.

8   Gail Jones, "Growing Small Wings: Walter Benjamin, Lola Ridge and the Political Affect of Modernism", *Affirmations: Of the Modern* 1, no. 2 (2014): 120–42; "A Dreaming, a Sauntering: Reimagining Critical Paradigms", *JASAL: Journal of the Association for the Study of Australian Literature*, no. 5 (2006): 11–24; "Turnings and Overturnings in Glebe", *Sydney Review of Books*, 9 February 2018, https://sydneyreviewofbooks.com/essay/turnings-and-over-turnings-in-glebe/

9   See https://www.westernsydney.edu.au/writing_and_society/postgraduate_study/ma_in_cultural_and_creative_practice/idea_time

one is positioned (be it a boat on the water for Galileo or a train moving past another for Einstein) is "still", and the world is moving around it.[10] One might argue for a play of inertial frames between characters in Gail Jones' works, most obviously in *Five Bells*, but also throughout her fiction. Yet the experience of time is still more complex. If Bergson sees our consciousness as an unbroken duration, Jones wishes to complicate this further, demonstrating (as Proust had before her in answering Bergson) that we inhabit several time frames at once. But as with Einstein there is no simultaneity between inertial frames, and no simultaneity between our remembered and experienced times. That is, the hard edges of time past burst into time present, rupturing its surface.

Little Is Known of Her Life …

Little by way of biographical information is currently on the public record for Gail Jones. She was born in the small town of Harvey, Western Australia, south of Perth, in 1955. She grew up in Broome (a coastal town built on the pearling industry involving rich mixtures of Aboriginal, Asian and European cultures) and Kalgoorlie (a rugged gold mining town), both vibrant, isolated communities, and memories of Broome in particular feature in her work. She briefly moved to Melbourne in the 1970s to study Fine Arts, underlining an interest in the visual arts that has never left her. She returned to Western Australia to undertake a BA majoring in English at the University of Western Australia. Her daughter Kyra Giorgi, who is also a writer, was born in Perth in 1977. Gail Jones completed her Bachelor of Arts with honours in 1980 and then worked for the University of Western Australia (UWA), Curtin and Murdoch universities in Perth as a casual tutor before being employed full time as a lecturer at Edith Cowan University in 1988. She began her PhD, entitled *Mimesis and Alterity: Postcolonialism, Ethnography and the Representation of Racial Others*, in 1990 and completed it in 1994 having also moved from Edith Cowan to a position of Lecturer in English at the University of Western Australia in 1993. Somehow at this time she also managed to emerge, almost fully formed, as a writer of fiction. She entered and won the T.A.G. Hungerford Award, an award set up to develop new writers in Western Australia who had not yet been published in book form, in 1991. The prize included the publication of the manuscript of *The House of Breathing*, a collection of fourteen short stories published by Fremantle Arts Press in 1992. Recognition of the quality of her writing soon followed as the collection won the F.A.W. Barbara

---

10   Albert Einstein, *Relativity: The Special and General Theory*, trans. Robert W. Lawson (New York: Three Rivers Press, 1961), 10–19.

Ramsden Award for book of the year, and the Western Australian Premier's Book Award for Fiction in 1992. This pattern has not altered, with many of her works winning major awards, including the Prime Minister's Literary Award for Fiction for *The Death of Noah Glass*, the South Australian Premier's Award, the Age Book of the Year and the ALS Gold Medal for *Sixty Lights*, the Nita Kibble Award for *Five Bells*, and the Colin Roderick Award for *A Guide to Berlin*. Indeed, all of her works have been shortlisted or longlisted for major awards including the Booker Prize, the International Dublin Literary Award, the Prix Femina Étranger, and the Miles Franklin Award. She was awarded the Philip Hodgins' Memorial Medal (for a body of work) and the PEN Sydney Award in 2011.

She published her second collection of short stories, *Fetish Lives*, in 1997, and this began another series, wherein her works began to be republished in the United Kingdom and the United States, and translated into multiple languages, including French, German, Polish, Czech, Spanish and Chinese. Yet if her early works were highly regarded short stories she is best known as a novelist of the twenty-first century. Her first novel, *Black Mirror*, was published in 2002, and since then she has published seven others: *Sixty Lights* (2004), *Dreams of Speaking* (2006), *Sorry* (2007), *Five Bells* (2011), *A Guide to Berlin* (2015), *The Death of Noah Glass* (2018) and *Our Shadows* (2020). The idea of place is essential to her work, and her career as a writer and academic has seen her take up residencies in London, Berlin, Shanghai and Rome, and to have travelled widely through Europe and North and South America. This idea is further apparent in her travelling in Australia: in 2008 she moved from Perth to Sydney to take up the position of Professor in Literature at the Writing and Society Research Centre at Western Sydney University (WSU). She retired from this position in 2020 but remains as a Professor Emerita at WSU.

Critical Reception

A good deal of critical writing has been dedicated to Gail Jones' work. At the time of writing, the AustLit Database lists sixty-three works of academic criticism focused on her works, and written by critics from Australia, Europe, North America, Japan and China. The first monograph dedicated to her work, by Tanya Dalziell, was published in 2020 by Sydney University Press. The novel that has attracted most international critical attention to date is *Sorry*, which has particularly drawn the attention of postcolonial critics through its engagement with problems of reconciliation between Aboriginal and Torres Strait Islander Australians and non-Indigenous Australians, yet critics like Valérie-Anne Belleflamme (who has a chapter in the current book) and Christopher Eagle approach the novel from different angles with Belleflamme considering questions of intertextuality and Eagle, who develops a comparative reading with the work of Philip Roth, examining the idea of "stuttering".[11] That Jones is taken seriously as a novelist of ideas, that is, one whose works themselves force us to think through complex problems, is demonstrated by the critical attention given to themes the novels set out to explore. For example, critics have written on the theme of modernism, space, mourning and mirroring in relation to *Black Mirror*,[12] photography and perception in relation to *Sixty Lights*,[13] modernity, time and

---

11 See, for example, Jie Huang, "'The Stolen Children' and the Unspeakable Repentance: Language as Metaphor in Gail Jones' *Sorry*" 不可言说的忏悔:"被偷走的孩子"与《抱歉》中语言的隐喻, *Foreign Literature Review*, no. 4 (2018): 135–52; Pilar Royo Grasa, "Looking for Othello's Pearl in Gail Jones' *Sorry* (2007): Symbolic and Intertextual Questioning of the Notion of 'Settler Envy'", *Journal of Postcolonial Writing*, 54, no. 2 (2018): 200–13; Sandra Regina Goulart Almeida, "A Story Told in a Whisper, or the Impossibility of Atonement", *Ilha Do Desterro: A Journal of English Language*, 69, no. 2 (2016); Liliana Zavaglia, *White Apology and Apologia: Australian Novels of Reconciliation* (Amherst: Cambria Press, 2016); Xing Chunli, "Becoming Indigenous: A Comparative Analysis of Patrick White's *A Fringe of Leaves* and Gail Jones' *Sorry*", *Australian Studies – Proceedings of the 14th International Conference of Australian Studies in China*, eds David Carter, Liang Zhongxian, Han Feng, (Shanghai: Shanghai Jiao Tong University Press, 2015), 123–31; Valerie-Anne Belleflamme, "Shakespeare Was Wrong: Counter-discursive Intertextuality in Gail Jones' *Sorry*", *Journal of Postcolonial Writing* 51, no. 6 (2015): 661–71; Diana Brydon, "'Difficult Forms of Knowing': Enquiry, Injury, and Translocated Relations of Postcolonial Responsibility", *Postcolonial Translocations: Cultural Representation and Critical Spatial Thinking*, eds Mark Stein, Markus Schmitz, Silke Stroh, Marga Munkelt (Amsterdam: Rodopi, 2013), 3–28; Christopher Eagle, "Angry Because She Stutters': Stuttering, Violence, and the Politics of Voice in *American Pastoral* and *Sorry*", *Philip Roth Studies* 8, no. 1 (2012): 17–30; M. Dolores Herrero, "The Australian Apology and Postcolonial Defamiliarization: Gail Jones' *Sorry*", *Journal of Postcolonial Writing* 47, no. 3 (2011): 283–95.
12 Robert Dixon, "Cosmopolitan Australians and Colonial Modernity: Alex Miller's *Conditions of Faith*, Gail Jones' *Black Mirror* and A.L. McCann's *The White Body of Evening*", *Westerly* 49 (2004): 122–37; Paul Genoni, "'Art Is the Windowpane': Novels of Australian Women and Modernism in Inter-war Europe", *JASAL: Journal of the Association for the Study of Australian Literature* 3 (2004): 159–72; Tanya Dalziell, "An Ethics of Mourning: Gail Jones' *Black Mirror*", *JASAL: Journal of the Association for the Study of Australian Literature* 4 (2005): 49–61; Fiona Roughley, "Spatialising Experience: Gail Jones' *Black Mirror* and the Contending of Postmodern Space", *Australian Literary Studies* 23, no. 2 (2007): 58–73; Naomi Oreb, "Mirroring, Depth and Inversion: Holding Gail Jones' *Black Mirror* Against Contemporary Australia", *Sydney Studies in English* 35 (2009).
13 Peter Davis, "Double Gazing and Novel Spaces – Examining Narrated and Manifest Photographs in the Novel", *Double Dialogues*, Winter, no. 7 (2007); Sukhmani Khorana, "Photography, Cinema and Time in Jane Campion's *The Piano* and Gail Jones' *Sixty Lights*", *Outskirts: Feminisms Along the Edge* 16 (2007); Kate Mitchell, "Ghostly Histories and Embodied Memories: Photography, Spectrality and Historical Fiction in Afterimage and *Sixty Lights*", *Neo-Victorian Studies* 1, no. 1 (2008): 81–109; Rosario Arias, "(Spirit) Photography and the Past in the Neo-Victorian Novel", *Literature Interpretation Theory* 20, no. 1–2 (2009): 92–107.

transnationalism in *Dreams of Speaking*,[14] and synchronicity and the sequential in *Five Bells*.[15]

The current collection is the first edited collection addressing her work and focuses almost exclusively on her novels. The chapters herein are arranged roughly chronologically in relation to her published works (although a few discuss several of her works). The collection draws on a range of critical expertise. Contributors include critics who have engaged with her work over many years (as the citations so far listed attest) in Tanya Dalziel and Robert Dixon; international critics in Valérie-Anne Belleflamme and Meg Samuelson; experts in Australian literature who have not previously published on her work in Elizabeth McMahon, Brigid Rooney and Tony Hughes-D'Aeth; and critics who have previously focused on modernist and contemporary fiction in James Gourley, Lou Jillett and myself.

Lou Jillett traces the motifs of space and time throughout Jones' fiction. She demonstrates how Jones works across different perspectives or concepts of space and time, to offer a kaleidoscopic representation of these fundamental themes. She particularly focuses on two ideas. First, the images of constellations in the night sky which are drawn into patterns of meaning that recur and resonate across Jones' body of works. Second, the image of phases of the moon which Jillett uses to situate the variable points of focus of each of Jones' novels.

Elizabeth McMahon also focuses on how Jones weaves metaphors through her works to generate meaning. McMahon focuses on *Sixty Lights* and the deliberately anachronistic concept of bioluminescence that Jones imagines back into the nineteenth century as the Australian character Lucy travels to London and India. McMahon argues that Jones' novel, in focusing on ideas of light, challenges the norms of our thought, unsettling the settled binaries that accompany standard accounts of Western "Enlightenment".

Tanya Dalziell chooses to examine a metaphorical logic that rarely comes to the surface in the manner of the metaphor of light. Sleep, Dalziell argues, is there, but often below the surface. She distinguishes sleep, as a kind of oblivion, from dreams, arguing that the former is not obvious in Jones' fiction while the latter

---

14 Robert Dixon, "Ghosts in the Machine: Modernity and the Unmodern", *JASAL: Journal of the Association for the Study of Australian Literature* 8 (2008): 121–37; Lydia Wevers, "Fold in the Map: Figuring Modernity in Gail Jones' *Dreams of Speaking* and Elizabeth Knox's *Dreamhunter*", *Australian Literary Studies* 23, no. 2 (2007): 187–98; Timothy Steains, "The Mixed Temporalities of Transnationalism in *Dreams of Speaking*", *Journal of Australian Studies* 41, no. 1 (2017): 32–46.

15 Ella Mudie, "The Synchronous City: Aural Geographies in Gail Jones' *Five Bells*", *New Scholar* 3, no. 2 (2014); Bridie McCarthy, "Ringing Out: *Five Bells* and Its Feedback Loops", *Telling Stories: Australian Life and Literature 1935–2012*, eds Tanya Dalziell and Paul Genoni (Clayton, VIC: Monash University Publishing, 2013), 44–50; Leigh Dale, "No More Boomerang? *Nigger's Leap* and *Five Bells*", *Journal of Australian Studies* 37, no. 1 (2013): 48–61; Dixon, "Invitation to the Voyage".

is. Yet the idea is nevertheless there, playing a crucial role. Dalziell begins by considering how this idea functions and hides in plain sight, in considering the cultural history of sleep. She applies this to readings of *Dreams of Speaking* and *The Death of Noah Glass*.

My chapter takes seriously the idea that literature is a kind of thinking and considers some of the ways in which Gail Jones' novels *Sorry* and *Five Bells* think about human experience and the idea of place. It traces points of resonance between these two novels which focuses on the difficulties of communication and the idea of coming to terms with past trauma. It draws upon ideas from Spinoza to set out a reading of the nature of fixation, and the problem of breaking away from fixation so as to again exist within a present moment that involves ongoing possibilities.

Valérie-Anne Belleflamme concentrates on the sections of *Five Bells* that concern the Chinese character Pei Xing, teasing out the complex sets of references to Chinese culture and aesthetics Jones develops in imagining this character. She demonstrates the depth of research Jones undertakes and the dialogues she enters into in relation to Chinese ideas of place and identity, which are contrasted with Western ideas in the novel.

Tony Hughes-D'Aeth turns to ideas drawn from the psychoanalytic theory of Jacques Lacan to shed light on Jones' work. He argues that Jones' idea of desire is fundamentally associated with ideas of difference, which leads to ambiguity and conflict, and shows how utopian ideals are in danger of collapse when faced with these forces of difference. He develops this in reading *A Guide to Berlin*, where a utopian and seemingly straightforward project of sharing responses to readings of the same books falls into chaos.

Brigid Rooney also reads *A Guide to Berlin* in examining still more closely the idea of communal reading. In *Sorry*, Gail Jones has a character claim that readers of the same book share a secret communion (144). Rooney considers the importance of literature itself to how we exist within and among communities and how we develop understandings of the world. She argues that this might challenge the dominant paradigms of global markets and commodities with the normative populist understandings they insist upon and impose.

Robert Dixon develops a detailed reading of ongoing relation between literary texts and art history in Gail Jones' work through a close analysis of *The Death of Noah Glass*. Dixon demonstrates that this text is steeped in forms of intermediality that already appear in certain of the works of Renaissance painting that are drawn into relation with this novel. He demonstrates how the novel applies and tests principles drawn from picture theory, showing how Jones is able to use fiction as a mode of theorising aesthetic ideas.

Meg Samuelson's chapter complements Dixon's and moves the ideas towards theories of light and colour, drawing us back to concerns McMahon underlines as already present in *Sixty Lights*. Samuelson develops a meditation on the colour blue, which weaves its way through an understanding of Jones' idea of art, and perception itself.

The chapters demonstrate the layers of depth and meaning revealed in Jones' texts, which open themselves to and reward close reading. They show us how far Jones' novels lead us into resonant spaces of knowledge, which, when we pause and pay attention, open worlds of feelings and understandings to us that help us in turn to come to terms with the complexities of our own worlds.

References

Arias, Rosario. "(Spirit) Photography and the Past in the Neo-Victorian Novel." *Literature Interpretation Theory* 20, no. 1–2 (2009): 92–107.

Almeida, Sandra Regina Goulart. "A Story Told in a Whisper, or the Impossibility of Atonement." *Ilha Do Desterro: A Journal of English Language* 69, no. 2 (2016).

Belleflamme, Valérie-Anne. "Shakespeare Was Wrong: Counter-discursive Intertextuality in Gail Jones' *Sorry*." *Journal of Postcolonial Writing* 51, no. 6 (2015): 661–71.

Boyd, Brian. *Nabokov: The Russian Years*. Princeton, NJ: Princeton University Press, 1990.

Brydon, Diana. "'Difficult Forms of Knowing': Enquiry, Injury, and Translocated Relations of Postcolonial Responsibility." In *Postcolonial Translocations: Cultural Representation and Critical Spatial Thinking*, edited by Marga Munkelt, Markus Schmitz, Mark Stein and Silke Stroh, 3–28. Amsterdam: Rodopi, 2013.

Chunli, Xing. "Becoming Indigenous: A Comparative Analysis of Patrick White's *A Fringe of Leaves* and Gail Jones' *Sorry*." In *Australian Studies – Proceedings of the 14th International Conference of Australian Studies in China*, edited by David Carter, Liang Zhongxian, Han Feng, 123–31. Shanghai: Shanghai Jiao Tong University Press, 2015.

Dale, Leigh. "No More Boomerang? *Nigger's Leap* and *Five Bells*." *Journal of Australian Studies* 37, no. 1 (2013): 48–61.

Dalziell, Tanya. "An Ethics of Mourning: Gail Jones' *Black Mirror*." *JASAL: Journal of the Association for the Study of Australian Literature* 4 (2005): 49–61.

Davis, Peter. "Double Gazing and Novel Spaces – Examining Narrated and Manifest Photographs in the Novel." *Double Dialogues* Winter, no. 7 (2007).

Dixon, Robert. "Cosmopolitan Australians and Colonial Modernity: Alex Miller's *Conditions of Faith*, Gail Jones' *Black Mirror* and A.L. McCann's *The White Body of Evening*." *Westerly* 49 (2004): 122–37.

———. "Ghosts in the Machine: Modernity and the Unmodern." *JASAL: Journal of the Association for the Study of Australian Literature* 8(2008): 121–37.

———. "Invitation to the Voyage: Reading Gail Jones' *Five Bells*." *JASAL: Journal of the Association for the Study of Australian Literature* 12, no. 3 (2012): 1–17.

Eagle, Christopher. "'Angry Because She Stutters': Stuttering, Violence, and the Politics of Voice in *American Pastoral* and *Sorry*." *Philip Roth Studies* 8, no. 1 (2012): 17–30.

Einstein, Albert. *Relativity: The Special and General Theory*, translated by Robert W. Lawson. New York: Three Rivers Press, 1961.

Eliot, T.S. "Ulysses, Order and Myth." *Selected Prose of T.S. Eliot*, edited by Frank Kermode. New York: Harvest, 1975.

Genoni, Paul. "'Art Is the Windowpane': Novels of Australian Women and Modernism in Inter-war Europe." *JASAL: Journal of the Association for the Study of Australian Literature* 3 (2004): 159–72.

Introduction

Grasa, Pilar Royo. "Looking for Othello's Pearl in Gail Jones' *Sorry* (2007): Symbolic and Intertextual Questioning of the Notion of 'Settler Envy.'" *Journal of Postcolonial Writing* 54, no. 2 (2018): 200–13.

Herrero, M. Dolores. "The Australian Apology and Postcolonial Defamiliarization: Gail Jones' *Sorry*." *Journal of Postcolonial Writing* 47, no. 3 (2011): 283–95.

Huang, Jie. "'The Stolen Children' and the Unspeakable Repentance: Language as Metaphor in Gail Jones' *Sorry*" 不可言说的忏悔:"被偷走的孩子"与《抱歉》中语言的隐喻. *Foreign Literature Review*, no. 4 (2018): 135–52.

Jones, Gail. *Black Mirror*. Sydney: Vintage, 2009 [2002].

——. *The Death of Noah Glass*. Melbourne, VIC: Text Publishing, 2018.

——. "A Dreaming, a Sauntering: Reimagining Critical Paradigms." *JASAL: Journal of the Association for the Study of Australian Literature*, no. 5 (2006): 11–24.

——. *Dreams of Speaking*. Milson's Point, NSW: Vintage, 2006.

——. *Fetish Lives*. South Fremantle, WA: Fremantle Arts Centre Press, 1997.

——. *Five Bells*. Milson's Point, NSW: Vintage, 2011.

——. "Growing Small Wings: Walter Benjamin, Lola Ridge and the Political Affect of Modernism." *Affirmations: Of the Modern* 1, no. 2 (2014): 120–42.

——. *A Guide to Berlin*. North Sydney, NSW: Penguin Random House, 2015.

——. *House of Breathing*. South Fremantle, WA: Fremantle Arts Centre Press, 1992.

——. *Our Shadows*. Melbourne, VIC: Text Publishing, 2020.

——. *Sixty Lights*. Sydney: Random, 2004.

——. *Sorry*. London: Harvill Secker, 2007.

——. "Turnings and Overturnings in Glebe." *Sydney Review of Books*, 9 February 2018, https://sydneyreviewofbooks.com/essay/turnings-and-over-turnings-in-glebe/

Khorana, Sukhmani. "Photography, Cinema and Time in Jane Campion's *The Piano* and Gail Jones' *Sixty Lights*." *Outskirts: Feminisms along the Edge* 16 (2007).

McCarthy, Bridie. "Ringing Out: *Five Bells* and Its Feedback Loops." *Telling Stories: Australian Life and Literature 1935–2012*, edited by Tanya Dalziell and Paul Genoni, 44–50. Clayton, VIC: Monash University Publishing, 2013.

Mitchell, Kate. "Ghostly Histories and Embodied Memories: Photography, Spectrality and Historical Fiction in Afterimage and *Sixty Lights*." *Neo-Victorian Studies* 1, no. 1 (2008): 81–109.

Mudie, Ella. "The Synchronous City: Aural Geographies in Gail Jones' *Five Bells*." *New Scholar* 3, no. 2 (2014).

Nikro, Norman Saadi. "Paratactic Stammers: Temporality in the Novels of Gail Jones." *JASAL: Journal of the Association for the Study of Australian Literature* 16, no. 1 (2016): 1–16.

Oreb, Naomi. "Mirroring, Depth and Inversion: Holding Gail Jones' *Black Mirror* Against Contemporary Australia." *Sydney Studies in English* 35 (2009).

Roughley, Fiona. "Spatialising Experience: Gail Jones' *Black Mirror* and the Contending of Postmodern Space." *Australian Literary Studies* 23, no. 2 (2007): 58–73.

Steains, Timothy. "The Mixed Temporalities of Transnationalism in *Dreams of Speaking*." *Journal of Australian Studies* 41, no. 1 (2017): 32–46.

Wevers, Lydia. "Fold in the Map: Figuring Modernity in Gail Jones' *Dreams of Speaking* and Elizabeth Knox's *Dreamhunter*." *Australian Literary Studies* 23, no. 2 (2007): 187–98.

Wood, Robert. "The Pleasure of Language Itself: An Interview with Gail Jones." *BLARB: Blog//Los Angeles Review of Books*, https://blog.lareviewofbooks.org/interviews/pleasure-language-interview-gail-jones/

Zavaglia, Liliana. *White Apology and Apologia: Australian Novels of Reconciliation*. Amherst, NY: Cambria Press, 2016.

1

Constellations of Light and Image | Contemplations on Deep Space: Apparent magnitude and scale

Lou Jillett

Space looms large in the work of Gail Jones. Not just the deep space of "out there", but also the spaces people occupy, the gaps between images, the hidden recesses of body and of mind. This chapter will explore the way time, space and scale inform Jones' broader cosmology, identifying astronomical and other interrelated spatial connections within and across her entire body of work. Through constellations of fragmented images – such as Lucy's Journal of "*Special Things Seen*" in *Sixty Lights* (2004), Alice and Mr Sakamoto's shared interest in the poetry of modern technologies and objects in *Dreams of Speaking* (2006), and the "speak-memories" of the Nabokovian circle in *A Guide to Berlin* (2015) – Jones constructs networks of meaning, showing objects and events from different perspectives in space and different perspectives in time. As with the Janus face of *Five Bells* (2011), the extremes of aloneness and togetherness, separation and union, inner and outer, surface and depth, are often conjoined, kept separate (physically) by mere layers of skin (overcome through the simple gesture of touch), and (emotionally) by a word spoken (or not spoken). Seemingly arbitrary convergences and divergences, and patterns of relation highlight the notion that joy and sorrow are, in fact, two sides of the same coin.

Constellations (among other spatial metaphors) manifest as a connecting principle in Jones' work in a variety of ways. There are the characters' references to specific known (and imagined) constellations and astronomical terms: the proliferation of stars and suns and moons and their various castings of light, shadow, reflection and refraction; but also the imagist poetics of Jones' prose, the particular memories that return to haunt us, coalescing into constellations of

Lou Jillett, Constellations of Light and Image | Contemplations on Deep Space: Apparent magnitude and scale. In *Inner and Outer Worlds: Gail Jones' Fiction*, edited by Anthony Uhlmann. Sydney: Sydney University Press, 2022. DOI: 10.30722/sup.9781743327791

Figure 1.1 Phases of the moon.

patterned meaning within and across texts. In *Sixty Lights*, Lucy, through the act of reading, observes that there "were sight-lines, image tokens, between people & people, between people & objects & words on a page, that knitted the whole world in the purest geometry of connections".[1]

One example of the ways I've drawn constellating patterns from across Jones' collected works (with the exception of *The Death of Noah Glass*) involves mapping the phases of the moon (Fig. 1.1).

I have attributed to each of her texts a particular moon phase, on the basis of its recurrence within that text's pages. Hence, by plotting these moon cycles, we see: *Black Mirror* (2002) as a new moon, *Sixty Lights* as a sickle (or crescent) moon,

---

1   Gail Jones, *Sixty Lights* (2004; London: Vintage, 2005), 114. All subsequent references are to this edition and appear in parentheses in the text.

Dreams of Speaking as the home of the woman in the moon – and *Fetish Lives*, by extension, the home of the man in the moon. *Sorry* (2007) is here represented as a three-quarter, or gibbous, moon, and *Five Bells* completes the cycle as the full moon. *House of Breathing* (1992) recalls us to the fact that the moon is, after all, merely a reflection of light from another source, having no generative light-giving power of its own, yet contains within itself the capacity for total eclipse.

Astronomical metaphors abound, on all levels of scale. From the fractal, the partial, the inter- and intra-personal, to the terrestrial, the universal, the celestial and theoretical, we find the infinite universe without: composed of individual stars, cometary and planetary orbits, binary and planetary systems, constellations, galaxies and nebula, dark matter and deep space – reflected by the infinite universe within: composed of memory, grief, loss, desire, sorrow and joy. These spirals, whorls, eddies and labyrinths refer equally to the human and elemental, the physical and metaphysical – the outer and other worlds of the cosmos and beyond – the inner world of cells, brain, organs and bones – and of circuitry, networks and electrical impulses. Though repulsed by the internet, its extensive reach and apparent claim, Alice, in *Dreams of Speaking*, explains that "there were galaxies of information in there, illimitable networks more complex than neural pathways, zapping multi-directionally … cluttered, schismatic, astronomical, microscopic".[2] Alice resists what she describes as the "technological subservience [of being seated at the] nexus of so many intervening sites", yet despite privileging the "latent forms of life [she sees] everywhere and [the] secret understandings" of these hidden worlds that she believes to be "richer than silicon", she recognises the value of describing their "inner geometry, their flight paths and havens" in cybernetic terms: "Hyperlinked without end" (103).

I began this chapter with the plan of investigating an astronomical theme within one of Jones' short stories, but soon became aware of a broader cosmology, and subsequently set about exploring the larger patterns at play. The following text contains a comprehensive list of the astronomical terms that I have encountered thus far across Jones' collected works (Fig. 1.2). The word "sky" alone rates 170 mentions (and counting), with descriptions ranging from: crystal, amethyst, turquoise and lapis, to cobalt, pink, silver and gold – and every other colour under the sun – from hazy, closed, smothering, low-ceilinged and weighty, to clear, open, gleaming, incandescent, extending and infinite.

---

2   Gail Jones, *Dreams of Speaking* (2006; London: Vintage, 2007), 136. All subsequent references are to this edition and appear in parentheses in the text.

acceleration, alien/s, alienation, astronaut/s, astronautical, astronomical, atomised, aura, beams, big bang, black hole, celestial, centrifuged, compass, conjunction, constellated, constellating, constellation/s, continuum, cosmic, cosmos, craters, creation, curvature, daylight, declension, degrees, dome, earth, earthrise, ebbing, eclipse, eclipsed, electromagnetism, element/s, elemental, elementary, elliptical, ellipses, emanation, emit, emitted, energy, escape, eternity, ether, extraterrestrial, firmament, flux, flying saucers, force-fields, galaxy, galaxies, geometry, global, globe, gravity, green ray, halo, heaven/s, heliotropic, hemisphere, horizon/s, illuminate, infinity, interplanetary, lens, luminosity, luminosities, lunar, magnet, magnetic, magnetism magnification, magnified, magnifying, magnitude, mars, martian, metaphysical, milky way, moon, moonbeam, mooners, moonlight, moonlit, moon shadow/s, moonshine, moonstruck, moony, nacred, nebulous, northern lights, oblique, occlude, occlusion, optics, orbit, orbited, orientated, orion, orrery, outer space, particles, penumbral, perpetual motion, planet/s, planetary, physics, ray/s, recursion, refracted, refraction/s, relativity, rocket-ships, satellite/s, saucer/s, singularity, sky, skylight, skyline, skyward, space/s, span, sphere, star/s, starburst, starfish, starless, starlit, starry, stellar, stereoscope, stereoscopic, sun, sundial, sundress, sunflower, sunlight, sunlit, sunrise, sunshine, sunny, telescope, terrestrial, time, time-travelling, transit, twilight, UFO, ultraviolet, universe, vault, velocity, waves, world, zenith

Figure 1.2 Glossary of astronomical terms.

One pattern that emerged early was Jones' characters' tendency to look up to the sky for solace, and by contrast, the sadness some characters attribute to the solitariness of space travel. "Grief is like spacewalking", thinks Alice, in the opening pages of *Dreams of Speaking* (36). "She saw herself a floaty astronaut strung in endless dark ... [Astronauts] belonged to moments of dismay and quiet estrangement. Alone in their silent worlds" (3).

The astronaut's perspective inverts our earthbound view of space. This topographical view is a recurring theme in every one of Jones' novels, with the distance from the earth's surface (as seen from the sky), and the relative speed of travel, dependent on the technology that was available at the time each novel was set. In *Sixty Lights*' nineteenth-century England, for instance, Lucy rides above London in a hot air balloon.

> When they bent to peer over the edge they saw London enflamed; the physical geography of the city had been remade by gas light, so that the main streets were

rivers of light and the Thames a pitch-dark canyon, and the shopping districts were redrawn in legends of gold. 'A fire map' was what the balloonist called it. (222)

Alice, in *Dreams of Speaking*, observes that "in photographs taken from the sky, cities resembled circuit boards" (111). Flying at night from one hemisphere to the other, "Alice saw a curve of endless black sky, and far below, a carpet of uneven lights, profuse and lovely. Bright forms constellated and slid beneath them. Patterns of flash, ardent glows, electrified destinations" (20). Narrowing the field of view to something a little closer to home, "In clear light, flights over Australia showed the continent as a crimson body" (189). Zooming in still further, in *Black Mirror*, Jones describes Victoria's early twentieth-century experience of flying over the Kalgoorlie mines in a biplane, close enough to the earth to see people waving back at her. "[S]he gazed down upon the earth and saw it sliding away. It was vermillion in the late light and pocked with mine-shafts – and little men – prospectors – left their labours to wave."[3]

In addition to these deep space contemplations, and topographical inversions, Jones' underground cartographies also present the labyrinthine worlds that exist beneath the earth's surface, through the mapping of mines and railways, of catacombs and rebellions, and of life on the margins. Reiterating these subterranean maps, on a human scale, are descriptions of the inner workings of a body or mind in decline, such as Lucy's perception of her consumptive body. As within, so without | As above, so below.

> At night she was assaulted by imaginings of her own inner body ... lungs like honeycomb ... She saw ... a kind of city, all caves and pipelines and underground tubes, rather like the ones engineers were now creating under the streets of London – the Metropolitan ... a dark new geography. (189)

Perdita, in *Sorry*, conceives of her mother's mind as undergoing a similarly degenerative process, "the honeycomb of dementia" described in terms of architectural ruin.

> By the time I was old enough to ask her, she was not interested in replying, and had already begun, in any case, to enter the honeycomb of dementia, the looped craters under-arching what might have been a memory, the brownish corridors to nowhere, the frail struts of something that had once been dense pillars of identity.[4]

---

3   Gail Jones, *Black Mirror* (2002; London: Vintage, 2009), 167. All subsequent references are to this edition and appear in parentheses in the text.
4   Gail Jones, *Sorry* (2007; London: Vintage, 2008), 75. All subsequent references are to this edition and appear in parentheses in the text.

Deleuze and Guattari, in their chapter on refrain from *One Thousand Plateaus*, describe "the literary or musical work" itself as being similarly architectural in structure.[5] In further rhizomal connections, James, at various points in *Five Bells*, describes the "cortical systems and webs that are our mysterious plumbing", the "trailing intricacies of the cells of the brain" viewed under the microscope, and "the sub-strata of his cells" as a space in which his first love still resides.[6] "The refrain is a prism", claim Deleuze and Guattari, "a crystal of space-time ...".[7] Jones' inner and outer worlds are not just mirrored, but replicated on ever increasing and decreasing orders of scale: stars, cells, and the whole expanding universe.

The significance of naming forms another constellation of sorts. The act of naming performs a crucial function in each of Jones' novels. From her first play on Anna's name in *Black Mirror* – "anachronistic", followed by analeptic, analytical, anaesthesia, anatomical, anagnorisis, and in a repetition with a slight difference, Anna-chronos – anachronism becomes a recurring theme, not just for Anna (and by extension, Victoria), but for several other characters and events throughout Jones' collected works (9, 62, 86, 118, 131, 213, 266, 276). In *Sixty Lights*, for example, Isaac Newton, who lived from 1643 to 1727, becomes Lucy's companion in 1860s India, and Lucy herself is increasingly presented as a woman out of time. "Someday", Lucy thinks, from her nineteenth-century perspective, "people will discover how to photograph the vast night sky"; "doctors [will] have an apparatus to photograph the inner body"; "They would even ... photograph the brain ... like newly discovered planets, remote, elaborate, drifting on glass plates like secrets unbroken" (183, 189, 190). This "out-of-time"-ness recalls Alice's description of astronauts in *Dreams of Speaking*, as being "beyond time itself", which in turn brings to mind Mr Sakamoto's anachronistic Spanish astronaut, that he explains was added to Salamanca's Renaissance-era cathedral during a period of restoration, some four hundred years after the cathedral was built (36). By the time Stella, in *Sorry*, arrives in remote north-western Australia, she has become firmly rooted in the world of sixteenth-century Shakespearean English, an anachronistic fixation that her daughter, Perdita, perceives to be a kind of madness, but which will ultimately be the source of the talking cure that will bring Perdita out of her own mute inner prison (185). Cass, in *A Guide to Berlin*, is attracted to Marco because of what she perceives to be his anachronistic charisma.[8]

---

5 Gilles Deleuze and Felix Guattari, "The Refrain", in *One Thousand Plateaus: Capitalism and Schizophrenia*, trans. Brian Massumi (Minneapolis: University of Minnesota Press, 1987), 329.
6 Gail Jones, *Five Bells* (2011; London: Vintage, 2012), 68 and 35. All subsequent references are to this edition and appear in parentheses in the text.
7 Deleuze and Guattari, *One Thousand Plateaus*, 348–49.
8 Gail Jones, *A Guide to Berlin* (North Sydney: Vintage, Random House, 2015), 36. All subsequent references are to this edition and appear in parentheses in the text.

Human bodies, like the planets Jones uses as metaphor, move in binary orbits around one another, in keeping with the laws of planetary motion and attraction. Encountering Thomas and Violet in a hallway embrace in *Sixty Lights*, for example, Lucy observes: "They were rapt and isolated. They were on their own planet ... [an] aloof orbit of just two" (180). Later, she describes "seduction ... [as] never face to face; [but rather] the side-by-side permission of inadvertent currents and connections. The galvanism of bodies alerted to each other. The prickling charge" (210). Bodies are beacons, guiding potential lovers with intimations of intimacy, yet hiding as much as they reveal, like the lighthouses employed as their metaphor.

It is not just the dynamics of binary systems that Jones is interested in. There are the constellations of far-flung family units, moving into and out of each other's orbits throughout a lifetime. "So this would be their pattern", thinks Alice in *Dreams of Speaking*, of her relationship with her sister, Norah. "They would zigzag in and out of closeness and distance ... For every far away time, or loss, there would be a return, there would be propinquity" (13). Nor is it just blood kinship that generates the ties that bind: "if there is a magnetic aspect to sensibility", thinks Alice, "it is evident in friendships" (60). Perdita in *Sorry*, too, understands the forces at play in the families we create: "Though she was the youngest and smallest, Perdita reached her arms around Mary and Billy and gathered them in; and their little group, like another family, inclined lovingly together" (56). Though her parents absent themselves for much of the narrative, "she learn[s] that she – Perdita – had been given a skin group ... included as a sister" within the local Indigenous community, named and claimed within the very kinship system that it was her father's aim to eradicate. "Perdita was both surprised and delighted. She knew herself suddenly implicated in a wider pattern, where there would always be someone, somewhere, to know of and look after her" (73). Later, in her speech therapy sessions with Dr Oblov, Perdita tells him: "There are other families ... not just the ones you are born with" (165).

Orreries appear in no less than three of the works, both as literal small-scale models of the solar system, such as we see in *Sorry*, and as figurative representations of the geometries of relation into which these various groupings coalesce. Jones describes the assemblage of loosely affiliated expats in *A Guide to Berlin*, for example, as a human orrery. "They were all orbiting each other ... The six eccentrics were swinging through deep space in close or faraway circles" (188). These close and faraway circles recall and mimic the familial bonds that proliferate elsewhere. Unfortunately, those ties of blood do become important in the eyes of the law. Characters find themselves barred entry to Kafkaesque castles, constrained by bureaucratic red tape as they navigate the absurd realms of legality, justice and governance, demonstrated at various stages by the impossibility of

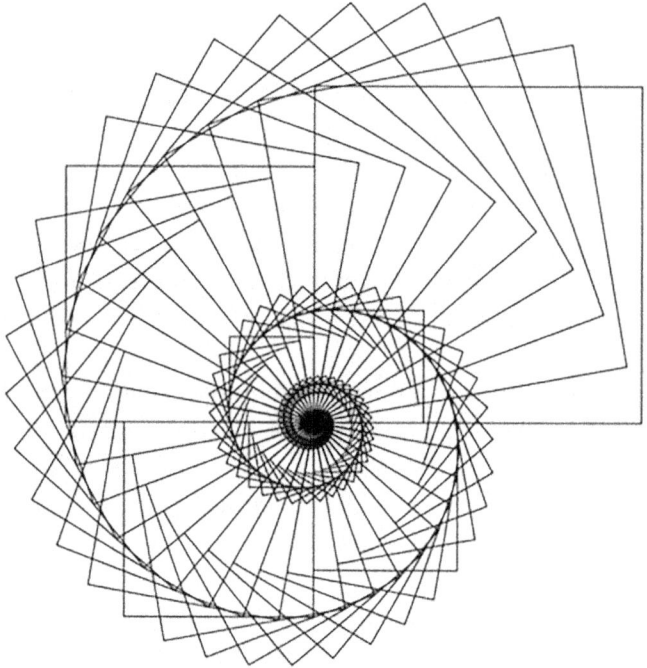

Figure 1.3 Nautilus spirals – the shape of the universe.

visiting non-relatives in prison and in hospital. "Only 'blood' relatives [are] permitted to visit", Billy, Pearl and Perdita are told, in *Sorry*, when they try to re-form their constellation of four in the new setting of Mary's women's prison (206). Alice encounters a similar stumbling block when she plans a surprise visit to Mr Sakamoto, in *Dreams of Speaking*, arriving in Japan unannounced, only to discover that he lies in hospital, having suffered a stroke from which he will not recover; and that only family may attend him there (171).

One way of thinking about these unremitting, arbitrary systems of rules – their ruptures and interventions – is to consider the fact that the other side of attraction, is, of course, repulsion. Just as the planetary metaphor is applied at all levels of scale, from the individual as a solitary star, to lovers locked in a binary spin, to constellations of connection and entire planetary systems in orbit around a central sun, so too does this fragmentation occur at each of these levels of scale.

New systems of relation bear the shape of the universe in embryonic form (Fig. 1.3). Nautilus spirals form another constellation across Jones' corpus, described at various points in terms of eddies, whorls, whirlpools, arabesques, gyres, Fibonacci sequences, vortices, conchometry and recursion. These connections, formed spontaneously out of a kind of universal harmonic, perhaps the music of the spheres, or what Mr Sakamoto in *Dreams of Speaking* describes as "sympathetic

1 Constellations of Light and Image

vibration" (189), Gino, in *A Guide to Berlin*, as "meaningful coincidence" (78), and Mitsuko as "matching time" (62), are sources of joy and happiness and friendship and love. Impediments, missed connections and miscommunications, however, cause the fragmentation of these new-formed constellations. Rendered broken, impaired or lost, they become discordant, out of sync, sources of sorrow and grief, folded within the deepest recesses of hidden selves.

All of Jones' stories depict these patterns of attraction and repulsion. We see it in the eclipse of the lover's turning away in "The Astronomer Tells of her Love",[9] in Lucy's refusal to marry Jacob in anticipation of her own impending eclipse (*Sixty Lights*, 237), and in Cass' shifting attitude to the other members of the speak-memory collective in *A Guide to Berlin* (246). The group – momentarily tight-knit – find themselves in a kind of free fall following the death of one of their members at the hands of another. Key sites of attraction and repulsion are also depicted in terms of gravity and anti-gravity. "The heaviest sediments", Jones tells us in *Sorry*, are "paradoxically ... produced by loss" (207). There is a gravity to grief in these worlds that has the capacity to warp the space-time continuum. In *Dreams of Speaking*, we find Hiroshi in 1972, "at last experiencing the grief of 1945" (73). There is a parallel here with Lucy and Thomas Strange's respective experiences of delayed grief in *Sixty Lights*, as well as the postponement of grief experienced by each of the principal characters in *Black Mirror*, who learn of the death of loved ones sometimes years after the deaths themselves have taken place. Similarly, in both *Five Bells* and *A Guide to Berlin*, we come to know that for some characters, grief is yet in store. As Alice tells us in *Dreams of Speaking*, "Anything in slow motion was intrinsically sorrowful" (3).

For every instance of the slowing and stretching of time in Jones' work, there is a corresponding acceleration, a compression, a time lapse. As well as the speeding up and slowing down of time, each of the novels includes some representation of the folding of space-time. For Pei, in *Five Bells*, it is a "fold in history, this diabolical return" (118). Lucy, in *Sixty Lights*, possesses sure knowledge "that time might distort like this, might loop lacily and suddenly fold over" (29). For Alice, in *Dreams of Speaking*, the mode of yesterday involves a "scooping of space ... [and a folding of] time" (36). Perdita, in *Sorry*, experiences time, not linearly, but as "recursion, fold, things revisiting out of time, the again and again" (182).

Lemniscate (Fig. 1.4), one of Cass' favourite words in *A Guide to Berlin*, discovered in the works of Nabokov, describes "the shape of infinity", another recurring symbol of these folds of time and space, seen also in Victoria's obsession

---

9   Gail Jones, "The Astronomer Tells of Her Love", in *The House of Breathing* (South Fremantle: Fremantle Arts Centre Press, 1993), 27.

Figure 1.4 Lemniscate.

Figure 1.5 Ampersand.

with the hourglass in *Black Mirror* (70). But not all journeys constitute a return. As Newton's first law of motion informs us, an object in motion will continue to move at a constant velocity unless acted upon by another external object or force. When connection between participants in a planetary system is broken, for instance; or, to bring things back to the human scale – such as we see in "The Astronomer Tells of Her Love" in *The House of Breathing* – when "the darkness push[es] between [lovers] like a dissevering wedge", each spins off into new infinities (27).

Which brings me to the ampersand, another symbol that forms constellations within and across several of Jones' worlds. (Fig. 1.5) Stella, who dwells outside the language, culture and company of the "little community constituted around her", in *Sorry*, senses familiar patterns, but does not understand, and so cannot participate in the refrain (26). "Something that might have been an ampersand, if it had a sound, repeated again and again, so that what she heard were connections and collusions affirmed: a bracelet of propositions, perhaps, or an extra logic of meanings, from which she was excluded" (26).

Stella *is* excluded from the extra logic of meanings that attend this series of images, as it is the logic of different worlds. Within the diegetic frame of the *Sorry* story-universe, it is a world governed by the logic of racial and cultural difference. Extra-diegetically, it is the world of *Black Mirror* and the logic of Rose's diary with its ampersand-strewn code, telling of her love (164–5). And it is the world

1 Constellations of Light and Image

Figure 1.6 Missed connections.

of *A Guide to Berlin*, and the logic of Cass' thwarted desire for connection. "She imagined invisible particles, twisting in ampersand with every slight movement of her body. *And, and, and*. This was the shape of her desire and its relentless wish for connection. She would never be satisfied" (110).

It is the ultimate marker of missed connection; rendered more tragic by the fact that an initial connection is made, with the first curve of the lemniscate complete (Fig. 1.6). The brief constellations we form in groups of two & three & four & more, all bear these signs of infinite potential, but the ampersand which joins us is simultaneously a symbol of conjunction & rupture, the sign of infinity that can never be achieved, representing the experiential joy of shared intimacy for a time, before criss-crossing into separate futures – sometimes as a result of a poor choice or a chance not taken, sometimes as a result of words not spoken, like Perdita's: "Sorry, my sister, oh my sister, sorry" (211).

Jones' writing evokes the vastness of the universe in the infinite distance that arises between estranged lovers, the arbitrariness of individual choice and chance, and the sheer wonder that we manage to cross paths at all on this spinning globe. "What accidental pattern of life delivers us our friends?" she asks in *Sixty Lights* (195). On a larger scale, we might ask, what accidental pattern of the universe delivers us life? Alice, in *Dreams of Speaking*, attempts to explain her interest in "machines and motion and invention" in response to Steven's query about where that curiosity began. "There are no beginnings", she tells him. "Only fragments. Only stories" (41). Nor, Jones shows, are there always adequate ends. Sometimes bodies simply disappear, spinning off into other orbits; other times their endings are more permanent, but the details remain unknown to the parties who need knowledge the most – in order to mourn – to properly grieve.

These unresolved disappearances are shown from the perspective of the bereaved, such as Pei's reflections in *Five Bells* on her parents' disappearance during the Chinese Cultural Revolution, only discovering much later that they "had been killed a week after they were taken" (154); and in Victoria's recollection of her Jewish lover, Jules, in *Black Mirror*, taken to the concentration camps during the Second World War, his final moments unknown. "Some limit", says Victoria, "will not allow any precise imagining of the camp" (266). Casual disappearances are also presented from the perspective of those who know of a person's death, but will never tell (such as we see in the complicity of the group in *A Guide to Berlin*); and from no known perspective, such as James' deliberate act of disappearance at the conclusion of *Five Bells*, the details of which may never come to the surface.

These multiple ways of viewing, and the inevitability of Ellie and James' broken connection, are foreshadowed in the Janus profiles described in the opening pages of *Five Bells*. "The ... profiles not matching. A simple image on the blackboard snagged at her feelings and Ellie loved it because it failed" (2). Janus, Ellie, informs us, "is the god of bridges, since bridges look both ways and are always double" (2). At various points over the course of the day, both Ellie and James will look to the Sydney Harbour Bridge and contemplate the view one would command from such a perspective, with Ellie looking westward to the mountains, and James, eastward, out to sea.

> Ellie looked across to the bridge and wondered if one day she might climb it. It must be a singular pleasure, with no end other than to rise, to see, to stand above the turquoise water and the green and yellow ferries and look out across the Harbour and the city spread between the ocean and the mountains. (95)

> He glanced up at the Sydney Harbour Bridge and could see a line of people, barely visible, climbing its bow. What must they see, he wondered. There would be the Harbour below them, and all the wake patterns on the water, there would be a bird's eye view of boats and of the meringue peaks of the Opera House, and perhaps there would be a view much further, out eastwards to the ocean. (200)

Though bound by the force of their mutual attraction, the passage of time, and the enormity of James' guilt and grief, generates a tyranny of distance, and like the failed image from the blackboard of her childhood – as symbolised by their irreconcilable perspectival positions – their love is rendered inert and ultimately destined to fail. Yet James will live on in Ellie's memory, returning to her again and again in her thoughts and recollections of their shared childhood experiences. This provides a positive counterpoint to the trauma of return experienced by James in the wake of his student's untimely death, which is itself an echo of that experienced by Perdita in *Sorry*.

In *A Guide to Berlin*, Jones presents memory as a thing with a semi-permeable membrane, like cells. Cass describes the manner in which:

memories of others had infiltrated and become her own; they exerted their influence as planets might, pulling time and space, oscillating in and out of far visibility, changing how the world itself appeared, and all that was inside it. Snowfall glistened and the sky outside sped away. The snow appeared as a maze of miniscule stars. (260)

In keeping with the logic of the Janus profiles, just as joy and grief are often co-mingled in our memories of lost loved ones, so too can life and death be conceived as two sides of the same coin, separated by the merest presence or absence of breath. And as with all other elements that I have explored in this chapter, the breath of life can also be identified at all orders of scale in Jones' cosmos. This rhythmic in and out is like a heartbeat, echoing across time and text. "For Aristotle", recalls James, in *Five Bells*, "*pneuma* was vitality, like the fifth element, ether, which makes up the stars" (142). Catherine, in the same textual world, finds pleasure in "eddying crowds and the wayward motions of human traffic, their tidal sweeps at traffic lights, their rhythmic currents of locomotion" (21). Alice, in *Dreams of Speaking*, describes a similar push-pull in her consideration of the perpetual flux of family relations "zigzag[ging] in and out of closeness and distance, retreating, converging, retreating and converging" (13). And Lucy, in *Sixty Lights*, who at times displays an uncanny knack for entering the various folds of the time-space continuum, experiences childbirth as an entry "into the dilations and contractions of time and space itself" (161).

The various interconnecting strata of Jones' cosmology, when the works are examined in conversation with one another, produce an orrery of sorts, a constellation, a map and guide to the living, breathing universe. Regardless of the size or detail of the map, though, some things will always remain hidden. Jones recalls us to the fact that our secret selves are manifold. That no matter how much is revealed, there is always more to discover. Rendered mute for much of their own narrative, I think it fitting that Perdita in *Sorry*, and by extension, Mary, have the last word: "She believed … that there are no cessations, that what is missing continues on, persisting somewhere else. Mary had taught her this, the principle of invisible presence, that one must always reckon on more than one sees" (145).

References

Deleuze, Gilles, and Felix Guattari. "The Refrain." In *One Thousand Plateaus: Capitalism and Schizophrenia*. (1987) Translated by Brian Massumi, 310–49. Minneapolis: University of Minnesota Press, 2005.
Jones, Gail. *Black Mirror*. (2002) London: Vintage, 2009.
– –. *The Death of Noah Glass*. Melbourne: Text Publishing, 2018.
– –. *Dreams of Speaking*. (2006) London: Vintage, 2007.

--. *Five Bells*. (2011) London: Vintage, 2012.
--. *Fetish Lives*. South Fremantle: Fremantle Arts Centre Press, 1997.
--. *A Guide to Berlin*. North Sydney: Vintage, Random House, 2015.
--. *The House of Breathing*. (1992) South Fremantle: Fremantle Arts Centre Press, 1993.
--. *Sixty Lights*. (2004) London: Vintage, 2005.
--. *Sorry*. (2007) London: Vintage, 2008.

2

Bioluminescence: Materiality, Metaphor and Trace in *Sixty Lights*

Elizabeth McMahon

Bioluminescence, the phosphorous cold light that emanates from living organisms,[1] is a central figure of Gail Jones' second novel *Sixty Lights* (2004). Bioluminescence is one light amongst many in this narrative, which traces the ancient and nascent fields of photography and, as Lyn Jacobs (2006) reminds us, there is an inherent ekphrasis that constructs the word *photograph* with its synthesis of *photo* (light) and *graph* (writing).[2] *Sixty Lights* announces itself as a venture in light writing by its title, the names of its characters (Isaac Newton and Lucy), its sixty-section album structure, narrative events and, ironically, its challenge to *Enlightenment* teleology and coherence. Within these collected illuminations, the figure of bioluminescence complicates the many structural and figural binaries in play in the text to show their inter-implication: light and shadow, image and word, presence and absence, subject and object, mind and body, organism and machine, masculine and feminine, life and death.

The particular ways bioluminescence unsettles binary oppositions propose both a riposte and an alternative to the monolithic category of the Western "Enlightenment".[3] The sixty scenes that comprise the novel accrete an array of knowledges and discourses of the Enlightenment as experienced in the Victorian

Elizabeth McMahon, Bioluminescence: Materiality, Metaphor and Trace in *Sixty Lights*. In *Inner and Outer Worlds: Gail Jones' Fiction*, edited by Anthony Uhlmann. Sydney: Sydney University Press, 2022. DOI: 10.30722/sup.9781743327791

---

1 See the Smithsonian site for an introduction to oceanic bioluminescence: https://ocean.si.edu/ocean-life/fish/bioluminescence. See also Kaan Biron, "Fireflies, Dead Fish and a Glowing Bunny: A Primer on Bioluminescence", *BioTeach Online Journal* 1 (Fall 2003), www.bioteach.ubc.ca
2 Lyn Janette Jacobs, "Gail Jones' 'light writing': Memory and the Photo-graph", *JASAL: Journal of the Association for the Study of Australian Literature* 5 (2006), https://openjournals.library.sydney.edu.au/index.php/JASAL/article/view/10180

era of the novel's setting: science and technology, historiography, literature and philosophy. In addition to its specific fields of meaning in individual and linked scenes in the novel, this chapter proposes that bioluminescence is at the centre of the novel's experiment with an alternative light to that of the "Enlightenment" and the structural binaries that underpin its logic and momentum. For bioluminescence literalises, re-embodies the light metaphor of the Enlightenment thereby reconnecting the fundamental split of body and mind that underpins Enlightenment thought.

The light metaphor that characterises the Enlightenment has a far longer history. As Jacques Derrida lays out in "Force and Signification", a certain understanding of light constitutes Western philosophy itself. This foundational relationship functions "not only because it is a photological one – and in this respect the entire history of our philosophy is a photology, the name given to a history of or a treatise on, light – but because it is a metaphor".[4] As Lindsey Kelley and Eva Hayward write, this function means that "sunlight as a materialising wave metaphorises into transcendent light, a heavenly light promising liberation from the flesh".[5] Understanding revelation and knowledge through this metaphor of light, therefore, simultaneously produces structures of binary logic, most profoundly, of mind and body. Bioluminescence is a form of corporeal light, and in *Sixty Lights* is the text's figure of the inseparability of mind and body as well as machine.

In its denial of mind/body dualism, bioluminescence also operates as the novel's aporia. For the novel's sixty scenes are structured around oppositions such as light and shade, materiality and immateriality; they detail and celebrate their interplay and effects, which are performed across the many levels of the novel's architectonics, narrative, characterisation and figuration. Yet bioluminescence complicates the very oppositionality that is fundamental to the novel. This essential contradiction, aporia, is integral to the novel's undoing and remaking of these structures and its revision of accepted relations between subjects, objects, and the energies of the created world.

Bioluminescence is almost literally central to *Sixty Lights* in that it appears for the first time towards the middle of the narrative when the young heroine Lucy Strange is voyaging from England to India. At sixteen years old, she is alone for the first time in her life "float[ing] away to a story that would be hers alone" (109).[6]

---

3   See James Schmidt's website of discussion and resources: Persistent Enlightenment: Notes on the Enlightenment as Historical Period and Continuing Project, https://persistentenlightenment.com/about-2/
4   Jacques Derrida, *Writing and Difference*, trans. Alan Bass (London: University of Chicago Press, 1978), 27.
5   Lindsay Kelley and Eva Hayward, "Carnal Light", *Parallax* 19, no. 1 (2013): 114.
6   Gail Jones, *Sixty Lights* (London: Vintage, 2005). All subsequent references are to this edition and appear in parentheses in the text.

2 Bioluminescence: Materiality, Metaphor and Trace in *Sixty Lights*

Bioluminescence is a causal and integral part of that new story. Lucy finds the "disquiet of ships" an "unending marvel" and she especially "love[s] the night" when she feels like she is sailing in the sky (109). Her experience of voyaging and the visions of the night promote in her a sense of "awe and impulse to artistry". The expanse of the oceans corresponds with and stimulates Lucy's own sense of expansive being. In this condition of receptivity and expansion, Lucy encounters the marvel of oceanic bioluminescence:

> One night when the ship was becalmed on a plain of black, she saw silvery threads of light in a thin film on a surface of the ocean. They followed the pattern of waves and looked like fluctuating stripes, breaking, reshaping, breaking again, reshaping. A hemline in a dance. A ribbon dropped from a sky gondola. A broken trace of moonbeam surfing the waves. Like and like and like and like. In truth it was like nothing she had ever seen before. It was of itself and radically particular. (110)

The spectacle challenges Lucy's capacities of description and she reaches into her past experience for generic touchstones through which to comprehend what she sees. These all fail. For Lucy at this point, the scene of "silvery threads of light in a thin film on the surface of the ocean" is "like nothing she has seen before. Of itself and radically particular".

A voice from behind her then speaks into the darkness and attaches a name to the wonder with taxonomical precision:

> "Bioluminescence".
> When Lucy turned to look, a little startled, she found a man standing close behind her, apparently peering at the ocean over her shoulder.
> "Plankton mostly. But underneath, down deep, there are fish that carry their own lights in spots on their cheeks, or in little pods dangling above their heads." (110)

Classification and definition can be understood as reducing the power of phenomena, of interrupting what is imagined as a direct connection between the viewer and the object or scene. According to this view, names and definitions diminish the force and charge of phenomena by locating and domesticating them within known structures of knowledge. Once located, they are no longer entirely of themselves and "radically particular" but relative units within an accepted system of understanding replete with its history and values. In the scene of Lucy's vision, the fullness of her experience of the phosphorous ocean, its "radical particular[ity]", is connected explicitly to its pre-defined status, its escape from known language. Crowley's naming of bioluminescence, a single technical word, is presented as a different order of being and knowing.

And yet, such oppositions between phenomena and language are refused here. Lucy is magnetically drawn to the speaker of the word, Captain William Crowley: "Perhaps, indeed she was seduced by him then, when he named a new light and stood obscured in shadow". Lucy also responds fully to the word itself, to both elements of the sign, signified and signifier, and the line between them is blurred. She is excited by the word that carries new knowledge and by its material properties of sound including its cascading polysyllables, and its syncretic construction, which combines science and poetry, past and future:

> Bioluminescence: it was a wonderful word. It was a word that sounded as if it had travelled from the future, from a completely new knowledge, from a new dimension of scrutability. (110)

Which, of course, it has. For neither "bioluminescence" nor "plankton" were coined at the time of the narrative. Hence the words, too, have an existence prior to their domestication within structures of knowledge. The proleptic use of words and knowledges from the next century is part of this scene's complex overlay of temporalities, all bound to the figure of bioluminescence. The novel's chronotope, the ascendant British Empire of the nineteenth century, is constructed by the superimposition of discourses in ways that reveal continuities and breaks in understanding in this period of radical change. The text gives and takes pleasure from details, facts and knowledges gained by characters, and by the access to the archive afforded the twenty-first century writer and reader. Bioluminescence is synecdochic of these connections and interruptions across and through the time of the novel. Sightings of what we now term bioluminescence have been recorded since antiquity but as noted by the great scholar of bioluminescence, E. Newton Harvey, it is in modern times that Western observers have recorded the spectacle in ecstatic terms.[7] The European Age of Sail (1571–1862) witnessed a proliferation of accounts: James Cook (11 June 1770), Georg Forster, Joseph Banks (4–5 January 1869) and Charles Darwin all record encounters in their journals; those of Forster and Darwin are especially poetic.[8] Bernard Smith (1956) provides a detailed study of the correspondences between the descriptions given

---

7   E. Newton Harvey, *A History of Luminescence: From the Earliest Times to 1900* (Philadelphia: American Philosophical Society, 1957) 508–509.
8   See Darwin's journal entry of 24 October 1832, as the *Beagle* approaches Cape Horn and he observes bioluminescent plankton: "The night was pitch dark, with a fresh breeze. – The sea from its extreme luminousness presented a wonderful & most beautiful appearance; every part of the water, which by day is seen as foam, glowed with a pale light. The vessel drove before her bows two billows of liquid phosphorus, & in her wake was a milky train. – As far as

2 Bioluminescence: Materiality, Metaphor and Trace in *Sixty Lights*

by Cook and Forster and Coleridge's description of the phosphorous ocean in "The Rime of the Ancient Mariner" (1798).[9]

> Beyond the shadow of the ship,
> I watched the water-snakes:
> They moved in tracks of shining white,
>   And when they reared, the elfish light
>   Fell off in hoary flakes.
>
> Within the shadow of the ship
> I watched their rich attire:
> Blue, glossy green, and velvet black,
>   They coiled and swam;
>   and every track
>   Was a flash of golden fire.

Coleridge's poem is directly referenced in *Sixty Lights* in the concluding section of the chapter that opens with the bioluminescent vision. The later scene, which "she later read[s] as an ill omen", includes the capture and slaughter of three albatross. Lucy witnesses the birds' "shocked dying eyes, glazed by betrayal" (113), just as Coleridge's Ancient Mariner betrays and kills the joyful albatross on his voyage. Betrayal is integral to both texts but the sequence of vision and betrayal is reversed; Lucy's vision of the bioluminescent ocean precedes the betrayal of the birds and of Lucy by Crawley, whereas the Mariner's vision is in the wake of his senseless killing.

The allusive engagement with Coleridge's iconic poem of bioluminescent vision, itself referent to the interconnections between science, discovery and poetry of the Enlightenment, traces the connected legacies into their Victorian heritage of the novel's setting and the time of the novel (2004) as well as the historical futures of all three. One of many such proleptic and analeptic manipulations in *Sixty Lights*, these processions through historical time draw lines of continuity between the pre- and post-industrial experience and understanding and between their organic and mechanical forms. Ironically, they also question narratives of progress, fundamental to the logic of modernity. From the Eduardo Cadava epigraph that prefaces part 1 of the novel, the technologies of modernity celebrated in *Sixty Lights* are located within their deep histories. Cadava writes: "There has never been a time without the photograph, without the residue and

---

    the eye reached, the crest of every wave was bright; & from the reflected light, the sky just above the horizon was not so utterly dark as the rest of the Heavens".

9   See also Arnd Bohm, "Georg Forster's A Voyage Round the World as a Source for 'The Rime of the Ancient Mariner': A Reconsideration", *ELH* 50, no. 2 (1983): 363–77.

writing of light".[10] So, too, Lucy is presented as having always been a photographer well before she encounters or practises photography. As a child she experiments by burning holes with her magnifying glass. Later in time but recorded earlier in the novel, she awakes from a night terror after witnessing a man falling to his death from a building, pierced with a large piece of glass. This anachronistic moment "greets her with the blinding flash of a magnesium ribbon" (5).[11]

The anachronistic use of the word bioluminescence extends the text's reach across time into futurity. In her analysis of *Sixty Lights* alongside Jane Campion's *The Piano*, Sukhmani Khorana "frame[s] time such that the over-exposed past becomes the blank page of the future".[12] Punning on the photographic sense of *over-exposure*, where film is exposed to too much light, and its more general sense of over-use, "over-exposure" can also be understood in terms of the novel's saturation with information, allusions, intertexts and multiple generic forms. In this pun Khorana identifies the potential to re-write and re-imagine colonial and gendered history into new futures. Ironically, then, the placement of a word from the narrative's future does not merely anticipate that future but shapes it. This futural reach extends beyond the time of the word's actual coinage in the early twentieth century and into the reader's imagined futures as well. For it disrupts teleological linearity and performs instead a process in which multiple potential futures, at radical variance from expected progressions of the present, are imagined. For, as utopian writers and theorists have shown us, idealistic futures require the relentless *process* of this imagining *not* the pursuit of a defined static goal.[13] The proleptic naming of "bioluminescence" and its traversal of multiple temporalities – the narrative, the actual coinage, the times of writing and of reading *Sixty Lights* – releases the word "bioluminescence" from the limitations of historical discourse. Its futurity fends off the fetishisation and reification of the past by the acknowledged uncertainty and unrealised possibilities of projected time. Moreover, these irresolutions and possibilities fold back into the temporalities of past and present. This process leads us to another ironic prolepsis that post-dates the text itself. For *Sixty Lights*, published in 2004, accords its

---

10 Eduardo Cadava, *Words of Light: Theses on the Photography of History* (Princeton, NJ: Princeton University Press, 2018) 11.
11 For a history of the development of magnesium ribbon for photography, see A.S. Darling, "Non-Ferrous Metals", in *An Encyclopedia of the History of Technology*, ed. Ian McNeil (London: Routledge, 2002), 113–116.
12 Sukhmani Khorana, "Photography, Cinema and Time in Jane Campion's *The Piano* and Gail Jones' *Sixty Lights*", Outskirts: Feminisms Along the Edge 16 (2007), http://www.chloe.uwa.edu.au/outskirts/archive/volume16/khorana
13 For two key analyses of utopian thought and method, see Louis Marin, "Frontiers of Utopia. Past and Present", *Critical Inquiry* 19, no. 3 (1993): 197–220, and Fredric Jameson, "Of Islands and Trenches: Neutralization and the Production of Utopian Discourse", *Diacritics* 7, no. 2 (Summer 1977): 2–21.

human subjects with the force of bioluminescence, five years before scientific research confirmed its existence using a highly sensitive imaging system by way of a cryogenic charge-coupled device (CCD) camera.[14]

As noted above in the comparison between Lucy and the Ancient Mariner's apprehension of the phosphorescent ocean, *Sixty Lights* experiments with the sequence, fracture and coalescence of experience in and over time from the moment to long histories. From the first fragment that opens the novel, in which the man falls to his death punctured by the glass mirror he held, the text records the non-alignment of immediate experience, emotion and understanding. Lucy's first involuntary response to the ghastly scene is to think of a photograph. It is only later that night that she "rise[s] in distress" (4). The photograph and fragment are the textual figures for the ways sequential experience can be held in a moment, an image or a trace. In this opening scene, the text also upscales this movement between compression and diffusion relative to the whole narrative by folding future events into the moment, including Lucy's own premature death in the penultimate chapter.

Sixty Lights insists on the imperatives of sequential experience and history while simultaneously undoing them, as in the scene of Lucy's bioluminescent vision. Lucy and the Ancient Mariner's respective apprehensions of the bioluminescent ocean mirror their particular and different conditions of being at the time of their experience. Sequence is also complicated by the related but distinctive conceptions of interactivity or reflexivity between subject or viewer and the natural phenomena they witness. For the Mariner, whose apprehension of phosphorus occurs after disaster has struck, he sees the lights as an effect of the "rotting sea". This analogue is a form of pathetic fallacy: "as a man is, so he sees", according to the great eighteenth-century poet of optics, William Blake:[15] "man" precedes the vision and determines its qualities.

The relationship between Lucy and the phenomenon she witnesses is tellingly different. The image of her standing on the ship's deck at night apprehending a vision of bioluminescence on the surface of the vast ocean presents a gendered

---

14 See M. Kobayashi, D. Kikuchi, H. Okamura, "Imaging of Ultraweak Spontaneous Photon Emission from Human Body Displaying Diurnal Rhythm", *PLoS ONE* 4, no. 7 (2009): e6256, https://doi.org/10.1371/journal.pone.0006256. "The human body literally glimmers. The intensity of the light emitted by the body is 1000 times lower than the sensitivity of our naked eyes. Ultraweak photon emission is known as the energy released as light through the changes in energy metabolism. We successfully imaged the diurnal change of this ultraweak photon emission with an improved highly sensitive imaging system using cryogenic charge-coupled device (CCD) camera. We found that the human body directly and rhythmically emits light. The diurnal changes in photon emission might be linked to changes in energy metabolism."

15 William Blake, Letter to Reverend Dr Trusler (1799), in *The Complete Poetry and Prose of William Blake*, eds David V. Erdman and Harold Bloom (New York: Double Day Anchor Books, 1988), 702.

reworking of the Romantic sublime. Akin to the iconic image of the sublime, Friedrich's Wanderer (1818), Lucy stands with her back to the viewer – including both Crawley and the reader – gazing out into the awesome expanse of light and obscurity. So, too, the sequence of her responses aligns with that theorised by Burke in his treatise on the sublime – in which he deploys the pervasive metaphor of light as clarity and reason.[16] In Burke's formulation the viewer's physical response to arresting phenomena at first prohibits articulation, as occurs for Lucy. In *Sixty Lights*, language at first fails to meet or explain the scene or her responses. The progression follows the logic and telos of sequential time: apprehension precedes comprehension, just as Crawley's verbal utterance names and answers Lucy's unuttered question regarding the phenomenon she observes. A year later in the narrative, Lucy is again voyaging by ship, now on her way home from India with her young baby, Ellen. She contemplates "what had been given to her to see" in this period of time. She feels that she has achieved "some degree of understanding … The word was bioluminescence" (117). She then catalogues instances of this experience. Here, then, is the comprehension that may follow prehension and apprehension.

In *Sixty Lights*, however, the relational dynamics of the scene differ profoundly from the Romantic schematic and its assumptions about being in the world. Lucy's state of being and her initial response is better described by what Alfred Whitehead termed "prehension", which he defines as an "uncognitive apprehension".[17] For Whitehead, "prehension" is not limited to living, self-conscious beings. Rather, it is a kind of conscious or unconscious perception that applies to living entities from humans to sub-atomic particles. As such, prehension differs markedly from the Romantic encounter between the human subject and Nature in which the human perceiver projects the self onto an aspect of natural phenomena to have that self-confirmed, magnified and returned to him (sic), as occurs with the Mariner.

In the shipboard scene, Lucy's expansive openness and receptivity contrasts with the projection or imposition of self onto the landscape. She is not seeking confirmation of selfhood. She is, rather, a subject in perpetual process, in a state of becoming, just as she is in transit on the voyage and on the threshold of

---

16 See Edmund Burke, *A Philosophical Enquiry into the Origin of Our Ideas of the Sublime and Beautiful of 1756* (Oxford: Oxford University Press, 2015). In addition to discussions of the role of light in predicting sublime effects in Sections XIV to XVIII (114–20), he refers multiple times to the "light of reason" and also to the "light and glory and that flows from the divine presence" (66).
17 The prehension refers to "pre-epistemic" experience in that it is yet to be located in a system of knowledge, see *Science in the Material World* (69), an operation Crawley achieves in part by the act of naming. See Alfred Whitehead, *Science and the Modern World* (New York: The Free Press, 1967), 69.

experience. She is intensely alive in and to the world. Her experience of the bioluminescence is interactive, a transmission between living organisms. One is not merely an analogue of the other for they are organically connected. The processual quality of this experience is also a kind of repetition as well as a sequence. In philosophical terms, the relationship between Lucy and the bioluminescent scene is akin to Deleuze and Guattari's concept of an assemblage or rhizome, which focuses on the relational structures between entities rather than their status as separate objects (1987). So, too, these assemblages can be understood as "multiplicities", structures that form and re-form without reference to a prior or future whole. We can read the relationship between Lucy and William Crawley in these terms. For it is another formation of bioluminescent exchange, now manifest in a sexual connection. As a relationship that breaches numerous social rules, that "has no future" according to conventional patterns, it does not refer to a prior or future whole.

Lucy's seduction in the wake – or midst – of bioluminescent prehension establishes the connection between the organic light of bioluminescence and sexual desire and experience, which is sustained throughout the novel. Lucy's oceanic vision is a prelude to her first sexual experience with Crawley and her sexual awakening. Making this link in a touching, cumbersome way, Lucy lies musing on the revelation of passion and of her own body after the first sexual encounter. She then whispers to her lover: "Tell me more … about bioluminescence" (112). He dismisses her request on the basis that she would not understand the requisite science, which is a discrete body of knowledge. For Lucy, however, new knowledge, which she is more than capable of understanding, is charged with desire not distinct from it.

Isaac Newton's parting gift to Lucy, as she leaves India to return to England, presents a related but distinctive kind of erotic, bioluminescent transmission. The painted miniature depicting the God Krishna and his consort Radha includes real beetle wings cut and fixed to Radha's chest. The beetle wings are literally bioluminescent and Lucy is surprised by the eroticism of the gift, speculating that the gift may be "freighted with the passion he wished to express". Again, organic bioluminescence is directly connected with eros, though in this expression it is stylised into that most objectified of objects – a miniature. This miniature is a metonym of converted or translated "passion" and the conduit of this expression between Isaac and Lucy. This miniature artwork, itself a translation of a sacred narrative, contains the literal trace of organic bioluminescence. This image in its "radical particularity", but others also in theirs, may carry organic bioluminescent charge, creative transmittable energy.

Finally, towards the end of the novel when Lucy imagines seducing her lover Jacob, she contemplates the mutual pleasure of "teach[ing] him all the forms of bioluminescence" (219) and this is the single word she speaks to him when she later does so (232). In addition to sexual tuition in this context, "all the forms of bioluminescence" refers to the wide range of creative energies Lucy lists on the voyage from India to England. Enraptured by her baby and re-examining the miniature of Krishna, Lucy has come to understand:

> The word was bioluminescence. There was in every living thing this elusive capacity. In lovers. In the newborn. In the congregation at a temple. In the man who was killed by a mirror and lay on his back looking at death. Every person was a lighthouse, a signal of presence. This was nothing sentimental: it was the single wise thing that she utterly knew. It was the knowledge that would carry her through a night of deathly terror – when the ship pitched fearfully, the timbers groaned, objects shattered everywhere and dangerously flew, many sailors wept with fear and called out to Heaven – to the surprising egg yellow of a dawn becalmed. (171)

Bioluminescence is a "capacity" in "every living thing". As an "elusive capacity", it needs to be discovered and activated. It is also a "signal of presence", an immanence. This immanent and corporeal knowledge is gained in the transmissions between minds and bodies, between the relentless interconnections between material and psychic domains, between Being and Knowledge and between all living matter. In key ways these qualities and operations recall the medieval philosophical concept of haecceity, the "thisness" or "radical particularity" of each thing,[18] which directly informed Gerard Manley Hopkins' formulation of inscape and instress, the enactment and the recognition of the individual design of creation.[19] It later informed Deleuze and Guattari's formulation of the assemblage and multiplicity discussed above.[20] I hear a literal

---

18 See Richard Cross, "Medieval Theories of Haecceity", in *Stanford Encyclopedia of Philosophy*, ed. Edward N. Zalta (Summer 2014 Edition), https://plato.stanford.edu/archives/sum2014/entries/medieval-haecceity/
19 Stephen Greenblatt et al., ed., "Gerard Manley Hopkins". *The Norton Anthology of English Literature*, 8th ed, vol. 2 (New York, London: W.W. Norton & Company, 2006), 2159. "[Hopkins] felt that everything in the universe was characterized by what he called *inscape*, the distinctive design that constitutes individual identity. This identity is not static but dynamic. Each being in the universe 'selves,' that is, enacts its identity. And the human being, the most highly selved, the most individually distinctive being in the universe, recognizes the inscape of other beings in an act that Hopkins calls *instress*, the apprehension of an object in an intense thrust of energy toward it that enables one to realize specific distinctiveness. Ultimately, the instress of inscape leads one to Christ, for the individual identity of any object is the stamp of divine creation on it."
20 See "Memories of a Haecceity", in Gilles Deleuze and F. Guattari, *A Thousand Plateaus*, trans. Brian Massumi (Minneapolis: University of Minnesota Press, 1987), 261. "[H]ere is a mode of individuation very different from that of a person, subject, thing, or substance. We reserve the

echo between the cadence and meaning of "every living thing" (above) and Hopkins' sonnet "As Kingfishers Catch Fire, Dragonflies Draw Flame": "*Each mortal thing* does one thing and the same:/ Deals out that being indoors each one dwells;" (Hopkins 65, italics mine).[21]

Other echoes are summoned by the repeated statement "The word was bioluminescence". The assertion can stress either subject or object. If the object is stressed, the sense is that "the word [best fit to describe this phenomenon or experience] is bioluminescence". If the subject is stressed, the sentence focuses on the relationship between the *word* bioluminescence and the "elusive capacity" of a life force. The invitation of this second sense is provocative because, as we have learned from structuralism onwards, language is a cultural structure, in which every word is a form of metaphor by dint of the way it stands in for something else. Moreover, the repeated claim "The word was bioluminescence" echoes the assertion of the Logos that opens St John's gospel: "In the beginning was the Word, and the Word was with God, and the *Word was God*" (italics mine). Does *Sixty Lights* replace God with bioluminescence as an originary metaphor or assert that the word has presence in and of itself?

If the two senses are both considered, the statement works to destabilise the opposition between language and nature. As Vicki Kirby astutely observes in her rethinking of structuralism in *Becoming Flesh*, "once you are seriously displacing the nature/language opposition, you have to be arguing that nature, far from being written on, and insofar as it cannot be said to 'lack language', must be articulate".[22] Conversely, Derrida argues for the "animality of the letter", as "the primary and infinite equivocality of the signifier as Life".

As noted above, *Sixty Lights* refuses the linear telos of chronology and narrative as the main direction or path towards meaning by presaging Lucy's death in precise terms in the first chapter. Although bioluminescent light is quite commonly observed in some dead fish – the effect of living bacteria on the fish – *Sixty Lights* explicitly refuses the connection between bioluminescence and death. When in India, Lucy is moved to try and re-experience bioluminescence when she reads news of a dead elephant. "If there is light visible in posthumous flesh, she reasoned, then it will be visible on this scale with this mountainous beast" (143). What she witnesses is a grotesque travesty of emanating organic light:

---

name haecceity for it. A season, a winter, a summer, an hour, a date have a perfect individuality lacking nothing, even though this individuality is different from that of a thing or a subject. They are haecceities in the sense that they consist entirely of relations of movement and rest between molecules or particles, capacities to affect and be affected."

21 Gerard Manley Hopkins, *The Poems of Gerard Manley Hopkins*, eds W.H. Gardner and N.H. MacKenzie, 4th ed. (London: Oxford University Press, 1967), 90.
22 Kirby, Vicki. *Telling Flesh: The Substance of the Corporeal*. (London and New York: Routledge, 1997), 90.

There was no shine but that of viscera; there was nothing lovely and bright. There was no redeeming conversion of death into luminescent surface. It was only a mass of putrescence, a butchered mess. (144)

Lucy corrects this absence and death in a dream that same night. In the dream she photographs the elephant. Through her viewfinder she sees into the elephant's body to a beating heart. As she takes the photograph, the elephant rises and shuffles away, alive. Her wish is fulfilled by a photograph taken in a dream. The photograph restores life albeit in another dimension of being.

Lucy's body, too, becomes host to bacteria, *mycobacterium tuberculosis*, which kills her. This luminous heroine is framed by her death from the outset. In this way, the text refuses the fundamental opposition of life and death. As a photographer, Lucy re-animates the dead and the past, while showing us the image of death. So, too, death is a part of life not an opposition to it, as for Epicurus. And finally, it is an immersion in and return to light. The text's reworking of the originary photological metaphor of philosophy, knowledge and clarity does not reverse the dying of the light of reason with the light of redemptive non-consciousness but presents the continuance of their multiplicities.

References

Banks, Joseph. *The Endeavour Journal of Sir Joseph Banks*, 25 August 1768–12 July 1771.
Biron, Kaan. "Fireflies, Dead Fish and a Glowing Bunny: a Primer on Bioluminescence." *BioTeach Online Journal*. 1 (Fall 2003) www.bioteach.ubc.ca
Bohm, Arnd. "Georg Forster's *A Voyage Round the World* as a Source for 'The Rime of the Ancient Mariner': A Reconsideration." *ELH* 50, no. 2 (1983): 363–77.
Cadava, Eduardo. *Words of Light: Theses on the Photography of History*. Princeton, NJ: Princeton University Press, 2018.
Deleuze, Gilles and Félix Guattari. *A Thousand Plateaus*. (1991) Translated by Brian Massumi. Minneapolis: University of Minnesota Press, 1994.
Derrida, Jacques. "Force and Signification." In *Writing and Difference*, translated by Alan Bass, 3–30. Chicago: Chicago University Press, 1980.
Greenblatt, Stephen. "Gerard Manley Hopkins." *The Norton Anthology of English Literature*. 8th ed. Vol. 2. New York, London: W.W. Norton & Company, 2006, 2145–2160.
Forster, Georg. *A Voyage Round the World*. London: B. White, J. Robson, P. Elmsly and G. Robertson. 1777. Gale Eighteenth Century Collections Online.
Hopkins, Gerard Manley. *The Poems of Gerard Manley Hopkins*, edited by W.H. Gardner and N.H. MacKenzie. 4th ed. London: Oxford University Press, 1967.
Jacobs, Lyn Janette. "Gail Jones' 'light writing': Memory and the Photo-graph." *JASAL: Journal of the Association for the Study of Australian Literature* 5 (2006). https://openjournals.library.sydney.edu.au/index.php/JASAL/article/view/10180
Jameson, Fredric. "Of Islands and Trenches: Neutralization and the Production of Utopian Discourse." *Diacritics* 7, no. 2 (Summer 1977): 2–21.
Jones, Gail. *Sixty Lights*. London: Vintage, 2005.

Kelley, Lindsay and Eva Hayward. "Carnal Light." *Parallax* 19, no. 1 (2013): 114–27.
Kirby, Vicki. *Telling Flesh: The Substance of the Corporeal*. London and New York: Routledge, 1997.
Kobayashi, Masaki, Daisuke Kikuchi and Hitoshi Okamura. "Imaging of Ultraweak Spontaneous Photon Emission from Human Body Displaying Diurnal Rhythm." *PLoS ONE* 4, no. 7 (2009): e6256. https://doi.org/10.1371/journal.pone.0006256
Khorana, Sukhmani. "Photography, Cinema and Time in Jane Campion's *The Piano* and Gail Jones' *Sixty Lights*." *Outskirts: Feminisms Along the Edge* 16 (2007). http://www.chloe.uwa.edu.au/outskirts/archive/volume16/khorana
Marin, Louis. "Frontiers of Utopia. Past and Present." *Critical Inquiry* 19, no. 3 (1993): 197–220.
Smith, Bernard. "Coleridge's Ancient Mariner and Cook's Second Voyage." *Journal of the Warburg and Courtauld Institutes* 19, no. 1–2 (1956): 117–54.
Whitehead, Alfred. *Science and the Modern World*. New York: The Free Press, 1967.

3

Gail Jones' Novel Modernism: *Sixty Lights* and Literary Tradition

James Gourley

While it is not possible to pin Gail Jones down, as novelist and scholar, to any one particular aesthetic-intellectual category of interest or writerly methodology, it is possible to document her consistent engagement with modernism broadly construed. Jones' novels, for instance, include engagement with various elements of modernism: in *Black Mirror* (2002), the presence of Surrealists such as André Breton; in *Dreams of Speaking* (2006), Alice Black's work on the "poetics of modernity"; and, *A Guide to Berlin*'s (2015) focus on the stories and novels of Vladimir Nabokov. Jones' scholarship broadly addresses modernity and acknowledges a range of modernist interlocutors, including Franz Kafka and Walter Benjamin.[1] Jones has also spoken specifically of her commitment to modernism; in a 2012 interview with Maria del Pilar Royo Grasa, she said: "I think of myself as a modernist writer … The assumptions that I make about where meaning lies, and how writing matters are probably high modernist".[2]

The focus of this chapter is Jones' second novel, *Sixty Lights* (2004). The novel takes place primarily in the 1860s, set in London (a city, as Lucy Strange calls it, of "radical modernity"), but also in the colonial "peripheries" of Melbourne in Australia and Bombay in India.[3] *Sixty Lights* is a novel imbued with the electric innovation of modernism: the novel's sixty sections build up, non-chronologically,

---

James Gourley, Gail Jones' Novel Modernism: *Sixty Lights* and Literary Tradition. In *Inner and Outer Worlds: Gail Jones' Fiction*, edited by Anthony Uhlmann. Sydney: Sydney University Press, 2022. DOI: 10.30722/sup.9781743327791

---

1 See Gail Jones, "A Dreaming, A Sauntering: Re-Imagining Critical Paradigms", *JASAL: Journal of the Association for the Study of Australian Literature* 5 (2006): 11–24; Gail Jones, "'Growing Small Wings': Walter Benjamin, Lola Ridge, and the Political Affect of Modernism", *Affirmations: Of The Modern* 1, no. 2 (Spring 2014): 120–42.
2 Maria del Pilar Royo Grasa, "In Conversation with Gail Jones", *JASAL: Journal of the Association for the Study of Australian Literature* 12, no. 3 (2012): 6.

the story of Lucy Strange; her parents, her brother, her life. The novel is shot through with temporal manipulation: Lucy's death, for instance, is presaged on the novel's second page. *Sixty Lights*' focus upon the various emergent technologies of photography links to its reflections upon time, and manipulations therein, which is surely one of the most notable of modernist preoccupations. In a 2005 interview, Jones described *Sixty Lights* as "anachronistic … it has a mimicry of Victorian time but in fact is a modernist text".[4] Considering the modernism that appears integral to parts of *Sixty Lights*, and that the author herself ascribes it, this chapter considers the question of *Sixty Lights*' apparently anachronistic modernism: how is a novel set in the nineteenth century modernist? How is a novel whose primary intertexts are popular Victorian novels (Charlotte Brontë's *Jane Eyre* [1847] and Charles Dickens' *Great Expectations* [1860–1]) modernist? How does a novel which focuses so thoroughly on the Victorian trope of inheritance perform its modernism? What exactly is the modernism that Jones attributes to *Sixty Lights*?

There are straightforward responses to these questions which it is necessary to acknowledge and set to the side before commencing. First, while modernism can be defined as a series of intermingling but separate intellectual and artistic movements occurring in Europe and America roughly in the period between the two world wars, a large body of scholarship points out that modernism is not a single movement or moment, and that it is not bound to a particular time or place.[5] In this sense, *Sixty Lights* is easily spoken of as modernist; this does not, however, address Jones' avowed commitment to "high" modernism, which appears contradictory, especially considering the role of Victorian themes and texts in *Sixty Lights*.

Second, an alternative approach might be to read *Sixty Lights* as a postmodernist text; one that takes the aesthetic and conceptual material of the Victorian period and repurposes it for the twenty-first century (readings of the novel which consider it an appropriation of *Jane Eyre*, for instance, might be understood as developing this reading, if only by implication).[6] The major theoretical touchstone for this approach is Linda Hutcheon's "historiographical

---

3   Gail Jones, *Sixty Lights* (2004; London: Vintage, 2005), 184. All subsequent references are to this edition and appear in parentheses in the text.
4   ABC Radio National, "Gail Jones", Interview and reading, 27 March 2005. https://www.abc.net.au/radionational/programs/archived/booksandwriting/gail-jones/3630050#transcript.
5   For an overview of this scholarship, see Douglas Mao and Rebecca L. Walkowitz, "The New Modernist Studies", *Publications of the Modern Language Association* 123, no. 3 (May 2008): 737–48.
6   See, for instance, Alexandra Lewis, "The Ethics of Appropriation; Or, the 'Mere Spectre' of Jane Eyre: Emma Tennant's *Thornfield Hall*, Jasper Fforde's *The Eyre Affair* and Gail Jones' *Sixty Lights*", in *Charlotte Brontë: Legacies and Afterlives*, ed. Amber K. Regis and Deborah Wynne (Manchester: Manchester University Press, 2017), 197–220.

metafiction" developed in *A Poetics of Postmodernism* (1988). While it is possible to read *Sixty Lights* in relation to historiographic metafiction, Jones' novel is very different to those texts that truly fit Hutcheon's classification. Hutcheon's analysis is focused on postmodern texts which "use and abuse ... intertextual echoes, inscribing their powerful allusions and then subverting that power through irony".[7] *Sixty Lights* is not ironic in this way, and, in fact, partakes of a modernist sincerity for the work of art, which is exactly what Hutcheon positions historiographic metafiction against.[8] My position accords with that proposed by Kate Mitchell in her discussion of the role of Victorian literary texts in *History and Cultural Memory in Neo-Victorian Fiction* (2010). There Mitchell notes the function of Hutcheon's historiographic metafiction is to privilege "those texts that focus on the constructedness of representation and renders any attempt to non-ironically revive the past as nostalgic, and critically suspect".[9] Rather, as Mitchell argues, *Sixty Lights* and other "Neo-Victorian" novels that re-read Victorian texts do so without irony, seeing these texts as "a cultural memory, to be re-membered, and imaginatively re-created, not revised or understood".[10] Again, this chapter sets these postmodern questions aside, whether regarding historiographic metafiction or Neo-Victorian fiction, because they do not satisfactorily address Jones' career-long preoccupation with modernism, nor her statements about *Sixty Lights*' modernism.

Before proceeding, it is necessary to outline the chapter's animating questions and its broad thesis. It asks, what is the modernism that Jones attributes to *Sixty Lights*? How might this identification of *Sixty Lights* as modernist clarify the understanding of what modernism is and what it does? This chapter pursues these questions by proposing that *Sixty Lights* amalgamates a nineteenth-century frame of literary reference with a twentieth-century technological-theoretical apparatus (i.e. photography as well as more routinely modernist temporal manipulation within the narrative), so as to present a contemporary text which is a "maculate" version of both traditions. In doing so, it relates the Victorian novel tradition to the modernist texts that came after it, and illustrates the modernist orientation that can be seen in texts like *Jane Eyre* and *Great Expectations*, which are rarely engaged with outside their Victorian context.

In short, if *Sixty Lights* is a novel engaged with modernism and modernity, then its modernism is novel; and I hope to evoke two senses of this word.

---

7 Linda Hutcheon, *A Poetics of Postmodernism: History, Theory, Fiction* (New York: Routledge, 1988), 118.
8 Hutcheon, *A Poetics of Postmodernism*, 118.
9 Kate Mitchell, *History and Cultural Memory in Neo-Victorian Fiction* (Houndmills: Palgrave Macmillan, 2010), 33.
10 Mitchell, *History and Cultural Memory in Neo-Victorian Fiction*, 7.

First, *Sixty Lights*' modernism is novel, in the sense of being new, a departure, in its acknowledgement of modernism's nineteenth-century precursors and its post–World War Two endurance. Second, *Sixty Lights*' modernism is derived from the novel form itself, from the "novel tradition" as Ian Watt calls it; that is, *Sixty Lights* treats the nineteenth-century novel like it does photography. The Victorian novel tradition is *Sixty Light*'s own particular generative technology; a technology of modernity which prompts *Sixty Lights* to its experimental twenty-first century modernism.

Emotional Inheritance in Sixty Lights

Both *Jane Eyre* and *Great Expectations* enter the lives of *Sixty Lights*' characters via inheritance. This is especially appropriate considering that inheritance is a key theme in both these Victorian classics: Jane remains without inheritance until the final chapters of *Jane Eyre* and it is only after her good character has been confirmed that her changed financial circumstances are revealed. The origin of Pip's inheritance is the major mystery of *Great Expectations*, and Pip's easy access to money is a key moral challenge in the narrative. Inheritance is also a primary focus for scholars addressing Victorian texts' attitudes to gender and colonialism, as well as literary-aesthetic questions regarding the reception and influence of Victorian texts in contemporary literature. Writing on Victorian sensation fiction, but with broad application, Jessica Cox states: "[i]nheritance, then, serves as a means of exploring a range of issues in the Victorian sensation novel, including social hierarchies, identity, madness, and women's rights".[11] Cox also notes: "[t]he pervasiveness of the inheritance theme in Victorian sensation fiction marks it out as a defining motif of the genre and reflects broader Victorian concerns about law, identity, origins, justice, and shifting social orders".[12] While adapting elements from *Jane Eyre* and *Great Expectations*, *Sixty Lights* is also the beneficiary of its Victorian inheritance. Jones' novel questions and rejects rigid Victorian hierarchies. In doing so, it endorses a more unruly vision of Victorian texts and thus claims a progressive legacy – aesthetic and political – for the Victorian novel.

In *Sixty Lights*, *Jane Eyre* follows a matrilineal path of inheritance; Brontë's novel is Honoria Brady's, then is passed on to her daughter, Lucy, and then on to Violet Strange, Thomas' wife and the surrogate mother of Lucy's daughter, Ellen. The reader expects, in the narrative's future, that Ellen will take solace from *Jane Eyre*'s story: of inner good enduring and thriving despite the challenge of

---

11 Jessica Cox, *Neo-Victorianism and Sensation Fiction* (Cham: Palgrave Macmillan, 2019), 197.
12 Cox, *Neo-Victorianism and Sensation Fiction*, 197.

a parent's death. *Great Expectations* is passed on to Lucy and Thomas in a less conventional fashion: it is, in effect, the first true gift their uncle, Neville Brady, is able to give them. *Great Expectations* is a gift that imparts on both Lucy and Thomas the love of reading and of stories, and is allied to their gradual realisation of Neville's happy suitability in the role of foster-father. The linking of love – for the novel and for Neville – is performed in the family's shared joy in Joe Gargery's humble phrase, "partickler when he see the ghost", a joke they will repeat throughout their lives (85). The inheritance Lucy and Thomas accept as a consequence of their parents' deaths is particularly literary; revealingly, this inheritance relates specifically to their own lives: they inherit two novels about parentless children. Both books are sentimental favourites and thus evoked and re-evoked throughout their lives and *Sixty Lights*.

The reader first encounters *Jane Eyre* through Honoria Strange's passionate experience of it. Brontë's novel is encapsulating: "No thing distracted [Honoria] … She travelled *Jane Eyre* … *I am Jane Eyre*, she secretly told herself" (12; italics original). The reader discovers that on the first night of their marriage "Honoria told her lover Arthur Strange the entire plot of Charlotte Brontë's famous novel, *Jane Eyre*. Her triangle-shaped face lit up as she spoke. She was impassioned, fixated; she knew whole paragraphs by heart" (16). Indeed, *Jane Eyre* underpins all that we discover of Honoria Brady. It constitutes both her youthful joys and her later disappointments:

> What Honoria could not tell Arthur was that the world, since Italy, had been terribly disappointing. Her reading had established great expectations: books led her to believe that adventure was everywhere to be had, that catastrophes, coincidences and conjugal excitations abounded, that lives were melodramatically enhanced and symbolically underwritten. After their metaphoric beginning … their lives had become rather literal and prosaic … In the coach she had been another Jane Eyre, full of self-righteous destiny and bound-for-glory; but now she thought, with ridiculous intensity, of the locked-away madwoman. She was assailed by an indistinct sense of imprisonment and remembered almost daily the character who chose immolation. How could she tell Arthur that he had confined and immobilised her? (61–2)

While by the time of her death Honoria Brady remains ensconced within Brontë's universe, it is Rochester's first wife, rather than Jane, that is her literary interlocutor. Constrained, dominated, and unhappy, *Jane Eyre* presages her death.

In addition to Lucy's inheritance of Honoria's passionate admiration for Brontë's novel, Lucy also inherits the specific object as well. In the wake of her mother's death, Lucy discovers a cache of "mother-things", which includes a "copy of *Jane Eyre*, with passages underlined" (45). Lucy is also described in relation to Jane Eyre. When this occurs, the novel determinedly points out that Lucy *is not* Jane: as a young woman, Lucy is "not well educated enough to apply for work as a governess", and upon her arrival in Bombay, Isaac Newton feels "embarrassed and put-upon, and inwardly cursed Neville Brady, who in his letter had promised a mature woman of thirty, chaste and well educated. A governess, he had written, a governess, chaste and well educated, as in a Brontë novel" (99; 128). *Jane Eyre* returns to the fore in *Sixty Light*'s final stages, as Lucy moves towards her death. Lucy's thoughts turn to her parents, and she "remember[s] Honoria's] inordinate fondness for the novel *Jane Eyre* …". Lucy, despite suffering from tuberculosis, "read[s] aloud to [Violet] from the sentimental novel, *Jane Eyre*" while Ellen listens and plays on the floor, an act of willed inheritance (228). *Jane Eyre* is presented as a story integral to generations; a novel orientational in its consequence for the independent women of the Strange family.

Lucy and Thomas Strange inherit *Great Expectations* from their uncle and father-substitute, Neville Brady, after their parents' deaths. Unlike Lucy's inheritance of *Jane Eyre*, which takes places after Honoria's death, Lucy and Thomas inherit *Great Expectations* from Neville at the point that he is transformed into a parent, Dickens' novel revealing previously "hidden resources of play as well as parenthood" (85). Before their familial bonding over *Great Expectations*, Neville is generally unsatisfactory as a parent; he is untrustworthy and unable to meet the requirements placed upon him. And yet, when both children are ill, he is transformed in his reading of Dickens' story:

> [Neville] waited at their bedsides with handkerchiefs and balm, told funny stories about his childhood, and read aloud from Dickens as the invalids settled for bedtime. The brand-new serial, *Great Expectations*, unfolded each night – "his best yet!" – a story driven by the tremulous anxiety of destiny unknown. Thomas called himself Pip for a while, but Lucy too wanted to be Pip and resented his claim. The novel made London seem altogether more actual and they were all delighted that Dickens had mentioned Australia: it validated an existence others here took as vague conjecture. (83–4)

As with *Jane Eyre*, the details of the narrative are key to what Lucy and Thomas inherit. They inherit an ability to embody the *Great Expectations* story; not just to enjoy it, but to exist imaginatively within the narrative, as Pip. *Great Expectations* is not only an important inheritance for the Strange children because of the bond it solidifies between children and foster-father; it also makes the children perceive their life in London as more convincing, more real: only pages before they reflect upon their experience in this new city: "The Houses of Parliament,

London Bridge, the Tower of London: each was too monumental to be anything other than fictitious" (82). Seeing their new home portrayed in fiction allows the Stranges to perceive the place as "altogether more actual", just as hearing the references to Australia confirms for them the reality and the consequence of their previous existence (82).

Both novels exist shadowed by the parents' deaths, but also aid in Lucy and Thomas' attempts at mediating other losses. Thomas is alone in London at the time of Neville's sad accident which leads to his death. (Prior to his death, Neville had been speaking companionably of his hopes for Lucy's unborn child: Neville imagines Lucy nursing a boy with "Great Expectations: he would make a fortune by the time he was eighteen years old" [182].) Thomas does not describe his active mourning for Neville; instead, he describes his participation in the mourning of Charles Dickens' death instead – "a small act of self-protection" – where Thomas "stood in a line with thousands of others filing into Westminster Abbey, and felt the dignity of the occasion, and its ceremony, and its historical importance" (172). While Neville's death does not have these features, Thomas mourns Dickens and Neville together. After Violet Strange's miscarriage – which activates again for Lucy all her repressed memories of Honoria Brady's death during childbirth – "Lucy read[s] aloud to [Violet] from the sentimental novel *Jane Eyre*" (228). As *Great Expectations* does for Thomas, *Jane Eyre* provides a means of catharsis for both Violet and Lucy, while at the same time facilitating a community between the sisters-in-law.

It is *Great Expectations* that is the more consistent recourse for Lucy and Thomas in times of loss. Lucy relies on *Great Expectations* during the late days of her affair with William Crowley, on the boat from London to Bombay. She discovers Dickens in the "ship's small library" (114), and as the affair grinds to a saddening halt (but before the lovers go their separate ways upon reaching Bombay), Lucy thinks through the relationship in its relation to Dickens' novel:

> In *Great Expectations* Pip is in love with Estella, a woman incapable of returning, or even understanding, his feelings. This does not diminish his love, but renders it a form of despair, a strain in the throat, a slow *disheartening* as the heart remains unconfirmed. Lucy's remnant philosophies were all derived from fiction: she had no-one to whom she could confess, and could not write to her brother or uncle of what occurred. How could she describe the changes wrought within her by unprecedented touch? (117)

Lucy understands that she is embodying Pip, undergoing similar experiences to those he undergoes in his torturous desire for Estella. And just like her eventual non-correspondence with Jane Eyre, Lucy is remade by the experience and exceeds Pip's limits. Rather than disheartened, Lucy steps off the boat in Bombay Harbour emboldened and self-aware, ready for her encounter with Isaac Newton, and with motherhood.

> In the wake of Lucy's death at *Sixty Lights*' end, Thomas takes to bed "to re-read *Great Expectations*" (249). The novel takes him back in time:
>> He read as carefully as possible, saturated by memories, and by the afternoon of the second day he was at the death-bed scene, in which the character Pip farewells his benefactor, the criminal, Magwitch ... Thomas began to cry. He cried for his parents, for Neville and for Mrs Minchin. He cried for his cherished, irreplaceable sister, Lucy. He felt that the whole world was drenched in grief, and was unmanned, a boy again, a boy naked with a candle, fearing what might be screened unbidden on mirrors, or in dreams. (249)

Thomas feels himself alone and vulnerable, holding a candle. This is a memory from his own childhood (in the period between his parents' deaths and his departure for London), but it is also another embodying of Pip, who in visiting Miss Havisham is constantly questing towards the light of a candle, whether it be held by Estella or in Miss Havisham's room. While *Jane Eyre* and *Great Expectations* are both a means for Lucy to manage grief, Thomas' moment with *Great Expectations* is more ambivalent; doubly so because it is the final moment of *Sixty Lights*. After "moving beyond the vehemence of sobbing, [and] just entering that state of calm and pause", Lucy's daughter, Ellen, enters the room "seeking him out" (249). Rather than inaugurating Ellen into the family inheritance of both novels, Ellen is the agent here. She senses "with an innate and precocious delicacy" that what she had observed was private, and backs out of the room, leaving Thomas to his grief (249). This action allows the emotional consequence of this scene to settle back on Lucy rather than look ahead to Ellen, thus suggesting the personal power these books have for Lucy and Thomas over all others. What is clear is that *Sixty Lights* presents these two canonical novels as of particular emotional consequence because of their inherited status. *Jane Eyre* and *Great Expectations* are important for Lucy and Thomas throughout their lives.

Literary Inheritance in *Sixty Lights*

In the same interview in which she identified *Sixty Lights* as a "modernist text", Jones spoke of her interest "in using the Victorian novel as a kind of paradigm to unpick". She continued:

3 Gail Jones' Novel Modernism: *Sixty Lights* and Literary Tradition

I'm interested in the idea of inheritance, and what we inherit, I think, apart from physical and obvious material inheritances like objects, we also inherit stories, and these stories might come to us unbidden, as it were … So it's the inheritance of story that I'm trying got [sic] get at, but also the way that stories circulate between families or lovers that we reconfigure them to suit ourselves in strange ways."[13]

As part of a continually evolving novel tradition, *Sixty Lights* itself inherits elements of novelistic mode and storytelling form from *Jane Eyre* and *Great Expectations*. Inheritance, for Jones, while situated primarily in the interpersonal (the inheritance of stories "circulat[ing] between families and lovers") is at the same time a literary question, "a paradigm to unpick". The second section of this chapter looks at the inheritance *Sixty Lights* takes from *Jane Eyre* and *Great Expectations*, and from the Victorian novel generally. In doing so, it argues that inherent to *Sixty Lights*' modernism is an acknowledgement of its inheritance from the Victorian novel, and an argument that *Jane Eyre* and *Great Expectations* are themselves proto-modernist.[14]

The inaugurating English-language critic of the novel tradition is Ian Watt, author of *The Rise of the Novel* (1957). Watt argues that the novel tradition, which he identifies as emerging in the eighteenth-century prose texts of Daniel Defoe, Samuel Richardson and Henry Fielding, facilitated and tracked a change in society and humanity: these British writers were writing novels for a community of readers that were increasingly interested in an individual's experience, and less interested in a mode of existence in which the individual was "universalised", especially in its relation to church and state.[15] Thus, Watt reads the emergent novel tradition as experimenting with various means to convincingly depict the "truth of individual experience", performing a "kind of correspondence between life and literature".[16] Understood in this way, nineteenth-century novels such as *Jane Eyre* and *Great Expectations*, which follow in the footsteps of Defoe, Richardson and Fielding, continue on in the pursuit of a literary aesthetic (often referred to as

---

13 ABC Radio National, "Gail Jones".
14 It is clear from Jones' comments cited above that there is an important relation between the Victorian period and modernism that is approached or worked out in *Sixty Lights*. Some of these elements are not within the remit of this chapter, especially the technological innovation of photography and its aesthetic and temporal consequences for the novel and for modernism itself. Note that Lyn Jacobs documents Jones' oeuvre's engagement with photography in its intersection with modernity and modernism. Referring specifically to *Sixty Lights*, Jacobs writes: "photography function[s] … as a refraction of feminist, modernist, pioneering innovation" (202). See Lyn Jacobs, "Gail Jones's 'light writing': Memory and the Photo-graph", *JASAL: Journal of the Association for the Study of Australian Literature* 5 (2006): 191–208.
15 Ian Watt, *The Rise of the Novel: Studies in Defoe, Richardson and Fielding*, 2nd ed. (Berkeley: University of California Press, 2001), 12.
16 Watt, *The Rise of the Novel*, 13; 12.

realism) in which the individual and their experience is key (especially, both Brontë's and Dickens' novels' focus on one particular character throughout: their *bildungsroman* scope). There is, then, a clear relation between the Victorian novel and its modernist successor: while the Victorian novel represents the experience of an individual from an external (and notionally objective) viewpoint, modernism, while rejecting realism, sought to represent this internal experience faithfully, while at the same time emphasising the fallibility of claiming absolute veracity in doing so.[17]

It is possible to understand *Sixty Lights*' modernist inheritance from *Jane Eyre* and *Great Expectations* as a conceptual orientation to modernity's turn-of-the-century emphasis on the individual's internal, embodied experience, instead of, say, an inheritance of modernist style. This view is corroborated by contemporary scholarship on the novel tradition which reads both Dickens' and Brontë's novels as exemplary texts which, preceding modernism, test out the novel's possibilities for a sustained focus on individual experience without yet delving within a character's mind. Thus, both *Great Expectations* and *Jane Eyre* have been recently interpreted as engaging with the emancipatory politics of their time, positioning each novel as a precursor to the greater individual freedoms of the twentieth century.

In *Great Expectations*, this proto-modernity has been perceived especially in relation to the novel's sceptical and particular description of its setting. This amounts to a Weberian disenchantment, in which the gods and ghosts of a pre-modern time have been exorcised and replaced with a new faith in human observation. This is akin to what Lucy and Thomas experience in reading Dickens' novel, where the novel itself makes London "altogether more actual". For Luke Thurston, the famous scene where Pip discovers Magwitch escaped from prison and lurking in the mists of the marshes is key:

> A fearful man, all in coarse grey, with a great iron on his leg. A man with no hat, and with broken shoes, and with an old rag tied round his head. A man who had been soaked in water, and smothered in mud, and lamed by stones, and cut by flints, and stung by nettles, and torn by briars; who limped, and shivered, and glared and growled; and whose teeth chattered in his head as he seized me by the chin.[18]

This is a preparatory moment where the Victorian novel develops the grounds for a modernist rejection of enchantment and ghostliness.[19] The passage's repeated

---

17 On modernism's interiority, see Peter Childs, *Modernism*, 3rd ed. (Milton Park: Routledge, 2017), 6ff; 82–91.
18 Charles Dickens, *Great Expectations* (1860–61; London: Penguin, 2003), 4.

3 Gail Jones' Novel Modernism: *Sixty Lights* and Literary Tradition

identification of Magwitch as a "man" (in the face of Pip's youth, and his palpable fear) emphasises his reality and his humanity, as does the detailed and familiar history (of prison barks and transportation) attributed to him. Despite the fantastic elements of *Great Expectations*' narrative (for both Pip and Magwitch), the sympathy both characters produce is key in the continuing evolution of the novel tradition.

Reading *Great Expectations* as proto-modernist is relatively more recent; *Jane Eyre* has been considered a radical precursor to some elements of modernity for longer. This reading is primarily focused on *Jane Eyre*'s feminism. In this approach to the novel, Jane's self-determination in its final volume, as well as her position of authority over the blinded Rochester, are key. But Jane's feminism does not accrue to her only in the novel's final volume; it constitutes her identity throughout the novel, famously expressed in volume one. Brontë writes:

> It is in vain to say human beings ought to be satisfied with tranquillity: they must have action; and they will make it if they cannot find it. Millions are condemned to a stiller doom than mine, and millions are in silent revolt against their lot. Nobody knows how many rebellions besides political rebellions ferment in the masses of life which people earth. Women are supposed to be very calm generally; but women feel just as men feel; they need exercise for their faculties, and a field for their efforts as much as their brothers do; they suffer from too rigid a restraint, too absolute a stagnation, precisely as men would suffer; and it is narrow-minded in their more privileged fellow-creatures to say that they ought to confine themselves to making puddings and knitting stockings, to playing on the piano and embroidering bags. It is thoughtless to condemn them, or laugh at them, if they seek to do more or learn more than custom has pronounced necessary for their sex.[20]

Adrienne Rich famously called this passage Jane's "feminist manifesto" which "is still having to be written over and over today".[21] It advocates a vision for women in collective political action, an idea rarely encountered in the Victorian novel. But there is more of relevance here than simply noting the anachronistic nature of Jane's feminism. In assessing the novel, Rich observes that *Jane Eyre* does not have a conventional *bildungsroman* structure; instead, *Jane Eyre*/Jane Eyre exceeds the *bildungsroman* because "she feels so unalterably herself".[22] This self-possession

---

19 See Luke Thurston, *Literary Ghosts from the Victorians to Modernism: The Haunting Interval* (New York: Routledge, 2012), 58–59.
20 Charlotte Brontë, *Jane Eyre* (1847; London: Penguin, 2006), 129–30.
21 Adrienne Rich, "Jane Eyre: The Temptations of a Motherless Woman", in *On Lies, Secrets, and Silence: Selected Prose 1966-1978* (New York: Norton, 1979), 97.

clarifies *Jane Eyre*'s proto-modernism: it depicts a character who is not bound by generic assumptions, but who evolves into new versions of womanhood. The same, of course, goes for Lucy Strange in *Sixty Lights*.

Indeed, both Lucy's and Thomas' individuality in *Sixty Lights* develops via their respective and shared commitment to a sceptical and politically progressive world view. Even as children, both share a tolerantly resigned attitude to Neville's boyish excitement in mediums, spirits and messages from their parents. This is despite their wistful desire to believe: while agreeing that Neville's first medium, "Madame Esperance", was "specious, fraudulent, and probably down-right criminal", both must tally their desire to believe with a sceptical viewpoint which will now allow them to (95). Similarly, while still a child and working at the albumen factory, Lucy asserts an outstanding belief in equality between the sexes. In the midst of her co-worker Rose being harangued by her husband, Lucy steps in to confront the man. She insists he stop harassing Rose and leave; the husband assaults Lucy and departs. After the moment, Lucy is inducted into the community of "female knowledge", and "experience[s] deliberate tenderness and everyday solidarity" (103). This is a defining moment for Lucy, who is committed to self-determination for herself and her female companions hereon.

Detailed attention is also paid throughout *Sixty Lights* to the way *Great Expectations* and *Jane Eyre* are described. This attention lends additional confirmation to this chapter's assessment that Jones' novel actively thinks its way through the nature and consequence of its literary inheritance from the Victorian novel tradition. Of the seven times that *Jane Eyre* is mentioned by title in *Sixty Lights*, it is described specifically as a "novel" six times (once as a "famous novel" and once as a "sentimental novel"; 12, 16, 47, 181, 227, 228). *Sixty Lights* is unequivocal in assessing *Great Expectations*; while I term it a novel, it is mentioned by title four times, and only once described. In this one instance where *Sixty Lights* is specific, rather than a novel, *Great Expectations* is "the brand-new serial *Great Expectations*" (84). In doing so, *Sixty Lights* adverts its knowledge of the publishing history of both novels (*Jane Eyre* was published as a novel, whereas *Great Expectations* was initially published serially, then in its entirety) thus illustrating an investment in the various elements of the Victorian novel tradition it inherits, and maintaining this historical distinction.

Beyond the care *Sixty Lights* shows in describing *Jane Eyre* and *Great Expectations*, it is clear that both novels play a role beyond their centrality to the narrative. That is to say, they have a metatextual function as well as an intertextual one, with the Victorian novel a clear structural influence upon *Sixty Lights*. Jones' novel, with its three-part structure, adapts and updates the "triple-decker"

---

22   Rich, "Jane Eyre: The Temptations of a Motherless Woman", 91.

(three-volume) structure both *Jane Eyre* and *Great Expectations* possess. Perhaps even more revealingly, *Sixty Lights*' twenty sections per part almost exactly replicates the structure of *Great Expectations*, which comprises nineteen chapters in the first volume, and twenty chapters in each of volumes two and three, for fifty-nine chapters in total. This correspondence evokes Lucy Strange's insistence on the role of the maculate – "spotted, stained, blemished" – in her photography, and in art more generally (146). In this example, however, it is *Great Expectations* that is "maculate", while *Sixty Lights* is immaculately symmetrical.

What does this correspondence suggest? An almost but not exact structural correspondence between *Great Expectations* and *Sixty Lights*; a mother and daughter that both initially identify with Jane Eyre (Honoria thinks to herself "*I am Jane Eyre*," while Lucy thinks she will identify herself as an orphan just like Jane [12; 76]), but who both eventually discard the correspondence (Honoria, unhappy in marriage, identifies with Bertha Mason rather than Jane; Lucy's life experience means that Isaac Newton and others will never identify her as Jane [62; 128]); and an improvised family that while delighting in *Great Expectations* as fantasy, never experience the same:

> 'Strange,' [Lucy] said to Thomas, 'how fiction predicts.'
>
> In *Great Expectations* there is an episode in which Pip, having newly come into his fortune, goes to a tailor to have a fine suit fitted. A boy there, Trabb's boy, treats him with insolence, sweeping the floor by banging the broom at every corner, scowling, getting in the way, physically dissenting from and mocking the hero's changed circumstances. Lucy thought of this episode when she began work at the albumen factory, except that her own situation was a kind of reversal. (102)

This passage is key: the predictive function that Lucy Strange identifies in *Great Expectations* functions differently to what the reader may anticipate. Rather than Lucy's life replicating Pip's, Lucy sees the prediction in the negative, an evocation which accords with the novel's abundant focus upon photography. It is as if both Lucy's and Thomas' lives are developed, at points, as negatives of *Great Expectations* and *Jane Eyre*. *Sixty Lights*' inheritance of the Victorian novel tradition exists, finally, in the way that it extends itself beyond the loved stories of those two novels. These two novels provide a certain generative technology, a means for Lucy and Thomas Strange to live their own modern lives. The novel modernism that characterises *Sixty Lights* acknowledges the significance of Victorian novels like *Jane Eyre* and *Great Expectations*, but also sees these texts as offering opportunities for new, and alternate, stories: rather than Jane Eyre's minor interest, for instance, in drawing, Lucy Strange is a full-blown artist, albeit one not acknowledged by the "Royal College of Photographers" (240).

This generative energy is particularly notable during key moments, especially when Lucy departs from the conventional sentimental narrative of the nineteenth-century triple-decker, and determines her own life's course. During her work at the albumen factory, Lucy reflects upon one of the great joys of her work:

> Once a week each contributed a farthing to hire a reader, who sat alongside them, reading aloud from serials, or newspapers, or collections of short stories. Words circulated in the air like a new kind of energy, in waves and particles, focused and diffuse, showing and obscuring what might exist in the world. (100)

The novel, then, is explicit about the energy, the modern creative impulse, it locates in the storytelling traditions of the nineteenth century. Similarly, when Lucy decides to accept Neville's proposal, and to travel to India to meet Isaac Newton (a negative reflection of Jane Eyre's own decision *not* to travel to India with St John), she is described, in her departure, as also leaving the tried and tested stories of nineteenth-century fiction: "she float[s] away into a story that would be hers alone" (108). Lucy Strange – and *Sixty Lights* – is freed from whatever remained of the coercive power of the Victorian novel. Rather than the conventional conclusions of *Jane Eyre* and *Great Expectations*, Lucy Strange's death is a twenty-first century conclusion to a novel dedicated to the nineteenth century. In this sense, *Sixty Lights* presents a combination of the modernising nineteenth-century novel form, alongside modernism's twentieth-century conceptual (and temporal) pyrotechnics, resulting in a twenty-first century hybrid recommitting itself to the novel tradition it develops from.

References

Brontë, Charlotte. *Jane Eyre*. (1847) London: Penguin, 2006.
Childs, Peter. *Modernism*, 3rd ed. Milton Park: Routledge, 2017.
Dickens, Charles. *Great Expectations*. (1860–61) London: Penguin, 2003.
Hutcheon, Linda. *A Poetics of Postmodernism: History, Theory, Fiction*. New York: Routledge, 1988.
Jacobs, Lyn. "Gail Jones's 'light writing': Memory and the Photo-graph." *JASAL: Journal of the Association for the Study of Australian Literature* 5 (2006): 191–208.
Jones, Gail. "A Dreaming, A Sauntering: Re-Imagining Critical Paradigms." *JASAL: Journal of the Association for the Study of Australian Literature* 5 (2006): 11–24.
––. "'Growing small wings': Walter Benjamin, Lola Ridge, and the Political Affect of Modernism." *Affirmations: of the Modern* 1, no. 2 (Spring 2014): 120–42.
––. *Sixty Lights*. London: Vintage, 2005.
Lewis, Alexandra. "The Ethics of Appropriation; Or, the 'Mere Spectre' of Jane Eyre: Emma Tennant's Thornfield Hall, Jasper Fforde's The Eyre Affair and Gail Jones' Sixty Lights." In *Charlotte Brontë: Legacies and Afterlives*, edited by Amber K. Regis and Deborah Wynne, 197–220. Manchester: Manchester University Press, 2017.

Mao, Douglas and Rebecca L. Walkowitz. "The New Modernist Studies", *Publications of the Modern Language Association*, 123, no. 3 (May 2008): 737–48.

Mitchell, Kate. *History and Cultural Memory in Neo-Victorian Fiction*. Houndsmills: Palgrave Macmillan, 2010.

Pilar Royo Grasa, Maria del. "In Conversation with Gail Jones", *Journal of the Association for the Study of Australian Literature*, 12, no. 3 (2012): 1–12.

Rich, Adrienne. "Jane Eyre: The Temptations of a Motherless Woman". In *On Lies, Secrets, and Silence: Selected Prose 1966–1978*, 89–106. New York: Norton, 1979.

Thurston, Luke. *Literary Ghosts from the Victorians to Modernism: The Haunting Interval*. New York: Routledge, 2012.

Watt, Ian. *The Rise of the Novel: Studies in Defoe, Richardson and Fielding*, 2nd ed. Berkeley: University of California Press, 2001.

4
Sleep's Sweet Relief

Tanya Dalziell

At one moment in *Dreams of Speaking* (2006), Gail Jones has her character, the bibliophile Alice Black, ruminate on books and, more slightly, sleep:

> She loved the feel of books, their integrity as objects … Random flicking of pages, inscriptions, dog-ears. She loved … Inherited books. Books as gifts. Books as objects flung across the room in a lover's argument. Books (this most of all) taken into the warm sexual space of the bed, held upon the lap, entered like another body, companionable, close, interconnecting with innermost things. Those bed books that chart the route between waking and sleeping, that are a venture of almost hypnogogic power. Those enticements. Adventures. Corridors of words. Capsules. Secrets.[1]

Alice's thoughts subtly hint at the complex relationships between sleep, subjectivity and representation that I would like to contemplate in Jones' long-form fiction. As Alice intimates, narratives might be read before going to sleep, they might induce sleep, or be formally attuned to the suggestion of sleepy states. The actual moment when sleep comes, though, eludes those "corridors of words" because the awareness needed to recognise it is necessarily absent. Sleep is a catachresis; it does not ensure knowledge of the entity it names even as Jones' narrative, at this moment, formally approximates hypnagogia's threshold consciousness and comes tellingly to rest on "Secrets". What I would like to

Tanya Dalziell, Sleep's Sweet Relief. In *Inner and Outer Worlds: Gail Jones' Fiction*, edited by Anthony Uhlmann. Sydney: Sydney University Press, 2022. DOI: 10.30722/sup.9781743327791

---

[1] Gail Jones, *Dreams of Speaking* (North Sydney: Vintage, 2006), 136–37. All subsequent references are to this edition and appear in parentheses in the text.

suggest is that Jones' novels are interested in sleep in part because of the very challenges it poses to the narrative form in which such enquiries are expressed.

Sleep is certainly not an obvious feature of Jones' fiction. The more apparent nocturnal interests of her writing are dreams. This inclination is signalled, possibly, in the title of *Dreams of Speaking*, although that novel is concerned more overtly with the promise of ethical connections than with those involuntary images and sensations that constitute sleep's imaginings.[2] And yet, this possibility commences in a dreamlike state as the simile that comes to Alice's drowsy mind suggests, "like a cradle, gently rocking", while she travels at night to the "maternal rhythm" of a train (58). The friendship between Alice and Mr Sakamoto, which is at the centre of the novel, commences on this night-ride and in this space-between, with each character experiencing sleepiness. The beginning of these characters' mutual recognition is conveyed through their shared responses to the music they unexpectedly hear and whose description – "posthumous and unearthly" (58) – educes both their mutual liminal states and the half-heard snatches of recorded sound.

When more recognisable dreams are told of elsewhere in Jones' writing, they license a break with dutiful realism and afford access to the unconscious. They also offer alternative ontologies and are mythopoetic spaces where what is impossible in waking life can be imagined. In *Sorry* (2007), for example, Stella Keene, unhappily exiled to a remote, outback town in wartime Western Australia, dreams of snow falling in the desert "[a]s if beneath a plastic dome".[3] In *Black Mirror* (2002), lost lovers are returned to the Surrealist painter, Victoria Morell, in her dreams: "I dreamed frequently of Louis and Jules, often in conflation, and could see them again beneath my eyelids, youthful, sexually present, ablaze with optimism".[4] And on board a boat to colonial Bombay, Lucy Strange in *Sixty Lights* (2004) dreams "unaccountably" of a peaceful marriage between herself and her cousin all the while "dimly aware of the sound of the ocean ... as though the ocean itself constituted the knitted patterns of dreams".[5]

And it is dreams that continue to be enthusiastically conceived of more broadly as content-rich; sleep at best forms the nondescript backdrop to this nightly display.[6] Jacqueline Rose (inadvertently) sums up this position in an essay on sleep and the dream interpreter *par excellence*, Sigmund Freud. In her reading,

---

2   See my chapter "Modernity" in *Gail Jones: Word, Image, Ethics* (Sydney: Sydney University Press, 2020), 141–67.
3   Gail Jones, *Sorry* (North Sydney: Vintage, 2007), 19. All subsequent references are to this edition and appear in parentheses in the text.
4   Gail Jones, *Black Mirror* (Sydney: Picador, 2002), 244. All subsequent references are to this edition and appear in parentheses in the text.
5   Gail Jones, *Sixty Lights* (London: Harvill Press, 2004), 118. All subsequent references are to this edition and appear in parentheses in the text.

Freud determines dreaming to be characterised by a "*productive*' nature" and "[o]nce you start thinking of it [dreaming] like this, then sleep appears, less as a metaphor for, more a pathway *into*, something else".[7] Sleep makes itself known as a dream conduit; otherwise, it slips out of view.

Sleep, then, is not quite so inviting of interpretation in the way that dreams are. Admittedly, *Sixty Lights* is disposed to leave off dreams as unfathomable, just as Roland Barthes, of whom Jones writes approvingly elsewhere[8] and whose thinking on photography is an intellectual companion to that novel,[9] paused cautiously before the enterprise of dream interpretation, determining that activity to subsume the confounding idleness of sleep for the graft of meaning. Pressed into the service of psychoanalysis and other interpretive modes, Barthes argues, "not only does it [sleep] restore, 'regain,' 'recuperate,' it also transforms, labors: it is productive, rescued from the disgrace of the 'good for nothing'".[10] Barthes is wholly unapproving of that circumstance, valuing instead sleep's sweetness, which he thinks of as a crucial condition for ethical living: "I would suggest calling the nonviolent refusal of reduction, the parrying of generality by inventive, unexpected, nonparadigmatizable behavior, the elegant and discreet flight in the face of dogmatism, in short, the principle of tact, I would call it, all being said: sweetness", he writes.[11] The capacity of sleep to elude assertion is what Barthes admires and to which Jones' texts attest. If we read for sleep in Jones' writing, rather than read to go to sleep, then aspects of Jones' texts that seek to make sleep apparent emerge to offer glimpses or "twinklings", to evoke Barthes' phrase,[12] into the otherwise inaccessible territory of somnolent interiority, as well as ruminations on time and representation.

In particular, I would like to consider sleep in Jones' novel *The Death of Noah Glass* (2018), a text that has its main characters expressly, if briefly, discuss this state and hint at how sleep might be conceived of as something other than a necessary life function. Before turning to that novel, however, I would like to grant that I broach the subject of sleep in Jones' writing in the knowledge that while sleep might not be an overt preoccupation of her fiction, it is certainly a hot topic

---

6   See, for example, Herschel Farbman, *The Other Night: Dreaming, Writing, and Restlessness in Twentieth-Century Literature* (New York: Fordham University Press, 2008).
7   Jacqueline Rose, *On Not Being Able to Sleep: Psychoanalysis and the Modern World* (London: Chatto & Windus, 2003), 110.
8   See, for example, Gail Jones, "The Heart Beating Across the Room (On Possessing Someone Else's Photographs)", *Australian Book Review* 173 (August 1995): 38.
9   Roland Barthes, *Camera Lucida: Reflections on Photography*, trans. Richard Howard (New York: Hill & Wang, 1981).
10 Roland Barthes, *The Neutral: Lecture Course at the College de France (1977–1978)*, trans. Rosalind Krauss and Denis Hollier (New York: Columbia University Press, 2005), 39.
11 Barthes, *The Neutral*, 36.
12 Barthes, *The Neutral*, 10.

in the wider world – in the popular media and in positivistic science. Hardly a day goes by without a news story telling of the importance of sleep, counsel that seems particularly pressing in the era of late capitalism. With shopping opportunities and information making claims on our attention twenty-four hours a day, and technologies of modernity – from the light bulb to the iPhone's blue light – feared to be damaging our slumber irreparably, natural sleep is deemed to be under threat. And this peril raises the implicit question as to how natural sleep might actually be. As debates over how much sleep we need fill column inches, they also point to how sleep is social and historical, and subject to meaning-making. If sleep might be ideally consolidated into seven or eight-hour blocks of time at night; take place in a bedroom, in a bed and in pyjamas; and be thought of as a battery-charging activity designed for ensuring daily productivity, as many commentators suggest, then this apprehension only underscores how this realm of human experience is perhaps not as natural as it might first appear.

A. Roger Ekirch describes in his study on the British Isles' medieval past, for example, the practice of segmented sleep, which saw people sleep following dinner for a few hours, only to wake after midnight to lie in contemplative repose, pray and/or have sex, and then resume their slumber until sunrise.[13] In his work on sleep and capitalism, Jonathan Crary argues that the Enlightenment and industrialisation saw the sleep Ekirch details undergo a radical change; that by "the mid seventeenth century, sleep ... became devalued in the face of a privileging of consciousness and volition, of notions of utility, objectivity, and self-interested agency".[14] And in our contemporary times, when an average adult "sleeps approximately six and a half hours a night, an erosion from eight hours a generation ago and ... down from the ten hours in the early twentieth century", any claims to being natural that might be made for sleep are very much undone by the presiding conceptualisation of it "as a variable but managed function that can only be defined instrumentally and physiologically".[15] Yet, in the face of this operationalisation of our circadian rhythms, Crary nevertheless singles out sleep as the last bastion against capitalism's profit-making logic:

> In its profound uselessness and intrinsic passivity ... Sleep is an uncompromising interruption of the theft of time from us by capitalism. Most of the seemingly irreducible necessities of human life – hunger, thirst, sexual desire, and recently the need for friendship – have been remade into commodified or financialized forms. Sleep poses the idea of a human need and interval of time that cannot be

---

13 A. Roger Ekirch, *At Day's Close: Night in Times Past* (New York: Norton, 2005).
14 Jonathan Crary, *24/7: Late Capitalism and the Ends of Sleep* (London: Verso, 2013), 12.
15 Crary, *24/7*, 11, 13.

colonised and harnessed to a massive engine of profitability, and thus remains an incongruous anomaly and site of crisis in the global present. In spite of all the scientific research in this area, it frustrates and confounds any strategies to exploit or reshape it. The stunning, inconceivable reality is that nothing of value can be extracted from it.[16]

Sleep apps, which have proven to be more than capable of monetising the need Crary singles out as heroically resistant to the dark league of science and capitalism,[17] were seemingly not on the historian's mind. But what Crary's argument calls forth is a pervasive idea about sleep, namely that it is an attenuated state, a cognitive shutdown, a nothingness, especially when compared to watchful consciousness. That wakefulness has to be evoked to get some kind of grip on sleep's slippery contours suggests that sleep itself is not a stand-alone subject of knowledge or experience. Fernando Pessoa, who gives the title and epigraph to *Dreams of Speaking*, suggests as much when he writes, as Bernardo Soares in *The Book of Disquiet* (1982), "I sleep and I unsleep", highlighting the mutually constitutive states that his fragmentary prose renders both suggestive and uncertain.[18]

With the aid of MRI scans, sleep scientists today now insist that sleep is not passive, as Crary seems to assume, but rather active and dynamic both neurologically and physiologically.[19] This is something that other historians of sleep would agree with, albeit through a different epistemological lens.[20] Yet, Crary's protest is levelled at exactly this way of scientific knowing, which would presume to observe and understand sleep; Jones' novels are sympathetic to his concern and also alert to a claim made for sleep by the philosopher Jean-Luc Nancy. "Sleep, perhaps, has never been philosophical",[21] Nancy forwards, not least because of philosophy's tendency to lean on sleep as a placeholder for all that snoozy unthinkingness and useless negativity (which Crary contrarily sees as sleep's strength and appeal) that it wants to distance itself from and define itself against. And there is also sleep's persistent conundrum; that it shows of itself

---

16 Crary, *24/7*, 10–11.
17 Marijn Sax, Natali Helberger, Nadine Bol, "Health as a Means Towards Profitable Ends: mHealth Apps, User Autonomy, and Unfair Commercial Practices", *Journal of Consumer Policy* 41 (2018): 103–34.
18 Fernando Pessoa, *The Book of Disquiet*, trans. Richard Zenith (1982; London: Penguin, 2015), 34.
19 Wallace B. Mendelson, *The Science of Sleep: What It Is, How It Works, and Why It Matters* (Chicago: University of Chicago Press, 2017).
20 See, for example, Sasha Handley, *Sleep in Early Modern England* (New Haven, CT: Yale University Press, 2016).
21 Jean-Luc Nancy, *The Birth to Presence*, trans. Brian Holmes et al. (Stanford, CA: Stanford University Press, 1994), 13.

"only in its disappearance, its burrowing and its concealment",[22] undoing both subjectivity and the possibility of phenomenology. "I fall asleep", Nancy writes, "and at the same time I vanish as an 'I'."[23] Nancy strives to counter what he sees as philosophy's neglect of sleep by turning, much like Alice in *Dreams of Speaking*, to the image of the rocking cradle to suggest a philosophical "awakening to sleep".[24] Writing more like a poet than a philosopher, he proposes that:

> Rocking movements put us to sleep because sleep in its essence is itself a rocking, not a stable, motionless state. [Rocking is a matter] of the initial beat between something and nothing, between the world and the void, which also means between the world and itself ... Nothing but the swaying of the world makes the cradle or rather cradling within which everything awakens – awakening to sleep as well as waking, awakening to self as to throbbing and rocking in general.[25]

In *The Death of Noah Glass*, Evie Glass, a former academic philosopher, is asked by her adult brother, Martin, as to whether sleep is "in or out of time".[26] The habits of philosophy are evident in Evie's response. She summons wide-awake reason to declare that, "My first response would be that there is no time without consciousness" (237), only to be then swept up unexpectedly by a childhood memory that comes unbidden to her otherwise logical mind. Another interpretation of sleep and the self which Evie intuits elsewhere in the novel recalls both Barthes' tropes and an apprehension of sleep proposed by Emmanuel Levinas. (In this regard, Levinas and Barthes, along with Nancy, are philosophers who prove to be the exception to the rule in that they do not shy away from sleep but rather write movingly about it.) For Levinas, sleep – "a soft languor of lassitude" – is subjectivity's refuge from rationality.[27] Evie thinks of sleep in a similar way as she reflects on the somnolence she experiences following her father's funeral: "To be nothing for thirteen hours: what sweet relief it had been" (15). At this point in the novel, sleep for Evie is less a flight from the alienating rationality that concerned Levinas, however, than a momentary release from her mourning. While representing seriously Evie's rational ideas about time and consciousness, Jones' novels also submit that the kind of logically rigorous

---

22   Jean-Luc Nancy, *The Fall to Sleep*, trans. Charlotte Mandell (New York: Fordham University Press, 2009), 13.
23   Nancy, *Fall*, 11.
24   Nancy, *Fall*, 31.
25   Nancy, *Fall*, 31.
26   Gail Jones, *The Death of Noah Glass* (Melbourne: Text, 2018), 237. All subsequent references are to this edition and appear in parentheses in the text.
27   Emmanuel Levinas, *Existence and Existents*, trans. Alphonso Lingis (Pittsburgh, PA: Duquesne University Press, 1978), 19.

argument largely favoured by philosophy can be met by the more oblique approach that philosophers of sleep recommend, and to which imaginative literature might seem ideally suited.

But, in addition to an awareness of sleep eluding us because it involves an absence of consciousness that is required for knowledge of the experience, sleep poses a further narrative challenge that Jones' texts admit: the sleeper would seem to do little that drives or interests character-focused storytelling. Of course, sleep is not without drama. In *Macbeth*, one of the Shakespearean plays Stella Keene recites in *Sorry* (most notably "while her husband bleeds to death" at the hand of her traumatised daughter [124]), a sleeping King Duncan is murdered by the play's titular character. Sharing his contemporaries' view that a quiet mind leads to restful somnolence, and that sleep heals, Shakespeare meaningfully deprives the treacherous Macbeth of slumber:

> Methought I heard a voice cry, "Sleep no more!
> Macbeth does murder sleep," – the innocent sleep,
> Sleep that knits up the ravell'd sleave of care,
> The death of each day's life, sore labour's bath,
> Balm of hurt minds, great nature's second course,
> Chief nourisher in life's feast,– . . . Still it cried,
> "Sleep no more!" to all the house;
> "Glamis hath murder'd sleep, and therefore Cawdor
> Shall sleep no more; Macbeth shall sleep no more."[28]

And to underscore sleep's signifying potential, the playwright has Lady Macbeth later admit her guilt while sleepwalking. Before this somnolent confession, however, Lady Macbeth yokes death and sleep as she first demands of her husband the bloodied blades so that she might cast suspicion on the servants – "Give me the daggers: the sleeping and the dead / Are but as pictures".[29] In so doing, she emphasises the play's tropic repetitions, renders sleep a state of vulnerability, and casts the sleeper as devoid of voice, agency, mobility, consciousness, personality, moral conundrums, shifting states of mind, sexual intrigue, social context and, in the case of Duncan, ultimately life. But while Shakespeare might plumb sleep, or the lack of it, for its moral measure, many other authors appear well aware of the non-promising subject of sleep for narrative. Laurence Sterne, for one, has his hero of *Tristram Shandy* (1767) contemplate the writing of a chapter on sleep, only to give up after eight paragraphs with the declaration that, "I would

---

28 William Shakespeare, *Macbeth* in *The Complete Oxford Shakespeare: Tragedies*, general eds. Stanley Wells and Gary Taylor (1623; Oxford: Oxford University Press, 1990), 2.2, 33–41.
29 Shakespeare, *Macbeth*, 2.2, 51–52.

undertake to write a dozen chapters upon buttonholes, both quicker and with more fame, than a single chapter upon this".[30] Sleep is beyond even the reach of that notoriously digressive text. Over two hundred years later, Paul Valéry would also stumble before his efforts to write of a woman experiencing a cataleptic sleep that lasted for years. (Snow White and Sleeping Beauty underwent a similar experience, with their awakening from lengthy sleeps a supposed sign of sexual maturation. Valéry's abandoned *Agatha* was intended as a study on memory and consciousness.) As Peter Schwenger, in his study on literature and sleep, relates the author's exasperation, Valéry told André Gide that the enterprise was doomed: "I shall never finish it because it's too difficult", he admitted.[31]

If writing sleep is difficult, then in the worlds of Jones' novels sleep is made apparent because many of Jones' characters have trouble experiencing it. There is, of course, a rich literary history that celebrates the insomniac, and in particular the insomniac-artist, as a special type. I am thinking of the aesthete's insomnia celebrated and suffered by modernists such as Marcel Proust, Walter Benjamin, Virginia Woolf and Vladimir Nabokov, to whom Jones' writings are particularly attracted.

Proust, for whom Jones constructs an imaginary biography in her short story collection *Fetish Lives* (1997),[32] made the bed his office and subject, and opens his magnum opus *In Search of Lost Time* (1913–27) with his protagonist falling asleep (something Proust himself found elusive), only to be awakened by the thought that it was time to sleep. (Barthes writes approvingly of Proust's "half-waking" as a "good kind" of sleep in which "the logical carapace of Time is attacked"; "another logic, a logic of Vacillation, of Decompartmentalization" is suggested; and the third form, "neither Essay nor Novel", based on "a provocative principle: the disorganization of Time" is produced.)[33] Woolf, whose meeting with Freud Jones fictionally renders in the same short story collection, linked her creativity with sleepless nights, writing in her diary four and a half years before the famous psychoanalyst paid her a visit, "I think owing to the sudden rush of 2 wakeful nights … I see the end of Here & Now [*The Years*]".[34] Benjamin's thinking, which runs through Jones' fiction and provides an epigraph to part two of *Sixty Lights*, is founded on a dialectics of sleep and awakening that he believed was essential for the emergence of collective subjectivity. As a state of unproductive potentiality

---

30 Laurence Sterne, *The Life and Opinions of Tristram Shandy* (1767; Aberdeen: George Clark and Son, 1848), 146.
31 Peter Schwenger, *At the Borders of Sleep: On Liminal Literature* (Minneapolis: University of Minnesota Press, 2012), 41.
32 Gail Jones, *Fetish Lives* (Fremantle: Fremantle Arts Centre Press, 1997).
33 Barthes, *The Neutral*, 281.
34 Virginia Woolf, Diary entry of 17 August 1934, *The Diary of Virginia Woolf: Volume 4, 1931–35*, ed. Anne Olivier Bell (London: Penguin, 1983), 237.

sleep is the precondition of revolutionary awakening in Benjamin's philosophising. He writes:

> Life only seemed worth living where the threshold between waking and sleeping was worn away in everyone as by the steps of multitudinous images flooding back and forth, language only seemed itself where, sound and image, image and sound interpenetrated with automatic precision and such felicity that no chink was left for the penny-in-the-slot called "meaning".[35]

In notable contrast, Nabokov was especially scathing of sleep. His hyperbolic disgust for it was of such an order that he likened those who slept easily on trains and other communal places to those who freely defecate in public. Writing in his autobiographical *Speak, Memory* (1951), a text which is highly valued by Jones' characters in *A Guide to Berlin* (2015),[36] Nabokov determined that, "Sleep is the most moronic fraternity in the world, with the heaviest dues and the crudest rituals. It is a mental torture I find debasing … I simply cannot get used to the nightly betrayal of reason, humanity, genius".[37] Sleep, for Nabokov, was an affront to art and (his) intelligence.

Jones' novels are clearly aware of this modernist-insomniac legacy in a number of ways, not least with many of her writer, or would-be writer, protagonists singled out because of their sleeplessness. In *Black Mirror*, the biographer Anna Griffin lies in bed at 2 am, "insomniac, and agonised by yearning" (260), and in her sleepless state she considers the patterns of faint streetlight on the ceiling that "signify everything vague and uncertain" (261). (She also takes advantage of a sleeping Victoria Morrell; Anna snoops through her biographical subject's personal items as Victoria slumbers, searching for signs of her history and inner life.) *Sixty Lights* begins with its exceptional photographer figure, Lucy Strange, "stranded" in an "anachronistic moment", wide awake at midnight and recalling a man's death she had witnessed earlier in the day in terms specific to her newly found visual profession (5). If *Sixty Lights* commences with Lucy's sleeplessness, *Sorry* concludes with Perdita remembering her younger self recalling her mother's snow globe dreams because she is unable to sleep following her father's death. The sleep of Alice Black in *Dreams of Speaking* is repeatedly interrupted by "the signals of night-life unfolding and bodily processes" (34) and

---

35 Walter Benjamin, "Surrealism: The Last Snapshot of the European Intelligentsia", in *Selected Writings*, vol. 2, eds Michael W. Jennings, Howard Eiland and Gary Smith (1929; Cambridge, MA: Harvard University Press, 1999), 208, [207–21].
36 Gail Jones, *A Guide to Berlin* (North Sydney: Vintage, 2015). All subsequent references are to this edition and appear in parentheses in the text.
37 Vladimir Nabokov, *Speak, Memory: An Autobiography Revisited* (1951; London: Penguin, 2012), 77.

"the commotion" of an equally sleepless Paris (41). Further, Alice's claims to being somewhat apart from everyone else – suggested by her favoured trope of the weightless astronaut – are exemplified by her inability, or refusal, to sleep while travelling on an aeroplane. The metaphors used to describe the light transmitted by the screens built into the seat-backs – "a posthumous blue … over bodies, faces" (19) – affords a deathly association to the sleep to which other travellers succumb, leading Alice to wonder at "what form of modernity this might be, and how she might include it in her book" (18). For Cass Turner in *A Guide to Berlin*, who travels to Berlin with hopes of writing, her night-time awakenings are awash with "the flowing past" (184). And while not a writer, Martin Glass, an artist, experiences troubled sleep from the first pages of *The Death of Noah Glass*. That novel begins with Martin remembering a story, hypnopompically, on the morning of his father's funeral.

Before venturing further thoughts about sleep and *The Death of Noah Glass*, I would like to note first that it is in *Five Bells* (2011) that Jones' possibly worst sleeper is to be found. James deMello is awake at 3 am and is said to feel solidarity at a distance "with others awake at this time, the desperadoes of the city and its working drivers. The stragglers, lost and wandering. The sleepless".[38] When James finally sleeps, briefly, he does so tellingly out of time, in the afternoon when the tourists at Circular Quay are making the most of the sunny summer day. It is only in the night, Jones writes, "in this rainy, woeful darkness where he felt truly himself" (30).

James' sleeplessness brings to mind what Maurice Blanchot nominates "the *other* night".[39] The phrase is characteristically, for Blanchot, imprecise. But it gestures towards a night other than the day's conception of it. The "*other* night" is not the time for, or state of, rest, which recent sleep scientists are preoccupied with and which ostensibly serves day's active purposes. Rather, the other night is where, or when, or perhaps a nocturnal nowhere where "the incessant and the uninterrupted reign";[40] or, what Jones identifies on James' behalf as the "woeful darkness". Further, "the *other* night" is also a state that is necessarily marked by the sleeplessness James endures because, for Blanchot at least, sleep is understood to concentrate the self. Blanchot writes in *The Space of Literature* (1982), "Where I sleep I fix myself and I fix the world".[41] In the formless other night, the self experiences something of what it is like to be without a self, at least according to Blanchot, and James in *Five Bells* seems to intuit, and indeed embody, the

---

38   Gail Jones, *Five Bells* (North Sydney: Vintage, 2012), 29. All subsequent references are to this edition and appear in parentheses in the text.
39   Maurice Blanchot, *The Space of Literature*, trans. Ann Smock (Lincoln: University of Nebraska Press, 1982), 163.
40   Blanchot, *The Space of Literature*, 119.
41   Blanchot, *The Space of Literature*, 266.

philosophical and psychological implications of this "*other* night". Alongside the three main female characters of *Five Bells*, James is decidedly unfixed and disconnected. He is racked by guilt, grief and desire, and ultimately comes to extinguish himself in another instance of darkness, the depths of Sydney Harbour.

Noah Glass in *The Death of Noah Glass* also meets a watery end at the novel's beginning, albeit in very different circumstances. Yet, like James and the other characters mentioned already, he too has trouble sleeping at times: he experiences terrible jet-lag when smuggling a sculpture into Sydney as part of an art heist that forms one of the novel's storylines. Resurrected in narrative (the novel tells of Noah's life following his death), and unable to sleep, he retrieves from under his bed an image of his sleeping daughter, Evie, as a young teenager that was sketched by her brother, Martin. The image from the past of Evie's momentary release from time and consciousness is, for Noah, both "like a living thing" and ghostlike, his daughter's face "a spectre, disappearing" (298). Martin's image of her has moved through the time her sleeping seems to deny, and is received by the adult children's father with complicated, "powerful feelings" (298). This is so because the image, for Noah, evokes convergent ideas of time he carries as both a father of adult children and as an academic with a special interest in time's pictorial representations, particularly in the works of Piero della Francesca.

Jones' fascination with the image is evident throughout her writing, and in a piece in the *Sydney Review of Books* which acknowledges this abiding preoccupation, Robert Dixon makes express note of the cover of *The Death of Noah Glass*, which is derived from Piero's *The Dream of Constantine* (1464), (Fig. 4.1). He does so to present an argument about ekphrasis and intermediality in Jones' text. Dixon writes:

> *The Death of Noah Glass* is a virtuosic staging of this rich field or "problematic". The idea of a productive gap or rupture in representation is repeatedly invoked by the novel's explicit allusions to and staged, ekphrastic descriptions of paintings, films and other visual texts. These include quattrocento paintings, such as Piero's *The Baptism of Christ* and the Arezzo frescoes; ottocento sculpture, such as Vincenzo Ragusa's *Japanese Woman* (c. 1881); the precious icons and cheap religious artefacts of Roman Catholic worship; the double helix of intermediality represented by the Italian *giallo* novels and film adaptations of the 1950s and 1960s; and the proliferating screen culture of the internet. As each of these media and genres re-crosses time and space, from the Renaissance to the contemporary era, from Italy to Australia and back via Japan, Jones demonstrates not a quaint equivalence between the sister arts, but an unruly dynamic of disjunction, rupture, play and appropriation that sets off a force field of narrative and semiotic energies.[42]

My interest in Piero's painting is less sophisticated, and rests on the observation that it is a classic study of sleep. In Piero's image, Constantine is composed and restful, and presumably receptive to the heavenly message from God the angel – swooping down at speed from the upper left-hand corner – appears to be delivering. Sleep, the painting suggests (and it is hardly unique in making this claim), is the state in which the divine communes with chosen humans. The sentinels in the painting's foreground are seemingly unaware of God's angel or the light he brings. But unlike the foregrounded soldiers who are steadfastly awake, the attendant – the figure pictured on Jones' book (Fig. 4.2) – is somnolent. His sleepy gaze is hard to read; he may be oblivious to the light in which he is bathed or knowing of what the emperor sees but is yet to understand. Yet, his sleep-waking state is also arguably that of the painting itself, with its simultaneous visions of, and within, Constantine's sleep, and is a topic of philosophical discussion in the book the figure ostensibly introduces.

Sleep in *The Death of Noah Glass* is of interest not only to the novel's narrative, as it wonders at what artistic form, the written or the visual, might honour sleep's representational complexities, but also to its characters. Evie and Martin expressly discuss sleep at some length. These are siblings who often find themselves in erudite conversations. Talking about time, for example, is something that they have grown up doing as a consequence, and with a mix of gratitude and resentment, of their father's efforts to instruct them in art history and composition. So, speaking about sleep and time is not out of the ordinary for them. And their conversations afford the opportunity to parse further this novel's responses to the challenges sleep poses to its own representational form and how the characters' concern with sleep is also a concern with time.

The death of their father has thrown Evie and Martin into what the novel proposes from its opening pages as the temporality of mourning. Awake, and walking separately through the same streets the morning following their father's funeral, Evie and Martin both have a profound awareness of time and of being removed from the daily temporal rhythms of working life. Its importance for the book is highlighted as Evie expressly discusses time, as well as sleep, with Martin in their shared grief. The conversations the siblings have often occur on Skype, with each sibling in a different country and in a different time zone. Moreover, the technology they use to facilitate their discussion is itself imagined by Evie to be both transcendent and representative of their chosen subjects; Skype affords a "timelessness" that sees brother and sister meet virtually and meaningfully to talk about time and sleep (235).

---

42 Robert Dixon, "Figures in Geometry: *The Death of Noah Glass* by Gail Jones", *Sydney Review of Books*, 7 September 2018, https://sydneyreviewofbooks.com/death-noah-glass-jones/

4 Sleep's Sweet Relief

Figure 4.1 Piero della Francesca, *The Dream of Constantine* (1464).

Figure 4.2 W.H. Chong, cover art, *The Death of Noah Glass* (2018).

The prompt for their Skype ruminations on time is a plaque Martin saw in Palermo. It officially commemorates the place "where Garibaldi slept for two hours in 1869" but is additionally perceived by Martin as a "verification of weariness ... and time out of time" (231). His understanding of the sign contrasts with that of Frank Malone, the Sydney-based detective who has unexpectedly turned up in Palermo, pursuing leads relating to the art heist Noah Glass is accused of and with little time for this kind of rumination: "So what's the big deal?" he asks Martin (231). As far as the novel is concerned, the big deal about time is its connection with human vulnerability and consciousness, with sleep imagined as that which pulls together, and apart, these two states.

I have mentioned already that Evie responds to her brother's querying about time by declaring the centrality to it of consciousness. Yet, the novel suggests that her brother had formed his own aesthetic response as a teenage artist, raising the question as to how narratives, the sequencing of their words wedded with linear time, might faithfully represent the proposed non-time of sleep. The answer the novel offers recalls comic-book depictions of dozing. In his early artistic efforts, Martin had drawn above the head of his sleeping sister "a scalloped dream cloud, and in the dream cloud Martin rendered her sleeping alphabetical: *zzzzz*" (298). It is a state into which Evie, as an adult, is said to slide away "darkly uncertain, on the inner surf of her zzzs" (37). On the evening after their father's funeral, Martin continues to watch his sister sleep with an artist's eye: "Her eyelids were cyan blue, her blotched skin was pasty ... her face was creased against the cushion" (12). The Glass men have an unsettling habit of staring at the women around them as though they are paintings. Yet, at the same time this gesture of looking at Evie recalls the long history of the paired figures of the sleep-watcher and the watched sleeper whose intimate interactions allegorise not only relations of power and trust but also what Michael Greaney recognises as "the philosophical problems that may bedevil any attempt to bring the otherness of sleep under the watchful jurisdiction of wakefulness".[43] For Evie, who internally recites compulsively but comforting word lists that run in an orderly fashion from A to Z, this depiction of sleep – slurring past the end time of the alphabet – supports graphically her philosophical position that she later confirms when listening to her lover, Benjamin, asleep at her side. She determines that sleep "is a sound without alphabet ... that arrives only with images" (311). As her teenage brother had understood, Evie too comes to think that it is the image that might honour sleep's sweetness.

Jones' novels suggest that sleep is much more than a period of rest in the service of the day's activities or a state discoverable by means of MRI scans. Sleep is rendered complex, and as a state that can assert, rather than dilute, notions of time and subjectivity. Jones' texts also acknowledge the quiet challenge to narrative itself that sleep poses. With Evie's turn to the image to imagine sleep, she proposes the principles of tact that distinguish Jones' writing.

---

43 Michael Greaney, *Sleep and the Novel: Fictions of Somnolence from Jane Austen to the Present* (London: Palgrave, 2018), 215.

References

Barthes, Roland. *Camera Lucida: Reflections on Photography*. Translated by Richard Howard. New York: Hill & Wang, 1981.
--. *The Neutral: Lecture Course at the College de France (1977-1978)*. Translated by Rosalind Krauss and Denis Hollier. New York: Columbia University Press, 2005.
Benjamin, Walter. "Surrealism: The Last Snapshot of the European Intelligentsia." 1929. In *Selected Writings, vol 2*. Edited by Michael W. Jennings, Howard Eiland and Gary Smith, 207–21. Cambridge, MA: Harvard University Press, 1999.
Crary, Jonathan. *24/7: Late Capitalism and the Ends of Sleep*. London: Verso, 2013.
Dalziell, Tanya. *Gail Jones: Word, Image, Ethics*. Sydney: Sydney University Press, 2020.
Ekirch, A. Roger. *At Day's Close: Night in Times Past*. New York: Norton, 2005.
Farbman, Herschel. *The Other Night: Dreaming, Writing, and Restlessness in Twentieth-Century Literature*. New York: Fordham University Press, 2008.
Greaney, Michael. *Sleep and the Novel: Fictions of Somnolence from Jane Austen to the Present*. London: Palgrave, 2018.
Handley, Sasha. *Sleep in Early Modern England*. New Haven, CT: Yale University Press, 2016.
Jones, Gail. *Black Mirror*. Sydney: Picador, 2002.
--. *The Death of Noah Glass*. Melbourne: Text, 2018.
--. *Dreams of Speaking*. North Sydney: Vintage, 2006.
--. *Fetish Lives*. Fremantle: Fremantle Arts Centre Press, 1997.
--. *Five Bells*. North Sydney: Vintage, 2011.
--. *A Guide to Berlin*. North Sydney: Vintage, 2015.
--. "The Heart Beating Across the Room (On Possessing Someone Else's Photographs)." *Australian Book Review* 173 (August 1995): 36–41.
--. *Sixty Lights*. London: Harvill Press, 2004.
--. *Sorry*. North Sydney: Vintage, 2007.
Levinas, Emmanuel. *Existence and Existents*. Translated by Alphonso Lingis. Pittsburgh, PA: Duquesne University Press, 1978.
Mendelson, Wallace B. *The Science of Sleep: What It Is, How It Works, and Why It Matters*. Chicago, IL: University of Chicago Press, 2017.
Nabokov, Vladimir. *Speak, Memory: An Autobiography Revisited*. 1951. London: Penguin, 2012.
Nancy, Jean-Luc. *The Fall to Sleep*. Translated by Charlotte Mandell. New York: Fordham University Press, 2009.
--. *The Birth to Presence*. Translated by Brian Holmes et al. Stanford: Stanford University Press, 1994.
Pessoa, Fernando. *The Book of Disquiet*. 1982. Translated by Richard Zenith. London: Penguin, 2015.
Rose, Jacqueline. *On Not Being Able to Sleep: Psychoanalysis and the Modern World*. London: Chatto & Windus, 2003.
Sax, Marijn, Natali Helberger, Nadine Bol. "Health as a Means Towards Profitable Ends: mHealth Apps, User Autonomy, and Unfair Commercial Practices." *Journal of Consumer Policy* 41 (2018): 103–34.
Schwenger, Peter. *At the Borders of Sleep: On Liminal Literature*. Minneapolis: University of Minnesota Press, 2012.
Shakespeare, William. *Macbeth*. In *The Complete Oxford Shakespeare: Tragedies*. 1623. General editors Stanley Wells and Gary Taylor, 1307–34. Oxford: Oxford University Press, 1990.
Sterne, Laurence. *The Life and Opinions of Tristram Shandy*. 1767. Aberdeen: George Clark and Son, 1848.
Woolf, Virginia. *The Diary of Virginia Woolf: Volume 4, 1931–35*. Edited by Anne Olivier Bell. London: Penguin, 1983.

5

Resisting Fixation in Gail Jones' *Sorry* and *Five Bells*

Anthony Uhlmann

This chapter engages with an Australian Research Council project, "Other Worlds: Forms of World Literature", which involved four writers, Gail Jones, Alexis Wright, J.M. Coetzee and Nicholas Jose, along with myself and Ben Etherington. It is therefore informed by two sets of ideas that underpin the project. The first is that literature is a kind of thinking, and that writers think seriously about the nature of the world through their creative practice. The second involves a provocation, first made by J.M. Coetzee in establishing a series of seminars at Universidad Nacional de San Martín (UNSAM) in Buenos Aires, Argentina, under the umbrella of a project called "Literatures of the South", but taken up by Gail Jones along with Coetzee in an event they co-convened in Sydney in April 2019 called "Writing from the South". This provocation involves the assertion that some kind of meaningful affinity might be drawn between writers based in the Southern Hemisphere.[1] Such an affinity might well be invented, (a kind of "worldmaking", as Chris Andrews contends),[2] or it might result from environmental and historical affinities, shared "biomes" (a term discussed by

Anthony Uhlmann, Resisting Fixation in Gail Jones' *Sorry* and *Five Bells*. In *Inner and Outer Worlds: Gail Jones' Fiction*, edited by Anthony Uhlmann. Sydney: Sydney University Press, 2022. DOI: 10.30722/sup.9781743327791

---

1 For information on "Literatures of the South", see http://www.unsam.edu.ar/english/catedra-coetzee.asp, and James Halford, "Southern Conversations: J. M. Coetzee in Buenos Aires", *Sydney Review of Books*, 28 February 2017, https://sydneyreviewofbooks.com/essay/southern-conversations-j-m-coetzee-in-buenos-aires/. For "Other Worlds" and "Writers from the South", see http://www.formsofworldliterature.com/writing-from-the-south/, and James Halford, "Southern Conversations 2: Writing the South in Sydney", *Sydney Review of Books*, 25 February 2020, https://sydneyreviewofbooks.com/essay/southern-conversations-2/.
2 Chris Andrews, "Publishing, Translating, Worldmaking", in *The Cambridge Companion to World Literature*, eds Ben Etherington and Jarad Zimblar (Cambridge: Cambridge University Press, 2018), 227–40.

Alexander Beecroft, in relation to the cultural contexts that allow certain kinds of works to emerge), or shared experiences of colonialisation, with its violent confrontations with Indigenous peoples, and the waves of immigration that followed (Halford "Coetzee in Buenos Aires"; Beecroft).

The first idea, that literature thinks about the world in particular ways and thereby allows insights that otherwise remain out of reach, once might have been taken for granted but now seems to need to be established. The second is a provocation rather than a concept: it asks us to think about things we might not have otherwise considered, and in part frames our responses, while never fully establishing the grounds from which the claim itself springs. There is a third element at stake in this chapter, too. This is well known and involves the recognition that as a critic one is always working within a critical frame or frames, even if they are not explicitly mentioned. One always approaches texts with some presuppositions, and perhaps more importantly, with techniques or methods one uses to interpret.

In this case the critical frame is drawn from work Moira Gatens and I have been developing relating Spinoza, and his philosophical system, to literature.[3] Yet, why would one relate Spinoza to Gail Jones, when, despite the fact that she is one of Australia's most philosophical novelists, there is no reference to Spinoza in either of the novels considered here?

The following responses are offered. First, Spinoza's influence, while occluded due to his iconoclasticism, has been transversal and ubiquitous, entering into Western literature through the importance of his work to German and English Romanticism, as well as to authors within the Victorian era, and nineteenth-century American literature.[4] Further, in part mediated by the influence Spinoza had on twentieth-century philosophy (Henri Bergson, Bertrand Russell, Wittgenstein, Deleuze and Guattari, Althusser, and others), psychology (William James, Sigmund Freud), and even physics (Einstein, Bohr), as well as directly being read by major figures (Joyce, Woolf, Beckett, T.S. Eliot) Spinoza's ideas can be traced through into modernist literature.[5]

---

3 Anthony Uhlmann and Moira Gatens, "Spinoza on Art and the Cultivation of a Disposition Toward Joyful Living", *Intellectual History Review*, 30, no. 3 (2020): 429–45, https://doi.org/10.1080/17496977.2020.1732705

4 See Jonathan I. Israel, *Radical Enlightenment: Philosophy and the Making of Modernity 1650–1750* (Oxford: Oxford University Press, 2001); David Bell, *Spinoza in Germany 1670 to the Age of Goethe* (London: Institute of Germanic Studies, University of London, 1984); Wayne Boucher, *Spinoza in English: A Bibliography*, 2nd ed. (Bristol: Thoemmes, 1999); Moira Gatens, "Cloud-Borne Angels, Prophets, and the Old Woman's Flower-pot: Reading George Eliot's realism alongside Spinoza's 'beings of the imagination'", *Australian Literary Studies* 28, no. 3 (2013): 1–14; William R. Hooton, III, "Wordsworth, Coleridge and the Politics of Pantheism", *Coleridge Bulletin: The Journal of the Friends of Coleridge*, (1999 Autumn): 14.

5 Resisting Fixation in Gail Jones' *Sorry* and *Five Bells*

It is possible, then, to see the influence of Spinoza, however occluded and deformed, coiled within modern and contemporary literature. The second justification attends to the ongoing power of Spinoza's ideas: his philosophy is built upon relations and relationality, and as such offers a description of the representational logics with which we form our understandings of the world. So, too, he develops a theory of the emotions that insists that our minds, which often seem to us to be separate from or cut off from the world we perceive, as a world within a world, are very much implicated within the world, responding and emerging just as everything else in the universe responds and emerges, through cause and effect. Ideas or images related to Spinoza's thought, then, (that God *is* Nature and is only revealed through Nature's laws, and Being is immanent rather than transcendent, and that there is a causal logic to the emotions that connects us to the world that forms us) have come to permeate our culture. So, too, Spinoza has been shown to be prescient by modern scientists: for example, his insistence that we think through the emotions as much as through reason resonates strongly with contemporary neuroscience and understandings of the workings of the brain, and these insights in turn are important to our understanding of writing creative works, which explicitly engage with both representations and presentations of conscious and unconscious thought.[6]

This chapter will offer readings of two novels Gail Jones wrote in the middle of her career, one after the other, *Sorry* (2007) and *Five Bells* (2011). One novel, *Sorry*, has Gail Jones' home of Western Australia, and the country around Broome, as its contextual frame, while *Five Bells* is set in the Sydney where she now lives and to which she had then recently moved.

Thinking in Literature

There are clear echoes between the two novels. First, the idea of communicating, or rather, of failing to communicate messages of apology is something that is

---

5   See Knox Peden, *Spinoza Contra Phenomenology: French Rationalism from Cavaillès to Deleuze* (Stanford, CA: Stanford University Press, 2014); Richard A. Cohen, "Philo, Spinoza, Bergson: The Rise of an Ecological Age", in *The New Bergson*, ed. John Mullarky (Manchester: Manchester University Press, 1999); Walter Bernard, "Freud and Spinoza", *Psychiatry: Interpersonal and Biological Processes*, 9, no. 2 (1946): 99–108; Marjorie Grene and Debra Nails (eds), *Spinoza and the Sciences*, Boston Studies in the Philosophy of Science (Amsterdam: Springer, 1986); Derek Ryan, "Entangled in Nature: Deleuze's Modernism, Woolf's Philosophy, and Spinoza's Ethology", in *Understanding Deleuze, Understanding Modernism*, ed. Paul Ardoin, S.E. Gontarski and Laci Mattison (New York: Bloomsbury, 2014), 151–68.
6   Antonio Damasio, *Looking for Spinoza: Joy, Sorrow, and the Feeling Brain* (New York; Harvest Book, 2003); Heidi Morrison Ravven, "Spinoza's Anticipation of Contemporary Affective Neuroscience", *Consciousness and Emotion* 4, no. 2 (2003): 257–90.

understood in particular personal terms on the one hand, and in general or political terms on the other in both novels. With *Sorry*, the context is Australia at the end of the Howard era, when an apology to Indigenous Australians for past and ongoing injustices was pointedly refused. With *Five Bells*, the context is Australia in the early days of the Rudd government, where his formal apology to Indigenous Australians seemed to offer a glimpse of hope for potential reconciliation.

A second echo involves how both novels insist upon the importance of works of fiction or art to our capacity to understand. Works of literature are essential sites of meaning for characters within the novels, and provide intertextual points of reference that help to structure each of them. Shakespeare's works in *Sorry* provide a method of achieving freedom for the central character Perdita on the one hand, and Shakespeare's plays (*The Winter's Tale* and *Macbeth*) are used as structuring elements for the novel as a whole. So, too, in *Five Bells* Kenneth Slessor's poem "Five Bells" and works by Boris Pasternak and James Joyce offer intertextual resonances for the work as a whole as well as resonating with characters. This importance of literature as something which might carry meaning for individuals and act as a bridge between the islands that individuals are in danger of becoming is underlined in *Sorry* where it is suggested that there is a secret communion between all the readers who have read the same book.[7]

There is more that can be said here, as this image of the importance of books has two sides: on the one hand, one can hide or escape within literature, as if cut off from the world, in one's own inner world. On the other hand, literature can also provide a means of connection to others, just as Perdita learns to overcome her stutter by reciting Shakespeare using the iambic pentameters of his poetry to find her own voice.

A third echo between the two novels tied to the idea of literature occurs in the image of snow. In *Sorry*, Perdita's mother, Stella, disconnected and discombobulated by her exile to Australia, dreams of snow falling over the new world she is forced to inhabit. This image is an image of comfort, of meaning somehow being forged or recovered among the ruins of her own capacity to feel adequately and understand. The image in turn is shared and adopted by her daughter Perdita. So too, in *Five Bells*, snow is an image that recurs among three of the four main protagonists, again as a site of meaning: Pei Xing remembers the snow in Pasternak's novel *Dr Zhivago*, which her father, who disappears during the Cultural Revolution in China, translates, while affirming as a kind of in-joke with the world that there are many words for snow. The Irish tourist Catherine Healy thinks of snow in relation to her dead brother, who dies meaninglessly in a car

---

7   Gail Jones, *Sorry* (North Sydney: Vintage, 2007), 144. All subsequent references are to this edition and appear in parentheses in the text.

accident, again relating the image to a work of literature, this time James Joyce's short story "The Dead", where snow falls. Here Jones has Catherine remember the final lines of Joyce's story:

> His soul swooned slowly as he heard the snow falling faintly through the universe and faintly falling, like the descent of their last end, upon all the living and the dead.[8]

James deMello, his mental health disintegrating just as his mother's had before him, thinks of the fog that attends his and her mental breakdowns as "snow". He also thinks of the snow domes she carried with her from her former life in Italy. The image of snow, then, like the idea of literature, paradoxically carries a sense both of enclosure or even imprisonment within one's self; a sense of enclosure tied to the impossibility of sharing one's innermost experiences and the world that formed them with others, and a sense of meaning, which offers a glimpse at least, of a shared world.

Of the four main protagonists in *Five Bells*, it is Ellie alone who does not think of snow, but, although she is unaware of her former lover James' suicide in the harbour, through a sympathy of images (that might be understood not to be random, since, as we have seen in *Sorry*, readers of the same books share something), at the end of the book, she is drawn to the idea of general rain, which is now falling over the living and the dead in Sydney.

Sorry ends with an allusion to snow which subtly invokes Joyce's "The Dead":

> Afraid of slumber agitation, or ghostly visits, I willed myself to think instead of Stella's snow dream: a field of flakes descending, the slow transformation of the shapes of the world, the slow inconclusive, obliteration. I saw a distant place, all forgetful white, reversing its presences. I saw Mary, and Billy, covered by snowflakes. I saw my mother's bare feet beneath the hem of her nightgown. Everything was losing definition and outline. Everything was disappearing under the gradual snow. Calmed, I looked at the sky and saw only a blank. Soft curtains coming down, a whiteness, a peace. (214)

The intertextual references confront what in *Five Bells* is called the "here-now" of the Australian setting. The snow that is imagined falling in *Sorry* stems from Stella's dreams, which uncannily bring together the time of Stella's European past that she mentally lays down over the present of Australia to allow her to be. In *Five*

---

8   James Joyce, "The Dead" (in *Dubliners*), quoted in narrative of Catherine Healy, in Gail Jones, *Five Bells* (North Sydney: Vintage, 2011), 58. All subsequent references are to this edition and appear in parentheses in the text.

Bells, Ellie is not an exile of Perdita's type. She too is tied to an idea of the past, but the here-now is a space she wants to occupy; a space she imagines to be still full of potential for her relationship with James, not yet knowing he has already drowned in Sydney Harbour, echoing the fate of Joe Lynch, who inspired Kenneth Slessor's poem "Five Bells".[9] The here-now of Sydney makes snow impossible, and in its place rain falls. The image that was an image of peace in *Sorry* now becomes one of a kind of obliviousness or ignorance, a momentary grace before one is forced to confront reality:

> Ellie is thinking of rainfall over the Opera House, thinking of the Harbour swept shining and mystical by rain light, thinking of the time lapse of all that she has known and read, and of James, and with James, ever and ever abiding. The night has gained an enormity with the coming of the storm and in the drench she imagines it out there, Circular Quay, the vast dark water, the rain-glazed tide, the Harbour buoys with their red flares tossing messages across the water, seabirds rising up and rain coming down and falling, falling upon the living and the dead, ever and ever abiding. There is the musical sound of rain on her roof and Ellie is thinking, so she will remember, *must ring James, must ring James, must ring, ring …* (216)

Other Worlds

Another element in common between the two novels is the understanding of time, as something that both moves and fails to move. Like water, time both flows and is still. That is, time is seen as a flow, or the lapping of waves (following Shakespeare and Virginia Woolf) but it is also understood, through the idea of memory that Jones addresses, to be fixed in place or still. The image that tries to come to terms with this is one of recursion or looping repetition. In both novels this is associated with an idea of Australia, which carries at once a conception of a space and time in the here-now, and relations to other times, other places. These other worlds might be spaces of memory, but for many characters they are also memories of other countries to which they are connected. There is a contrast, then, that might become a contradiction, between the somatic here-now of Australia and the psychological otherness overlaid upon it. In some instances, for Aboriginal characters, such as Mary in *Sorry*, the "here-now" can manifest as a perpetual present, extending to time immemorial through connection to place that, despite being viciously disrupted by colonisation, remains. In turn these

---

9   Kenneth Slessor, "Five Bells" in *Selected Poems* (1939) (Sydney: HarperCollins, 2014).

custodians are capable of communicating this eternal now to others they come into contact with such as Perdita, who glimpses it. At the other extreme there are characters such as Perdita's mother Stella, or Pei Xing in *Five Bells*, who cannot ever fully heal the gulf between the physical "here-now" of Australia and the psychological European or Asian histories they carry with them.

Yet the gap is not simply one between different places and times. It also involves memories of pasts within the same Australian place. Pasts which carry personal traumas (such as Perdita's experience and Mary's, and those of Ellie and James in *Five Bells*) and interpersonal traumas (such as the colonial wars that dispossessed and displaced Indigenous Australians) that haunt characters and the very place of Australia itself. These ideas bring into focus some of what is at stake in any "idea of the South". Complex and often traumatic relations to events which are both here-now (the eternal present of the land of Australia) and carried across from other times and places, scar and change the lands that were colonised by peoples of the Northern Hemisphere over a number of centuries. These processes form and deform the people who live in these "new worlds" both in an actual psychological present that is always in relation to psychological pasts, and in a "here-now" of the perpetual present of the places themselves.

Haecceity: What is the South?

Although the relations between elements are extremely complex, it is possible to attempt to set out what is at stake conceptually, and I will sketch this here drawing on ideas from philosophy. In *A Thousand Plateaus*, Deleuze and Guattari define a different kind of individuation, drawn from a concept first developed by the fourteenth-century Scholastic philosopher Duns Scotus, called "haecceity".[10]

Duns Scotus, like Spinoza, saw God as being immanent, rather than transcendent, and involving a univocity of being (where all things are one thing). "Haecceity" is taken from the Latin word "haecc", or "this", and is defined by the Oxford English Dictionary as "'thisness'; 'hereness and nowness'; that quality or mode of being in virtue of which a thing is or becomes a definite individual". As Deleuze and Guattari explain, haecceity might refer to a different kind of individuality, one that does not depend on the ideas of the subject, or the thing.

> A season, a winter, a summer, an hour, a date have a perfect individuality lacking nothing, even though this individuality is different from that of a thing or a subject. They are haecceities in the sense that they consist entirely of

---

10   Gilles Deleuze and Félix Guattari, *A Thousand Plateaus: Capitalism and Schizophrenia*, trans. Brian Massumi (Minneapolis: University of Minnesota Press, 1987).

relations of movement and rest between molecules or particles, capacities to affect and be affected.[11]

This concept brings to mind *Five Bells*, which, as the cover of the Random House edition states, is set on "one radiant Sydney day". Deleuze and Guattari's development of the concept might be better understood by attending to the particular use they make of "longitude" and "latitude". On the globe of the world, longitude connects us with the ever-changing time of our "now" on a north–south axis, and latitude with biomes or climate zones (tropical, temperate, polar, etc.), south to south and north to north. In the quotation above, longitude concerns those relations of movement and rest and latitude to the capacity to be affected that any individuated body has. They explicitly align the idea of "longitude" with Spinoza, who defines individuals as being comprised of the drawing together of elements arranged in a certain ratio of speeds and slowness. That is, all the extensive parts that determine that body: the molecules that comprise it, for example.

This idea of latitude is consistent both with Spinoza and with many Indigenous knowledge systems, including Australian Aboriginal understandings. It understands individuals not in terms of some ideal or form, such as a species (mankind), or function (doctor, or lawyer or quantitative psychologist); rather, the individual is defined by the capacities they have to affect and be affected by others through the relations they enter into.

For Spinoza, each body corresponds to a degree of power, but this is subject to change. That is, our power shifts as we grow weaker or stronger due to the relations we enter into. These shifts in our degree of power in turn are felt or sensed as affects. "Affects are becomings", as Deleuze and Guattari famously state: we change as we shift between one degree of power and the next. So too, for Spinoza, the more affects a body is capable of, the more it can do.

Haecceity involves both "longitude" and "latitude". On the one hand (longitude), it involves the complex sets of relations of smaller bodies that comprise our particular body. On the other hand (latitude), it involves the capacities open to us through our engagement with the world: what we can do.

This can be understood as much in relation to the entire planet as it can in relation to an individual person: polar regions are frozen and certain things are possible there. Very different things are possible at the equator among rainforests, or in the temperate regions of the South. At the same time, these possibilities are susceptible to change: as the climate changes different things become possible, or

---

11 Deleuze and Guattari, *Thousand Plateaus*, 261.

no longer possible. The possibilities open to a city without water differ from those open to a city with water security, for example.

Yet for beings such as ourselves, what is also at stake, what determines what we can do, involves our own dispositions, which open up or close off our potential to act. This in part is attitudinal; it involves how we respond to what happens to us; how the longitude that corresponds to a particular body made up of particular elements is empowered or rendered weaker through latitude, which corresponds to what a body is able to do.

Disposition: Breaking with Fixation

While she consistently returns to the "here-now" of continuous place, Jones focuses more intently on the temporal, psychological relations of the pasts that haunt her characters' present. In "Five Bells", Kenneth Slessor attends to the same problem. Time "is not of the clock", and "many lives are lived between five bells".

In *Sorry*, the child Perdita learns Shakespeare by heart so as to overcome stuttering brought on by the suppressed memory of murdering her father (a crime for which her Aboriginal friend Mary takes the blame and is wrongfully imprisoned). This process involves a deliberate attempt to alter her disposition, the way her body responds to words. She takes on the disposition of the poetry itself, allowing it to flow through her and open up possibilities that had become closed off. There is a recognition, here, of the power of art to situate us within worlds and increase our capacities. Yet it is not a simple matter of following the footsteps of great European forefathers. Perdita finds herself, in interpreting Shakespeare's "Sonnet 60",[12] in disagreement with Shakespeare's idea of time (in turn echoed by Virginia Woolf in *The Waves*):

> Like as the waves make towards the pebbled shore,
> So do our minutes hasten to their end;
> Each changing place with that which goes before,
> In sequent toil all forwards do contend.[13]

Perdita states: "I realised Shakespeare was wrong. There was no forward incessancy, like waves meeting waves, but recursion, fold, things revisiting out of time" (182). Perdita's mother Stella is stuck and breaks down over the failure to properly exist in the here-now of Australia; Perdita is stuck trying to come to

---

12   William Shakespeare, "Sonnet 60", *The Arden Shakespeare Complete Works* (London: Arden Shakespeare, 2002).
13   Shakespeare, "Sonnet 60", quoted in Jones, *Sorry*, 182.

terms with the failure to prevent or make right the awful injustice Mary has been made to bear on her behalf; a sacrifice that is echoed in the deep injustices done to all Indigenous Australians.

The same idea of being stuck structures *Five Bells*. The characters are doing all they can to exist in the here-now, and part of this involves embracing the flow of time that has passed through and remains in the place, yet they are all also constantly returning to memories that fixate them. James is fixated by the memory of the dead schoolgirl he failed to protect from drowning in Western Australia; Ellie is fixated by memories of her first love with James; Catherine is fixated by the death of her brother in Ireland; Pei Xing by the horrors of the Cultural Revolution in China. As such, their capacities to live, to be, to do things, are reduced.

Another element that serves to structure both novels is the importance of places; not just as backdrops in which situations and events might unfold, but as actors or agents in the scenes. Here place does not only frame the ideas and events, it enters into and informs the dispositions of the characters. To put this another way, the physical or longitudinal being of the here-now acts upon the latitudinal being of capacity.

Each of these structuring elements might be considered in relation to ideas of fixation and reconciliation (or understanding) that allow a moving on from fixation, an opening up of new potentials, new capacities. Both of these involve questions of disposition. All of these things, in turn, are approached in the two novels by techniques of characterisation, or by focusing on and developing the inner lives and the external contexts that give life to the characters in Jones' novels. They are also brought to light through structural or formal methods: particularly through kinds of intertextuality.

All of these elements concern, to a greater or lesser extent, a central problem, which involves kinds of fixation which prevent understanding, and keep the characters stuck, and reduce their capacities. They also all involve reflections upon either a failure to break out of this fixation, or efforts to break out of this fixation.

Both cases – both the failure to break out, and efforts to break out – relate to questions of disposition.[14] Disposition, ultimately, involves the attitude one has towards the possibility of understanding. One might be so disposed that understanding is impossible, in which case one will remain ignorant, locked off from possible understanding. On the contrary, it is possible to open oneself to understanding, and thereby open up one's capacities to act. This is central to the distinction between joyful passions and sad passions Spinoza sets out in *The Ethics* because joy *disposes us* towards understanding, while sadness *disposes us* towards being unable to understand. That is, Spinoza suggests that our disposition can

---

14   Uhlmann and Gatens, "Spinoza on Art", 2–8.

vary in relation to the affects we experience, and that we can organise the affects in such a way as to avoid sad passions and experience more joyful passions.

In 4P38 he states:

> Whatever so disposes the human body that it can be affected in a great many ways, or renders it capable of affecting external bodies in a great many ways, is useful to man; the more it renders the body capable of being affected in a great many ways, or of affecting other bodies, the more useful it is on the other hand, what renders the body less capable of these things is harmful.[15]

In 5P9 Spinoza states that an "affect is only evil, *or* harmful, insofar as it prevents the mind from being able to think". The harmful affect is that which prevents us from thinking by making us fixate on one object. He goes on to claim that insofar as we are able to understand, we have the capacity to change sad passive affects into joyful active affects. This does not mean we do not feel pain; rather, we understand what we are feeling and why, and aspects, at least, of how it has come about.

Of course, given the enormity of certain kinds of suffering, this is extremely difficult to achieve in practice. What is emphasised, rather, is the attempt to try to do this. In *Sorry* and *Five Bells*, we are shown characters that are fixated on particular events in their lives; memories which are like standing water, they recur and continue to re-occur and the danger is that one might become fixated upon and ultimately destroyed by these events.

Stella and Nicholas, Perdita's parents, have fixed ideas. These ideas in turn are involved with an inability to successfully move from one place to another, because the ideas of the former place take over and inhabit the new place, making it seem lesser and oppressive. The narrow disposition involved in this makes the whole world of the here-now seem small and stale, effectively driving Stella and Nicholas mad. Yet almost all the characters in these novels are asked to engage with the same problematic. How might it be possible to overcome fixations, which inhibit our capacities to communicate both with others and the very elements that comprise us in the here-now?

Perdita herself becomes a sign of this fixation, through which the evil brought into being by the violence she does to her father (in turn provoked by the violent

---

15 Benedictus de Spinoza, *The Ethics*, in *The Collected Works of Spinoza*, vol. I. trans. and ed. Edwin Curley (Princeton, NJ: Princeton University Press, 1985). Quotations from Spinoza are from Curley (1985). References follow the standard abbreviations for Spinoza's Ethics: E for the Ethics, Arabic numerals for the five parts, P for Proposition, S for Scholium, C for Corollary, Appen for Appendix, and DefAff for Definition of the Affects that appear at the end of E3.

rape of Mary he is engaged in as Perdita walks in) manifests itself through the symptom of her stutter. The psychological trauma causes her to suppress the memory of her part in her father's death, but the symptom of this trauma is a new inability to communicate.

While the source of the trauma is occluded, even from Perdita herself, or while it is not faced, she remains fixed in place, trapped, more or less, within an inability to communicate or understand. Through therapy, including the therapy of her taking on the disposition of the works of Shakespeare as she reads, she at last is able to recognise what it is exactly that has caused her to be fixed in place. This in turn leads to a new revelation: that she needs to make good, as far as this is possible, the damage she has caused, in particular to Mary, who is imprisoned for the crime Perdita has committed. The idea of making good, or breaking out of, or overcoming the traumatic event on which one is fixated, involves, in her case, the need to apologise, to be reconciled, both with her friend Mary and her mother Stella.

In both cases the efforts at reconciliation are frustrated. She is unable to help free Mary, and her mother remains locked within her own fixated self, unable to allow Perdita in. Yet the effort itself is valuable. It opens Perdita to the possibility of understanding what has happened and so, what might remain possible.

Similar stories are found in *Five Bells*: Pei Xing, in particular, as the oldest and wisest of the four main characters, has been the subject of wrongs, rather than the perpetrator of them. Yet she makes the effort to forgive the woman who tortured her in China, Dong Hua, who has now, through accidents of fate, also found her way to Australia. At first Pei Xing resists Dong Hua's efforts to apologise, but after a time she opens herself to them. It is a deliberate effort, and not one that seems necessarily rational. She is forced to justify it to her son, who does not see why she should forgive Dong Hua, given the gravity of the injustices done.

She thinks "this is how one lets go, in sympathetic reconciliation" (114). Yet none of this is represented as being simple or even successful. It is not as if reconciliation can be ultimately achieved, yet her character wishes to believe that this will allow her to live, to be alive in the here-now, even though the recurring nightmare of herself in a prison cell undergoing torture will never be effaced. It is not about effacing the trauma; rather, it is about shifting one's disposition, opening oneself to understanding.

In contrast, James finds himself racked with guilt for the death of the schoolgirl who was under his supervision during a school excursion. He tries to apologise but fails to find words adequate to this. His fixation ultimately leads to his suicide. James' fixation in turn is complicated by both mental illness and substance abuse. There is nothing straightforward in the movement from being fixed within a sad affect to finding a way to open oneself to positive understanding. James' tragedy, and Ellie's (though she is not yet aware of James' death as the book ends) is made more acute because Ellie might offer a way forward for him, a way back to the here-now, but he fails to see it.

Catherine too has not yet made her way out from the fixation on her beloved brother's death. At the end of the novel, indeed, even the optimism Pei Xing expresses is called into doubt. She finds herself falling back on "number superstition", wishing to change the number of protagonists (the four protagonists of the novel) who have all been photographed with a small girl who is missing, from four to five.

Four is "a bad luck number in Chinese, four was the homophone of 'death'" (197). Pei Xing must make it so that she thinks of the number five and not four. Yet she herself is aware that this spell might very well fail to work; that all might not turn out well for the little girl who is missing; that she might not be kept safe. Neither book, then, offers neat solutions. Spinoza too concedes that, after all, we might not be capable of attaining adequate knowledge, and thereby protecting ourselves from what befalls us and those we love, yet *The Ethics* offers a way, insofar as we are capable, of attempting to open our dispositions to understanding, and increase our capacities to both feel and act. Spinoza tells us, "a free man thinks of nothing less than of death, and his wisdom is a meditation of life, not on death" (4P67).

It becomes apparent that achieving such freedom is difficult, perhaps even impossible. Insofar as we fail to achieve it, however, he recommends a plan for living. Even if we have not achieved adequate knowledge that will allow us to live in accordance with reason, we can develop a plan for living and arrange the affects so that we are affected more by joyful affects than sad affects.

> It is the part of a wise man, I say, to refresh and restore himself in moderation with pleasant food and drink, with scents, with the beauty of green plants, with decoration, music, sports, the theatre, and other things of this kind, which anyone can use without injury to another. For the human body is composed of a great many parts of different natures, which constantly require new and varied nourishment, so that the whole body may be equally capable of all the things which can follow from its nature, and hence, so that the mind also may be equally capable of understandings many things at once. (4P45 Schol.)

That is, while it is certain that life involves suffering, we nevertheless need to focus on what is "here-now". This is the case even as death hovers over us, or haunts us. For Gail Jones in both novels, it is apparent that one way forward is to recognise the interconnected nature of things. One of the covers of *Sorry* refers to an image that is associated with Mary, the Aboriginal protagonist of *Sorry*: the cats-cradle.

Figure 5.1 Cover of *Sorry*.

This image carries an idea of the interrelatedness of all things. Here, Spinoza is in accord with ancient Aboriginal knowledge. Our only hope of understanding, and therefore of living well, even when faced with suffering, even when confronted by powerful forces and events that happen to sunder the connections that sustain us, is to recognise that everything is connected.

One has to break out of an internal fixation on one's self and open oneself to the world. Mary teaches Perdita this lesson when she first meets her, but underlines it when Perdita visits Mary in prison, where, rather than giving in to the sad passions generated by the injustices she has suffered, Mary thinks of her cell mates in prison, who she helps by teaching them how to read. Yet even this is not a ready-made solution. It is a particular response to a particular condition of suffering. The suffering itself is not somehow overridden or made to disappear; rather, Mary simply focuses on living and not death.

Yet death hovers in Gail Jones' works. I will end by returning to the final passages of each book which are cited above. Both novels address overwhelming sorrow. *Sorry* seems to offer the consolation of a space in which all separation is overcome, leaving only what is eternal. Note the effort Perdita makes to find this consolation, to come to terms with the sorrow: "I willed myself to think instead of Stella's snow dream … a whiteness, a peace" (214).

There is a different situation in *Five Bells*. Ellie too is feeling some consolation; yet it is overturned by dramatic irony, since we know, while she doesn't, that James is dead. She leaves us, as an emblem of this, with four rather than five rings: "*must ring James, must ring James, must ring, ring …*" (216). The bell sounds four times, signifying death.

For both novels, then, death is inescapable, even when we are unaware it is approaching us. Yet the formula, the plan, might remain. Try not to fixate upon this. Try to live as best as possible in the radiance of the here-now.

References

Andrews, Chris. "Publishing, Translating, Worldmaking." In *The Cambridge Companion to World Literature*, edited by Ben Etherington and Jarad Zimblar, 227–40. Cambridge: Cambridge University Press, 2018.

Beecroft, Alexander. *An Ecology of World Literature: From Antiquity to the Present*. London: Verso, 2015.

Bell, David. *Spinoza in Germany 1670 to the Age of Goethe*. London: Institute of Germanic Studies, University of London, 1984.

Bernard, Walter. "Freud and Spinoza." *Psychiatry: Interpersonal and Biological Processes* 9, no. 2 (1946): 99–108.

Boucher, Wayne. *Spinoza in English: A Bibliography*. London: Thoemmes; 2nd ed, 1999.

Cohen, Richard A. "Philo, Spinoza, Bergson: The Rise of an Ecological Age." In *The New Bergson*, edited by John Mullarky, 18–31. Manchester: Manchester University Press, 1999.

Damasio, Antonio. *Looking for Spinoza: Joy, Sorrow, and the Feeling Brain*. New York: Harvest Books, 2003.

Deleuze, Gilles and Félix Guattari. *A Thousand Plateaus: Capitalism and Schizophrenia*. Translated by Brian Massumi. Minneapolis: University of Minnesota Press, 1987.

Gatens, Moira. "Cloud-Borne Angels, Prophets, and the Old Woman's Flower-pot: Reading George Eliot's Realism Alongside Spinoza's 'Beings of the Imagination.'" *Australian Literary Studies* 28, no. 3 (2013): 1–14.

Grene, Marjorie and Debra Nails (eds.). *Spinoza and the Sciences, Boston Studies in the Philosophy of Science*. Amsterdam: Springer, 1986.

Halford, James. "Southern Conversations: J.M. Coetzee in Buenos Aires." *Sydney Review of Books*, 28 February 2017, https://sydneyreviewofbooks.com/essay/southern-conversations-j-m-coetzee-in-buenos-aires/

Halford, James. "Southern Conversations 2: Writing the South in Sydney." *Sydney Review of Books*, 25 February 2020, https://sydneyreviewofbooks.com/essay/southern-conversations-2/

Hooton, William R. III. "Wordsworth, Coleridge and the Politics of Pantheism." *Coleridge Bulletin: The Journal of the Friends of Coleridge*, no. 14 (1999 Autumn): 60–72.

Israel, Jonathan I. *Radical Enlightenment: Philosophy and the Making of Modernity 1650-1750*. Oxford: Oxford University Press, 2001.

Jones, Gail. *Five Bells*. North Sydney: Vintage, 2011.

—. *Sorry*. North Sydney: Vintage, 2007.

Joyce, James. *Dubliners*. New York: Norton, 2006.

Peden, Knox. *Spinoza Contra Phenomenology: French rationalism from Cavaillès to Deleuze*. Stanford, CA: Stanford University Press, 2014.

Ravven, Heidi Morrison. "Spinoza's Anticipation of Contemporary Affective Neuroscience." *Consciousness and Emotion* 4, no. 2 (2003): 257–90.

Ryan, Derek. "Entangled in Nature: Deleuze's Modernism, Woolf's Philosophy, and Spinoza's Ethology." In *Understanding Deleuze, Understanding Modernism*, edited by Paul Ardoin, S.E. Gontarski, Laci Mattison, 151–68. New York: Bloomsbury, 2014.

Shakespeare, William. *The Arden Shakespeare Complete Works* (1609). London: Arden Shakespeare, 2002.

Slessor, Kenneth. "Five Bells." In *Selected Poems*. Sydney: HarperCollins, 2014.

Spinoza, Benedictus de. *The Ethics*. In *The Collected Works of Spinoza*. Vol. I. Translated and edited by Edwin Curley. Princeton, NJ: Princeton University Press, 1985.

Uhlmann, Anthony and Moira Gatens. "Spinoza on Art and the Cultivation of a Disposition Toward Joyful Living." *Intellectual History Review* 30, no. 3 (2020): 429–45, https://doi.org/10.1080/17496977.2020.1732705

6

"Moving on Metaphorical Silk Roads of Intellectual Trade": Chinese Aesthetics in *Five Bells*

Valérie-Anne Belleflamme

In his essay exploring "The Chinese Attitude towards the Past", Simon Leys postulates that the Chinese past "seems to inhabit *the people* rather than the bricks and stones"; it is, as he puts it, "both spiritually active and physically invisible".[1] Indeed Chinese architecture "embodies a sort of 'in-built obsolescence'… [it is] essentially made of perishable and fragile materials … it decays rapidly and require[s] frequent rebuilding", whereas non-Chinese architecture "attempt[s] to challenge and overcome the erosion of time" by using "the strongest possible materials" as well as "techniques that will ensure maximum resilience".[2] As a result, Leys observes that, "in China, the taste for antiques has always remained closely – if not exclusively – related to the prestige of the *written word*".[3] In her 2016 essay entitled "'I am Chinese': Of Bodies and Walls, Of Boundaries and their Dissolution", Gail Jones takes her cue from Leys' "fascinating provocation" according to which there is in China not only "a strange physical absence of ancient monuments" but also "a native suspicion of history located in buildings and objects", which potentially legitimates the notion that "what is imperishable are ideas, the bridges of time within consciousness", while "the written word … supersedes the prestige of solid things". Written for inclusion into *Moving Worlds: A Journal of Transcultural Writings*, her essay is "a discontinuous meditation on occasions of creative encounter".[4] More specifically it considers "artistic

Valérie-Anne Belleflamme, "Moving on Metaphorical Silk Roads of Intellectual Trade": Chinese Aesthetics in *Five Bells*. In *Inner and Outer Worlds: Gail Jones' Fiction*, edited by Anthony Uhlmann. Sydney: Sydney University Press, 2022. DOI: 10.30722/sup.9781743327791

---

1   Simon Leys, *The Angel and the Octopus: Collected Essays, 1983–1998* (Sydney: Duffy & Snellgrove, 1999), 6.
2   Leys, 8.
3   Leys, 10.

encounters in relation to space, perspective, and scales of knowing and access" in four imaginative narratives: the Chinese folktale of Meng Jiangnu, Kafka's short story "The Great Wall of China" (written in 1917 but published posthumously in 1931), Michelangelo Antonioni's film *Chung Kuo, Cina* (1972), and in her own novel *Five Bells* (2011).[5] Both the local folktale and her self-critical commentary will serve as my focus of attention in this chapter and, consequently, be quoted from extensively.

In her Chinese essay, as I shall call it, Jones claims that the Great Wall of China, the most paradigmatic and "the most commonplace signifier of Chinese history … draws us to contemplate the trope of the monumental in our imaginative and intellectual rapprochements". Considered in popular belief as "a vertical grave, an unholy ossuary, a structure bolstered in its material substance by the bodies of its workers",[6] the Great Wall aestheticises what Leys identifies as the Chinese attitude towards the past.[7] Indeed, paradoxical though it may seem, this macabre myth of the Great Wall, in which "the workers becom[e] the monument",[8] literally and literarily materialises the Chinese past's immateriality.[9] In a parallel step, although there is no Great Wall in *Five Bells*, I wish to contend that Jones aestheticises the Chinese attitude towards the past in her fifth novel, namely through the character of Pei Xing.

Five Bells draws together four strangers (Australian ex-lovers Ellie and James, Irish tourist Catherine, and Shanghainese *émigré* Pei Xing) and makes them all converge on a single Saturday on Sydney's iconic Circular Quay, with its emblematic Opera House, its Museum of Contemporary Art, and its famous Harbour Bridge. This particular setting, which associates monuments in eclectic arrangements but is also, first and foremost, an Aboriginal site of memory,[10] encapsulates Jones' view of history as twofold: on the one hand, as she explains, "there is the history that seems to be unfolding and moving forward", while on the other hand there is a "plunging down into the interiority of the place, into its

---

4   Gail Jones, "'I am Chinese': Of Bodies and Walls, Of Boundaries and Their Dissolution", *Moving Worlds: A Journal of Transcultural Writing*, Imagining Asia, 16, no. 2 (2006): 80.
5   Gail Jones, *Five Bells* (North Sydney, NSW: Vintage Australia, 2011). All subsequent references are to this edition and appear in parentheses in the text.
6   Jones, "'I am Chinese'", 80, 81.
7   In this chapter, I will use this phrase to refer to the Chinese past that inhabits the people, not the buildings and monuments.
8   Jones, "'I am Chinese'", 82.
9   To be more specific, on the premise that the Chinese past inhabits the people, not the monuments, and is therefore immaterial, as the workers on the Great Wall have literally become the monument, somewhat paradoxically then, the monument comes to materialise the Chinese immaterial attitude towards the past.
10 It is marked as the place where Captain Arthur Phillip established the penal colony's first settlement in Australia.

lost history".[11] This is certainly reminiscent of what Merlin Coverley says about psychogeography, namely that it "increasingly contrasts a horizontal movement across the topography of the city with a vertical descent through its past".[12] Jones claims an interest in psychogeography, or "in the idea", as she puts it, "that we must walk around our own place with an active intelligence and with a degree of radical attention to what is there", as "within the material spaces of a city are these immaterial traces of something else". Taking Sydney as an example, she insists on the importance of looking at the city's "shapes, its motions", and of attending to its "sounds, corridors between spaces, the unexpected".[13]

In *Five Bells*, James, the novel's sole male protagonist, muses at the sight of the Opera House: "The monumental is never precisely what we expect" (5). In fact, as Jones interestingly declared at a reading in Cologne in 2014, in her novel, "the 'monuments' are the inner responses, not the icons".[14] In like manner, Robert Dixon argues that the characters in this novel "have their own peculiarities, responding to chance encounters and even to the same sights in utterly unique ways".[15] This then further ties in with what Jones said of the characters of *Five Bells* elsewhere in an interview, namely that, although "they've seen images", it is nonetheless "the presence of the monument [that] addresses them in some aesthetic moment". This "address of the monument", that is to say the retrieval of space "from its disparagement as superficial, glitzy pleasure", coupled with a "reinvention of aesthetic apprehension for a kind of liberating, emancipatory end", is indeed what she is interested in here.[16] *Five Bells* thus not only materialises the aesthetic architecture – the actual folds – of the Opera House in its own narrative folds (in the form of flashbacks and flashforwards, analogies and associations, patterns and recursions),[17] but it also dematerialises the solidity of this most iconic building (as well as of the Harbour Bridge and of the Museum of Contemporary Art) by focusing on Ellie's, James', Catherine's and Pei Xing's

---

11   Gail Jones, "*Five Bells* with Novelist Gail Jones", interview by Eleanor Wachtel, *CBC Radio*, 2012.
12   Merlin Coverley, *Psychogeography* (Harpenden: Pocket Essentials, 2010), 14.
13   Jones, "*Five Bells* with Novelist Gail Jones".
14   Gail Jones, Gail Jones beschreibt einen Samstag in Sydney, reading (Literaturhaus Köln, 20 November 2014).
15   Robert Dixon, "Invitation to the Voyage: Reading Gail Jones's *Five Bells*", *JASAL: Journal of the Association for the Study of Australian Literature* 12, no. 3 (2012): 6.
16   Gail Jones, "Novelist Gail Jones Explores Tacky Tourist Traps", interview by Catherine Keenan, *Sydney Morning Herald*, 5 February 2011.
17   The protagonists' aesthetic apprehensions of the Opera House are at once imbued with and the embodiment of narrative folds. Indeed, Ellie and Catherine describe the Opera House respectively as "an unfolding thing, shutters, a sequence of sorts … opened to circuit and flow" (3) and as "peaked shapes … derived from a bowl of white roses", "its folded forms stretching upwards, its petal life extending" (14). For Pei Xing, "the Sydney Opera House look[s] like folded paper" (186).

responses to this same monument. In her novel, in other words, Jones meta-discursively reflects on the icons' abilities to prompt inner responses that will displace the quality of the monumental from their own solidity to their viewers' sensibilities.

Consider how, at the sight of the Opera House, James wonders "why ... time shudder[s] in this way, and return[s] him always to this inadequate boy that he was, in short pants, and afraid, and seeing white teeth in a jagged vision" (6). Through this self-questioning, he raises his own consciousness and trains it to consider the bridges of time that the sight of the Opera House induces in him. His subsequent and somatic reaction is abruptly to "turn ..., pissed off by this ridiculous *memory-siege*" (6, emphasis mine). Catherine, Ellie and Pei Xing also make a turning movement in reaction to their inner responses to the monuments at Circular Quay: Catherine, for instance, "turn[s] away, almost tearful from a jumble of associations she could neither disentangle nor inspect. How confused this place had made her, this Circular Quay, turning on the curve of lost time and *unbidden recurrences*" (18, emphasis mine). As to Ellie, when seeing the Harbour Bridge, she recollects how her former schoolteacher Miss Morrison had drawn Janus, the god of bridges, on the blackboard, then "turn[s], like someone *remembering*, in the other direction" (3, emphasis mine). Unlike James, Catherine and Ellie, however, Pei Xing "turn[s], as one does when one *glimpses the future*" (11, emphasis mine). Moreover, it is not at the sight of the Opera House that she enacts this turning gesture, but after seeing death clouding her friend, the ice-cream vendor at Circular Quay, Aristos' eyes (11). It has always been her lot "to know things in advance, her particular burden"; sure enough, "even as a child she had known things, had seen death arrive early, had read what is yet to come written in the lines of a face" (11). This instance then singles her out, right from the outset, as the only character who can read the folds of time (i.e. the past but also the future) in people – as opposed to monuments and buildings. In other words, she is the only one who consciously deciphers her own personification, her own materialisation if you wish, and hence the aestheticisation of "the bridges of time within consciousness", as outlined earlier. In line with this, it is relevant that she sees herself "from the inside" in terms of "layers of self slowly, gently, time-travelling across the water":

> She saw her own folds and crevices. I have lived many lives. There was something reassuring in this, not to be single but many, not to be of one language but several, not to have but one discrete past but a skein, and multiple. (13)

This is indeed yet another striking portrayal of Pei Xing's allegorical status as an embodiment of the Chinese attitude towards the past, in which people become the repositories of the past, of the lives of others.

Elsewhere in her Chinese essay, Jones says of Pei Xing that she appears as "the moral centre of the text".[18] What makes her so, I wish to suggest, is her capacity to forgive her former jailor at the labour camp on Chongming Island, where she was forced to work during the Cultural Revolution, and to generate new, unexpected bonds with her, namely by reading in English to the now senile and mute Dong Hua. This I believe, is where one of the greatest ironies of *Five Bells* lies, namely in the fact that it is Boris Pasternak's *Doctor Zhivago* which acts as literary mediator between the two Chinese women. After all, for Dong Hua, it was a black book at the time of the Cultural Revolution that belonged to "the pile of books deemed ideologically treacherous" to be set aflame during the book-burnings (40). For Pei Xing, it was the book her father had spent years translating and which eventually condemned him and his family to disgrace or, worse still, to death. And yet, in spite of these literal and literary liquidations, this melting of the flesh of books and bodies, words at first offer Pei Xing a continuity of sorts: "The past never left her. Her parents were always there, always kneeling, the last time she saw them alive. The pile of books was perpetually burning" (41). The literary is everlasting, and so are her memories of her father:

> He had a Russian story handy for every occasion, a literary homily for all events. But his tale added beautifully to the memory of the day. It was there, years later, like breath on a pane of glass, a human trace to see through. (80)

The "subtle, persisting ways in which she would remember her father, long after he disappeared", are thus in a sense literary ones (80). This is because her father "believed in ideas, not things, words, not new overcoats" (83), so that he ends up incarnating the Chinese reliance on people and ideas as guardians of the past, as opposed to bricks and stones.

Nevertheless, under the Cultural Revolution, the Chinese past ends up being threatened with obliteration, for, as Pei Xing comes to realise, "possessions would be the least of the destruction" (83). Indeed, the Chinese traditions, as encapsulated by the Four Olds (Old Customs, Old Culture, Old Habits and Old Ideas), and incarnated by the people, are themselves put at risk. Accordingly, when Pei Xing is sent to prison after being denounced as an advocate of the Four Olds, she starts leading her own literary resistance:

---

18   Jones, "I am Chinese", 87.

Pei Xing was not permitted to write, but nothing could prevent her privately remembering. Over the weeks she slowly told herself the story of *Doctor Zhivago*, and when she had finished she began again, embellishing what she had earlier recalled, adding a few Chinese details of her own. *Doctor Zhivago* was her secret life, whispered not into the air, but into the cardinal recesses of her heart, held close as she had been held by her mother and her father. … In this way, and by small degrees, Pei Xing saved herself. In this way she kept alive in spirit what was dangerously impermissible and communed with her family, who were hungry ghosts before their time. (155-6)

Thus in *Doctor Zhivago*, Pei Xing finds literary salvation, but perhaps what saves her even more is her re-imagining of the Russian classic. What keeps her alive, and her family through her, belongs to the realm of ideas because they are, to take up again Jones' formulation, the last bastion of "what is imperishable" due to their function as "bridges of time within consciousness". By turning Pei Xing into a literal incarnation of the Four Olds, Jones then not only materialises the Chinese attitude towards the past in the flesh of a character – and on the pages of her novel – but she also, subtly and almost paradoxically, aestheticises its immateriality.

There is, however, yet another ironic dimension to Pei Xing's story and to what she has come to embody: when, for the second time in two years, she gets "bashed on the occasion of Mao Tse Tung's birthday" (156), her literary resistance – the immaterial level on which she keeps her parents alive by narrativising their lives – assists her own materiality, as the imperatives of bodily resistance eventually take precedence and she gives in to the beatings of her torturers. Convinced that her brother is abroad and safe, she "concoct[s] a story" in which she confesses his anti-revolutionary activities (156). This is when the ironic twist occurs, inasmuch as her literary-owed liberation from prison coincides with the moment when she is told of her parents' death. Not only is it ironic that the stories she invented to commune with her family will help her make up a story about her brother that will serve her own purposes while betraying and disgracing him, but by some even deeper irony her stories, which were meant to keep her parents alive, turn out to be just that, stories, for they do not prevent them from dying. For Pei Xing, reality and fiction get fused and confused, and she leaves prison "in the daze of one unsure of her own measure of reality, stepping into the streets of Shanghai clouded over, like a shadow of herself" (156). So it seems that, inside Pei Xing and in her flesh, the Four Olds have broken down after all. This double disintegration – of the physical body and of the former Chinese body politic – is further illustrated in Shanghai's doomed cityscape:

> Something was demolished that could never be rebuilt. Years later, when Shanghai was under reconstruction, when cars largely replaced bicycles and steel high-rise loomed everywhere, Pei Xing saw 'cui', 'destroy', written in white paint in a circle on the walls of condemned buildings. Everywhere she saw it: *cui, cui*. And felt as if she too was marked with such a sign. (156)

Interestingly here, while the writings on the wall foreshadow their own doom, for they will be erased with the destruction of the condemned buildings, the sign *cui* will live on in Pei Xing's memory and feeling of destruction, and her later telling about it. Once again, Pei Xing embodies, and as such she figuratively "materialises", this immaterial attitude towards the past; this time, however, it is the related process of physical destruction, and therefore a sort of literal *de*materialisation, that is made flesh in her.

After being told about her parents' death, Pei Xing is released from prison and sent to work on a farm on Chongming Island for re-education. There, in the country, grieving for her parents, she no longer tells herself stories from *Doctor Zhivago*: "She was lost to herself. The stories were gone. Her life was a repetitive cycle of brute hard labour, and she was often mistreated by cadre leaders because she was of 'the criminal class'" (157). Despite these physical hardships, however, "there was sky and wind and occasions of numinous delight", when a kind word was offered, or "solidarity expressed" (157), which makes Pei Xing "remember human gratitude and the scale of what might unfold" (158). Unlike in prison, where she needed to tell herself stories in order to remain in touch with her past and her humanity, out in the fields, where human encounters suddenly become possible again, it is the people, with their stories, who remind her of her own humanity. So it appears that in order to mourn the death of her parents and to rebuild herself in an attempt to bring her past and present together, Pei Xing will need both the personal and the literary; and she will find both in Wang Xun, her future husband and the father of her son.

Wang Xun is a junior cadre who comes to work in the provinces as a volunteer. On his arrival on the island, he is "wearing a badge that sa[ys] '*In the Service of Chairman Mao*'", yet strangely enough he "talk[s] not in Maoist slogans but in a kind of literary language":

> He talked, Pei Xing thought, as if words mattered, as if they might be relied upon to untie the tongue into praise songs to the worlds, to describe falling snow, perhaps, or the shifts in fluid light on the surface of the Huangpo River at the very moment at which a migratory flock of birds ascends. (158)

Xun translates the ordinary into the literary; his vision and expression of the world are sophisticated ones; and while "others [are] driven to silence by years of rural labour", as is the case for Pei Xing, "he retain[s] a chatty disposition and idealist convictions" (158). More significantly still, "he want[s] to be a writer, some day, and tell the daunting huge story of the great Chinese people" (159). Xun is thus yet another embodiment of the Chinese attitude towards the past and somebody who believes in and enacts to the letter sinologist Frederick Mote's statement that "*the only truly enduring embodiments of the eternal human moments are the literary ones*".[19] Prior to Leys, Mote had already argued that China's ancient cities were "repositories of the past in a very special way": many times destroyed and rebuilt – and therefore "'time free' as purely physical objects" – they "embodied or suggested associations whose value lay elsewhere. The past was a past of words not of stones".[20] In the face of destruction, what lives on in him as a person and through him as a writer are words and ideas, the Chinese past; and his materiality – by this I mean his presence and physicality – as well as his literary disposition appeal to Pei Xing. In the same manner, when he tells her that the only personal object he took with him when moving to the North West Provinces was "a favourite shuttlecock, a Swift Pigeon, slightly damaged, that he had kept from his childhood", she realises that she loves him, this man "with a handful of ragged feathers, invaluable, saved from the past" (160). Here, Jones creates an analogy between the shuttlecock and Pei Xing: both are slightly damaged, but they are also saved from the past, and with them, so are the memories of this past. Xun's story of the Swift Pigeon then correlates with Pei Xing's own story of dematerialisation, poignantly encoded as it is in *cui*, the ideograph for destruction.

By the same token, in his book *Ideographic Modernism: China, Writing, Media*, comparatist scholar Christopher Bush investigates "the relationships between text, context, and history" as imprinted in the ideograph.[21] His approach seeks to "enrich the terms in which we talk about cross-cultural or historical *representation*" by exploring the ways in which "China and Chinese writing have served as important means of reimagining the West's most basic traditions and technologies of representation".[22] Convinced that "there is history and meaning on the level of the letter", he proposes a "multivalent way of reading that can ... reopen the question of what is literal and what is figurative, occasionally asking readers to see what is on the page not instead of, but in addition to, reading for

---

19 Quoted in Leys, *The Angel and the Octopus*, 24.
20 Quoted in Leys, *The Angel and the Octopus*, 23.
21 Christopher Bush, *Ideographic Modernism: China, Writing, Media* (New York: Oxford University Press, 2012), xvi. As Bush observes, it is commonly understood as "Chinese writing as imagined in the West".
22 Bush, *Ideographic Modernism*, xxx.

meaning or metaphor".²³ His argument on the ideograph's material implications then adds an extra layer – ironic perhaps – to the written words' supplanting of the prestige of solid things. After all, the ideograph is "a figure of mediation (and/or its limits)", which functions "as a literary and critical topos with which to explore … the borderlands between word and image, the impersonality and materiality of language, and the force of collective memory".²⁴ His insistence on the written word/image's twofold nature, spanning the materiality of the ideograph and the immateriality of the message it conveys, finds an echo in Jones' *Five Bells* and especially in the character of Pei Xing as well as in her Tai Chi-performing body.

A case in point is the following passage, which Jones claims in a self-reflexive impulse is "a central moment in the text",²⁵ and which sees Pei Xing perform a Tai Chi gesture right after stepping from the ferry onto Kurraba Point Wharf on the North Shore of Sydney:

> And so, after placing her heavy handbag carefully to one side, she held out her right arm, lifted her left leg, leant sideways, swung back, swooping her arms in a restrained formal elegance before her, moving into eternity for a few precious seconds. She held the pose, staring at nothing. She felt the shape of her body and the fine balances it could achieve, muscles taut, or relaxed, or forming a woven pattern of crimson chords tucked deep inside her. The left leg down, the weight moved, the arc of her arms afloat on the air. *Qigong.* The life of breath. Then she began again, her arms upraised: the soft sway of a movement known as "cloud hands." Behind her the ferry lurched away with an animist tremor of departure. (112–13)

This passage brings horizontal/spatial Australia and vertical/temporal China together in the character of Pei Xing. In performing Tai Chi, she "both halts and aestheticizes time: in a novel based structurally on repetition, wake patterns and flow, she enters vertical time by entering her body, suspended above the water, and in an uncontained space".²⁶ What Pei Xing personifies is then not only the prestige of the literary but also its physicality and medi(t)ating quality. Tai Chi strikes Jones "as oddly both within and beyond the block shape the body makes (the ideogram of the body), a slo-mo series of breaking and remaking the implicit frame".²⁷ In her literal embodiment of the ideograph *Qigong*, Pei Xing then acts as a mediator: she creates multiple and new connections or "translations", not only physically by

---

23   Bush, xvi.
24   Bush, xvii.
25   Jones, "I am Chinese", 90.
26   Jones, 89–90.
27   Jones, 90.

mediating between the earth and the sky but also between countries and cultures, or between Australia's horizontal notion of space and China's vertical notion of time. "I wanted to evoke *wu ji* – the 'core reverting to stillness'", Jones self-critically comments, "and 'cloud hands' represents the vertical cycle of water (evaporation and precipitation), as opposed to the horizontal of travel and movement on ferries across the harbour".[28] "Cloud hands" in *Five Bells* thus represents Jones' twofold vision of history as an unfolding and moving forwards but also as a plunging down – ideographically: it aestheticises the prevalence of the written word or image inherent in the Chinese attitude towards the past, where the suspension of monumental materiality forms a prelude to successions of cultural translations or correlated alternative encodings.

At the end of the novel, Pei Xing finds herself remembering "old people performing *cloud hands*, swaying their bodies in the air, then walking backwards, stepping carefully, stepping beautifully solemn. It was another Tai Chi practice, walking backwards, backwards" (215–16). This is the moment when Pei Xing "realises this is her: some of us walk backwards, always seeing what lies behind" and acts out this ebbing movement, "revers[ing] into her own history, seeing her own childhood and what she has lost, walking backwards, and backwards, walking forwards backwards …" (216). In what appears to be a self-reflexive gesture of the text, Pei Xing realises that, like the Tai Chi practice of "cloud hands", which consists of forward-backward movements, she too carries the bridges of time within her inner self, in self-aware confirmation that she operates like an embodiment of the Chinese attitude towards the past.

In *Five Bells*, both in the character of Pei Xing and in her depiction of Tai Chi, Jones physically and metaphysically aestheticises her perception of the Chinese attitude towards the past, with its focus on personal and literary (as opposed to monumental) forms of materialisation. There is thus no Great Wall in *Five Bells*, but there are Circular Quay's most iconic monuments "configured explicitly not as tokens of national pride but as aesthetic objects, as *art historical* in phenomenological terms".[29]

Through this sort of displacement, Jones shifts historical representation from the material to the aesthetic and "perform[s] a kind of wall-collapsing labour" inseparable from the production of her own text.[30] "Literature", she argues, "has always been a mode of transportation and diffusion; has always imagined minds and bodies elsewhere, moving on metaphorical silk roads of intellectual trade".[31]

---

28 Jones, 89–90.
29 Jones, 89.
30 Jones, 82.
31 Jones, 91.

What then emerges from her fiction are new imaginings and alternative connections. This is, to quote one last time from the Chinese essay, "the modest insertion of a Chinese aesthetic into an Australian space".[32]

References

Bush, Christopher. *Ideographic Modernism: China, Writing, Media*. New York; Oxford: Oxford University Press, 2012.
Coverley, Merlin. *Psychogeography*. Harpenden: Pocket Essentials, 2010.
Dixon, Robert. "Invitation to the Voyage: Reading Gail Jones's *Five Bells*." *JASAL: Journal of the Association for the Study of Australian Literature* 12, no. 3 (2012): 1–17.
Jones, Gail. *Five Bells*. North Sydney, NSW: Vintage Australia, 2011.
--. "*Five Bells* with Novelist Gail Jones." Interview by Eleanor Wachtel. CBC Radio, 2012.
--. Gail Jones beschreibt einen Samstag in Sydney. Reading, Literaturhaus Köln, 20 November 2014.
--. "'I Am Chinese': Of Bodies and Walls, Of Boundaries and Their Dissolution." *Moving Worlds: A Journal of Transcultural Writing*, Imagining Asia, 16, no. 2 (2006): 80–108.
--. "Novelist Gail Jones Explores Tacky Tourist Traps." Interview by Catherine Keenan. *Sydney Morning Herald*, 5 February 2011. https://www.smh.com.au/entertainment/novelist-gail-jones-explores-tacky-tourist-traps-20110204-1agdg.html
Leys, Simon. *The Angel and the Octopus: Collected Essays, 1983–1998*. Sydney: Duffy & Snellgrove, 1999.

---

32 Jones, 90.

7
Utopia and Hysteria in *A Guide to Berlin*

Tony Hughes-d'Aeth

Reading Gail Jones' novel *A Guide to Berlin* (2015) sent me tumbling back to my memories of teaching with Gail at the University of Western Australia (UWA). In my first year as a lecturer at UWA in 2002, I was thrilled to be asked to teach into Gail Jones' first-year unit "Voicing Difference and Desire", which ran in the late 1990s and early 2000s. The unit was made very much in Gail's image: Toni Morrison's *Sula*, Marguerite Duras' *The Lover*, Jeanette Winterson's *The Passion*.[1] But the unit began by looking at Danny Boyle's film *The Beach* (2000), adapted from Alex Garland's cult novel, which was introduced to give the students a contemporary expression of utopia. In the film, a group of backpackers establish a commune on an idyllic Thai island.[2] Central to its allure was the fact that "the beach" was hidden, and its whereabouts a closely guarded secret. Not only was the island secreted within an extensive archipelago, but the beach had somehow formed on the "inside" of the island in a lagoon that connected to the ocean by a tunnel. In one of the first lectures in the unit, Gail set up Boyle's film with a typically mesmeric excursus on the idea of utopia, beginning with Thomas More, and modulating through time and place. She connected the idea of a social utopia with the unit's emphasis on voicing difference and desire. In utopias, differences appear to disappear, only to reappear, often traumatically. Gail's idea of desire thus turned on the ambiguities and ambivalences that attach to difference. On

---

Tony Hughes-d'Aeth, Utopia and Hysteria in *A Guide to Berlin*. In *Inner and Outer Worlds: Gail Jones' Fiction*, edited by Anthony Uhlmann. Sydney: Sydney University Press, 2022. DOI: 10.30722/sup.9781743327791

---

1   Toni Morrison, *Sula* (1973; New York: Vintage International, 2004); Marguerite Duras, *The Lover*, trans. Barbara Brey (1984; London: Harper Perennial, 2006); Jeanette Winterson, *The Passion* (1987; London: Vintage, 1996).
2   Danny Boyle (dir.), *The Beach* (2000).

the one hand, she noted, desire can be expressed as the wish for constitutive difference (class, race, sex) to disappear, but on the other hand, those very sources of difference were also the *cause* of desire. One of the brilliant features of Gail's unit was how it showed contemporary politics to be beset by these same ambivalences. For instance, cultural difference was to be respected, but this same impulse could also lead to a second-order imperialism, such as in orientalism, in which difference became a fetish object traded among the hegemony. These contradictions were neatly captured in the defining image of *The Beach*, an aerial shot of the mythical beach completely enclosed by a lagoon. This quintessentially utopian image depicts constitutive difference (figured as the interface of land and water, i.e. a beach) that has become internalised. In this image, the ocean is not a real ocean, open in its otherness, but a reduplicated faux ocean depleted of its threatening difference. It is thus no coincidence that the collapse of the utopian community in *The Beach* is precipitated by the unexpected appearance of a shark in the lagoon which fatally mauls one of the members of that community. In many ways, this is exactly what takes place in the novel *A Guide to Berlin* (2015), where a utopian community also comes to grief when an act of violence exposes the seams of difference that persist beneath a common and seemingly benign enterprise.

Speak-Memories

The scenario in *A Guide to Berlin* is unashamedly staged, and the narrative wastes no time in assembling its members around a utopian premise. A group of six Nabokov devotees fall in with each other one winter in Berlin. A young Japanese couple (Mitsuko and Yukio), two handsome Italian men (Marco and Gino), a Jewish-American man in late middle-age (Victor), and the heroine, Cass. Cass is a slender, slightly ethereal ingénue, and is a figure familiar to aficionados of Jones' work. Cass has boldly exchanged her life in a Sydney bookshop for the icy streets and ramified histories of Berlin, and it is her consciousness that provides the lens for the novel. Cass is not what she calls a "joiner" but finds herself drawn into this group nonetheless. Indeed, there is a self-consciously ceremonial quality to the meetings, "as if each were there to play a part".[3]

> Somehow each knew, even then, that their number would be no more than six. Theirs were a few circumstantial spokes, faint rays going nowhere. They could not last. They were adventitious. They were constructed essentially by happenstance and would be destroyed a few weeks later (8).

---

3   Gail Jones, *A Guide to Berlin* (Sydney: Penguin Random House Australia, 2015), 6. All subsequent references to this novel are to this edition and appear in parentheses in the text.

This coterie of expatriates – part pilgrimage, part salon, part therapy group, but most importantly, a quasi-family – decide to convene at a specific time each week to honour their literary hero. But rather than discussing Nabokov or his works, they agree instead to enact the title of the author's autobiography *Speak, Memory*.[4] Each undertakes to share with the group some moment that forms the epicentre of their being. As Cass explains it to Gino: "[S]ome historical story you like to tell that is the marvel that tells you" (149).

What stands out is the very particular way that the premise of the novel enjoins speech in its protagonists. It seems to go directly to the origin of speech – is it willed or is it compelled? We are told in the novel that the group members are bound by a "narrative pact" (16) or "narrative contract" (168), but we are also told that there was "no compulsion ... no pressure or obligation" (16–17). It seems impossible that both assertions could be true. This radical ambiguity at the heart of speech is what Jacques Lacan explores in his theory of discourse.[5] Lacan was concerned with the question of what makes us speak and what speech consists of. As Gérard Wajcman explains: "Lacan's concept of discourse is a specific formalization of the basic components of speech and its effects. It accounts for what is at stake when we first claim the right to speech."[6] For Lacan, discourse is understood as a particular dispensation between knowledge, power (mastery, the master signifier), pleasure (*jouissance*), loss (*objet petit a*) and truth (the real). In this chapter, I wish to draw on Lacan's theory of discourse to try and understand the enigma of speech which *A Guide to Berlin* addresses. Lacan outlined four discourses: Master, University, Hysteric, Analytic. For most of us, it will be the hysteric's discourse that will be closest to home. In popular parlance, the term "hysteric" is a pejorative and highly gendered term. But not for Lacan, who saw this as the most authentic of the four discourses, and as near to "normal" as anyone ever comes in psychoanalysis. As Patricia Gherovici puts it: "The hysteric's discourse pertains not only to a pathology but also to the essence of the speaking being."[7] Epistemologically, the being of the hysteric is characterised by the quest for truth. Indeed, for Lacan, true scientific endeavour, as well as progressive politics, takes place via the modality of the hysteric. Dissatisfied with the determinations of the symbolic order (the big Other, the "master") and the status quo, the hysteric demands answers for injustices, inconsistencies, contradictions,

---

4   Vladimir Nabokov, *Speak, Memory: An Autobiography Revisited* (London: Weidenfeld and Nicolson, 1967).
5   Jacques Lacan, *The Seminar of Jacques Lacan, Book XVII, 1969–70: The Other Side of Psychoanalysis*, trans. Russell Grigg (1991; New York: Norton, 2007), 9–83.
6   Gérard Wajcman, "The Hysteric's Discourse", *The Symptom: Online Journal for Lacan.com* 4 (Spring 2003), n.p. https://www.lacan.com/hystericdisc.htm.
7   Patricia Gherovici, "Where Have the Hysterics Gone? Lacan's Reinvention of Hysteria", *English Studies in Canada* 40, no. 1 (March 2014): 57.

and longs for a dispensation where such things will finally disappear – in short, the hysteric longs for utopia.

In terms of the novel, each of the six in the group does indeed deliver their speak-memories. Victor's story is a recollection of his childhood in Newark, son of two Auschwitz survivors. The elements are woven together in that mix of historical tragedy and quirky whimsy that is characteristic of magical realism. His father worked in an umbrella factory. His mother goes crazy. Victor goes off the rails and is rescued by a Russian widow who introduces him to Nabokov. Mitsuko tells about growing up in rural Japan. Her father was a potter and her village still produced pottery as it had for many generations. At sixteen, however, Mitsuko moves to Tokyo to live with an aunt. There, she comes to identify with a particular cosplay subculture based around the figure of Lolita and becomes, in an echo of the author's own fashion sensibilities in the 1990s, a "goth-Lolita". Mitsuko found work as a "rental sister", providing paid chaste company to socially awkward young men, particularly those who had taken to shutting themselves permanently in their bedrooms. This is how she came to meet Yukio, whose concerned parents had employed Mitsuko in a desperate effort to save their son from a life of social isolation. She eventually entices Yukio out of his room, wooing him with translations of Nabokov's stories slipped under the door. Yukio, in his speak-memory, traces his adolescent social anxiety to the 1995 Sarin gas attacks on the Tokyo subway, when he was ten years old. But he was also oppressed by his father and older brother, who seem to have withdrawn all the available masculine confidence from the family account.

Gino's speak-memory begins in 1980, when his father died as a result of injuries sustained in the bombing of Bologna's central railway station. Gino was five at the time and the father's death devastated his family and left him feeling rootless and unanchored. Intellectually gifted but irresolute, he went to Rome to study art history, and then literature, but failed to complete his doctorate on Calvino and Nabokov. He had come to Berlin, like Cass, with a nebulous wish to write. Marco's speak-memory, like Victor's, draws on his experience as the son of Holocaust survivors. Marco's mother was Jewish, and during the war, to spare her from execution, she was adopted by the Catholic family of a watchmaker. He promises his mother that "I will one day write the history of our family, and that there will be a recompense in words for those who come after" (121). Marco's father had abandoned the family when Marco was just eight. As the eldest son, he assumed the symbolic role of father but the burden of this being thrust upon him at such a tender age took a toll and becomes connected in Marco's memory with the onset of his epilepsy: "I suffered from epilepsy. It made me vulnerable, how shall I say, in almost feminine ways" (117). In other words, the epilepsy is regarded in the novel, as it traditionally was, as a form of hysteria, in which a psychic disturbance is somatised in the body: "I think I was seven when I had my first *grand mal* seizure, and in my childish mind thought for years that my father had left because of it" (117). In between these speak-memories being related, we follow Cass in her perambulations around Berlin, particularly on its subway system, with which she develops a fascination. Sometimes she is joined by Marco, and after meeting him at a museum, Marco has an epileptic fit, and both regard this event as a moment when a private shame is made public. Later, they commence, with a minimum of fuss, a sexual relationship. After they become intimate, Marco tells Cass that his friend Gino is a drug addict and that he is worried for him.

Speech and the Missing Father

The story ritual that the group inscribes as their founding principle institutes a particular circuitry for the intersubjective transit of desire. The articulation of traumatic incidents in their past within the confidential confines of a secret society becomes a kind of obscene glue which joins the members together.

> After Mitsuko's speech, they decided they were irrevocably committed, and that each remaining story should swiftly follow … Each would consent … to revelation … It was an acceleration of the usual process of friendship; it was a narrative artifice to which they might all pledge their mysteries. (55)

The novel stresses the group's strange sense of community. As Marco tells Cass, theirs "was a new kind of community, not academic, not social, but some new species linking words and bodies with an occult sense of the written word" (14). The utopia in *A Guide to Berlin* is linguistic and hermeneutic: a utopia of the signifier. In this group, instead of the signifier being based in constitutive difference, "words and bodies" would be "linked" together by a magic provided by "the written word" (specifically, in this case, Nabokov's texts), which would circumvent the miseries and misunderstandings of everyday life. This is the utopia of a pure speech, one that operates seamlessly with desire, where one's innermost thoughts are caught and perfectly understood by the other, who then hands them back gently in the sublimated and pacified form of a social bond experienced as a sense of belonging.

For Lacan, hysteria is inherently social because it is based on the wish to be the object of the other's desire. Even though this repeatedly fails, the hysteric is nevertheless located in the *field* of the other's desire. As Patricia Gherovici explains: "Lacan sees hysteria not just as a neurosis but as a structure, a 'discourse' that produces a particular social bond".[8] And this bond is based on a particular displacement of desire, or as Gherovici puts it: "For the hysteric, desire is established as the desire to be desired, as desire for desire – that is, desire of the Other's desire".⁹ In his seminar, Lacan reflected on the social dimension of hysteria in typically vivid fashion:

> What is the desire of my hysteric? It is what opens what I would not say is the universe, but a whole wide world of what we can call the vast dimension of the latent hysteria in every human being in the world ... Any hysteric echoes everything related to the question about desire as it appears in others, especially in the other hysteric, but also in someone that may not be hysteric, only occasionally, or even in a latent manner, insofar as he or she would manifest a hysteric modality of posing the question.¹⁰

The image presented in Lacan's description is of hysteria as a kind of choral subjectivity, and suggests that for him hysteria in the subject is always an incipient form of mass hysteria, a sociality defined by the invocation of a desire that is in the other, always deferred. The hysterical society is one based on a communal plea for love. As they await an ultimate love that will make good the difference – the difference between the love that exists in reality and the love they imagine will sanctify their existence – the hysterical community transact with tokens of this transcendental love, which exists in a state of permanent deferral. The resemblance to the contemporary financial system is difficult to deny. In *A Guide to Berlin*, it is the figure of Nabokov that the characters invoke to sustain their coexistence – the central banker, as it were, in this libidinal economy. The situation is captured precisely in the courtship of Mitsuko and Yukio, where Mitsuko slides her translations of Nabokov's stories under Yukio's door, who receives them as signs of her love, and rejoins society as a consequence. Although, significantly, it is not quite "society" at large, but its subcultural reduplication (Japanese cosplay).

But what exactly is the "figure" of Nabokov in the novel? Certainly, this figure seems to have little in common with the famously curmudgeonly author. Instead, the "Nabokov" that is operating in the novel is the imaginary figure implied by the beauty of the sentences he composed. As the narrator says of the leader, Marco: "He knew Nabokov's life, but mostly in a general outline. He was interested in the writing, he told them, *primarily the writing*" (10, original italics). It is this implied (ideal) point of linguistic inception that the group upholds

---

8   Gherovici, "Where Have the Hysterics Gone?", 63.
9   Gherovici, "Where Have the Hysterics Gone?", 62.
10 Jacques Lacan, *Le Séminaire: Livre V, Les formations de l'inconscient (1957-1958)*, ed. Jacques-Alain Miller (Paris: Seuil, 1998) 466-67, quoted in Gherovici, "Where Have the Hysterics Gone?", 61-62.

as their deity. What this distinction between the "real" and "ideal" Nabokov makes clear is the imbrication of love and the signifier. The group in the novel is bonded by their common discernment of a legitimating love in the *words* of Nabokov. When Mitsuko eventually comes to read *Lolita* (which is well after she had assumed the costumed identity of a goth-Lolita), she explains how she ignored the sexual component of the novel, and focused instead on the beauty of the author's language and "the peculiar, vivid way he knew about secret inner lives" (52). The careful sequestration of the narrative of illicit sexual seduction and its replacement with the act of being seduced by words replaces the (unbearable) real of sexuality with the ideal of an ineffable affirming gentleness. Indeed, the sibling quality of Mitsuko and Yukio's relationship, their twin-like uncanniness and infantile sexlessness, is part of an uneasy odour of incest that permeates many of the stories.

The question of speech – of speak-memories and their relationship to the meta-text of Nabokov's writing – is brought to an intriguing point of crisis when it is Cass' turn to speak. Because the novel is focalised through her we are given access not just to her actual spoken words, but to the umbra of self-talk rendered as free indirect discourse in the novel. Something interesting happens; namely, "she fails to convince herself". Like the others, Cass recounts her childhood, which took place just outside Broome in the far north of Western Australia. But while she speaks fluently, she is conscious of a certain hollowness in her speech. She offers up some traumatic baubles to the group. She contracted ringworm and had to have her head shaved. Her mum said it was from feral kittens, and then drowned the kittens in a hessian bag. But as she is speaking, Cass keeps upbraiding herself: "she was babbling … she was sounding literary when she wanted to sound more straightforward" (163). Then, a little bit later, she asks herself: "What was it that made this artificial tale-telling, once begun, veer into flowery declarations and indulgences?" (166). At last her story putters to a halt: "She could not go on. Cass was aware that her story was thin beside the others'. It was secretive, almost sham … It sounded invented, she knew, but it released her from speaking of more difficult things" (168).

> Cass could not help it: she was disappointed in herself. She knew she had somehow not fulfilled the narrative contract; the others were all less reserved, more confiding and more open. She was provincial, she was a failure. She perceived a radical lack of clarity. In not producing a coherent story, she was not possessed of those properties of necessity and fullness that make a plausible self. (168)

In this way, Cass' speak-memory, the moment assigned to her to substantiate her subjectivity through a narrative properly grounded in traumatic impossibility, evaporates before her eyes. In the place of a foundational narrative is a litany of lack in which the primary qualities are masquerade ("artificial", "thin", "sham", "invented", "flowery") and incoherence ("lack of clarity", "not … coherent"). This sensation is exemplary of the hysteric, as Vicente Palomera points out: "The most fundamental complaint of hysterics is that of their 'lack of identity'".[11]

The devaluation by Cass of her subjective legitimacy – her conviction about the poverty of her "story" – implies a fullness in the speak-memories of the others that may in fact be equally illusory. Intriguingly, while each person's speak-memory is meant to stand for them, their speeches can only allude to the existence of a void at the centre of their being. In the first instance, this void is generally given the clothing of historical tragedy – Auschwitz (Victor, Marco), the Tokyo subway gas attacks (Yukio), the Bologna railway station bombing (Gino). But as the novel pushes a bit further, the name of this void takes on a different visage – that of the (absent) father. Marco begins his speak-memory by explaining: "Like Gino, I grew up without a father. Mine was an enduring grief; he disappeared when I was eight and never returned" (115). The family, particularly Marco and his sisters, were united by their absent father: "We entertained each other with our endlessly disappearing father" (119). It is significant, in this respect, that the missing father becomes the central element of Jones' most recent and most complete novel, *The Death of Noah Glass*. The search for an ideal father (or master signifier) also typifies the hysteric. As Gherovici explains: "What the hysteric is searching for is not her father, but an improved and revised version of him – the complete mythical father. In this sense, we can understand that the hysteric is looking for a perfect Master".[12] In *A Guide to Berlin*, it is clear that it is the figure of Nabokov that becomes the substitute for the missing paternal signifier, the missing father that haunts the speak-memories of each of the speakers. The idealised Nabokov, after all, provides the imaginary ground of their social bond, even authorising the love affair between Cass and Marco. As noted above, Cass believed "she was not possessed of those properties of necessity and fullness that make a plausible self". The anchorage and gravity ("necessity and fullness") that Cass longs for is another way of designating the missing (but not foreclosed) paternal signifier.

---

11 Vicente Palomera, "The Ethics of Hysteria and of Psychoanalysis", in *Reading Seminars I and II: Lacan's Return to Freud*, eds Richard Feldstein, Bruce Fink and Maire Jaanus (Albany, NY: State University of New York Press, 1996), 387.
12 Gherovici, "Where Have the Hysterics Gone?", 59.

7 Utopia and Hysteria in *A Guide to Berlin*

The Dissolution of the Nabokov Complex

After the stories are all shared, the novel stalls briefly before taking a new turn that comes about quite suddenly. Having lost access to their regular meeting place, Cass offers to host the group in her small rented apartment. During this meeting, Marco's drug-addled friend Gino appears on edge and increasingly surly, before turning on the group in a dramatic fashion:

> We are all shits, my friends. We are all literary snobs in this vicarious little room of our own, dilettantish, smug, hidden from the fucked-up world. We are enslaved to the folly and the whirlpool of our own obsessions. Why do we meet for this writer … we adore … because we find some cracked mirror there, we think that words will save us, that a fine description will drag us away from our own disappointments, and offer consolation, or explanation … We want to cancel our nothingness with a vigour of incarnation, we want to believe, truly believe, in literary salvation. (201)

It is a brilliant moment in the novel, because it up-ends the whole basis for the sociality that had formed the novel's substance until that moment. The whole enterprise is suddenly called out in all its well-meaning absurdity. This coy dance of carefully edited tragic self-revelation, what is it in aid of, demands Gino? What the hell is it we think we are doing? What are we soliciting with our little displays of picturesque shame?

After his tirade, Gino is ushered out onto the balcony by Victor, and the rest of the group watches through the glass door as Victor does his best to mollify Gino. The group, still taken aback by this sudden spilling over of actual passion in the here-and-now of their salon, then watches on helplessly as Gino throws Victor over the balcony, where he plummets several storeys to his death. They watch on, mute spectators to a primal scene. As if he intuited there was only one way to prove his point, Gino kills Victor before the assembled group in the manner of an object lesson. The remainder of the novel then transpires in a different mode. Instead of calling the police, the group decides to conceal the body. They enlist the shady son of Cass' landlord and travel together in a ute to a frozen river. They weight Victor's body with a heavy chain and struggle to break through the surface of the ice to consign his body to the deep. It is a Hitchcockean scene, particularly the awful awkwardness of trying to make the body disappear. Until then, the utopian community of hysterical speakers were imagining that they were living a protected life, with the figure of Nabokov authorising their pseudo-confessions and their exquisitely poignant relationships. Before, they had all "felt" guilty, but their speeches were elaborate denials of responsibility. Now, they were all "genuinely guilty". What happens next? Not much. Nothing is particularly resolved after this point. Gino ends up committing suicide, and everyone else drifts back into their own lives.

Perhaps the best way to process the bifurcation in the novel – the utopian community of literary pilgrims in the first part, and then the obscene gang bent on liquidating the corpse of their most senior member, in the latter part – is to imagine it happening in reverse. If we do that, we get the basic communal structure that Freud outlines in *Totem and Taboo* and *Moses and Monotheism* – in other words, the assassination of the primal father by the primal horde, and his restitution as master signifier.[13] For Freud, Christianity was the exemplary religion in this regard, because Christians worship the God they murdered, and eat a piece of him each time they take communion. In the novel, it is the hapless and ironically named Victor who finds himself in the position of the primal (i.e. real) father, and it is Nabokov that is installed in the place of the paternal signifier. In this specific way, and to put it in blunt Lacanian terms, "Nabokov" becomes, for the group, the name-of-the-father. But the basic problem of the novel is that "Nabokov" fails to work. He does not function as the master signifier he is meant to be; he does not deliver the requisite symbolic efficiency. On the one hand, as an ideal, the figure of Nabokov does convene the group and sustain it through a speech ritual that brings them together. But on the other hand, it collapses in the most spectacular and macabre way imaginable. The failure is once again typical of the hysteric whom Lacan defined as "a subject who cannot constitute the other as a Big Other or the Other as the locus of language and law".[14]

It is worth asking why Nabokov fails in the role of paternal signifier that is assigned to him by the group. One answer might be that the "Nabokov" the group invokes is not so much a paternal signifier, as its denial. The paternal signifier is, in the first instance, a limit, a primordial "no" or foundational prohibition.[15] But the Nabokov the group worships never says "no" – he is instead, a "yes", a permissive signifier. The law, however, depends on a foundational duality, where its sanctioning of licit action is premised on the prohibition of illicit action. Indeed, if as Freud suggests, the law begins with the taboo on incest and murder, then in *A Guide to Berlin* it is exactly these two phenomena that erupt in the place of the utopia its members had sought. The quasi-family bond between the

---

13   Sigmund Freud, *Totem and Taboo: Some Points of Agreement Between the Mental Lives of Savages and Neurotics* (1913; London: Routledge, 1950); *Moses and Monotheism* (New York: Knopf, 1939).
14   Gherovici, "Where Have the Hysterics Gone?", 61.
15   For a discussion of the paternal metaphor as interdiction, see Megan Williams, "Father Love: From Oedipus Complex to Paternal Metaphor", in *Studying Lacan's Seminars IV and V: From Lack to Desire*, eds Carol Owens and Nadeshda Almqvist (Routledge: London, 2019), especially 168–70.

members gives to all of their relationships, particularly that between Mitsuko and Yukio, but even that of Cass and Marco, an incestuous quality. And then, the group's confessional intimacy is shattered by the violent murder of Victor.

The Four Discourses: Hysteric, University, Analyst, Master

The modulations in the novel closely follow the Lacanian theory of discourses (Fig. 7.1). Intriguingly, while the group bonds hysterically, their mode of speech is not the hysteric's discourse. In the hysteric's discourse, the subject, motivated by lack, goes after the master, trying to expose his shortcomings, and creates knowledge as a product. Their alternative society is premised on the excision of the "master" (i.e. the normal rules of society with its brutal assignations of identity and value) and instead installs the figure of Nabokov as a pseudo-master. We can tell that "Nabokov" is not a true (i.e. symbolically efficient) master, because an entire group of hysterics have not a single bad word to say about him. If he was really a master, then the group would waste no time exposing his manifold failings.[16] Instead of the hysteric's discourse, what gets established as the mode of speech inside the group is what Lacan called "the university discourse". In the discourse of the university, the active element is actually knowledge itself, which is powered by the master (i.e. draws its sustenance and support from the master signifier), and seeks to strip the world of its contaminating desire. In trying to deplete knowledge of desire (i.e. achieve "objectivity"), the university produces the split subject, replete with lack. Anyone who has worked in a university knows the strong current of imposter-anxiety that runs through the veins of its hapless denizens.

The structure of the speak-memories matches that of university discourse: the speech is powered by the master (Nabokov) and addresses itself to the lack in the subject – their constitutive trauma. But, instead of removing lack, the university discourse produces *the subject in their lack*. Thus, with Cass, while she thinks her speak-memory will give her "necessity and fullness" (i.e. remove her lack), what in fact occurs is an acute accentuation of her own lack, the conviction that she is "hollow" and lacks the substance the others have. Like a university academic, Cass, even as she speaks, is assailed by the fact she is an imposter. In psychoanalysis, the remedial dialectic to the discourse of the hysteric is the discourse of the analyst. Indeed, the advent of psychoanalysis is concomitant with

---

16 "The hysteric demands that the Master produce an answer. Once this happens, the hysteric will render this answer incomplete or inconsistent. The question ultimately is aimed at exposing where the Master's knowledge is lacking." Gherovici, "Where Have the Hysterics Gone?", 63.

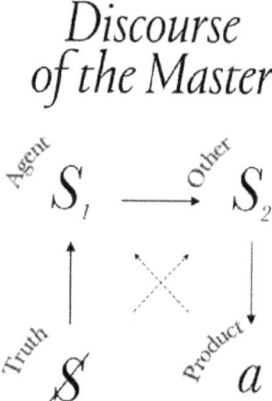
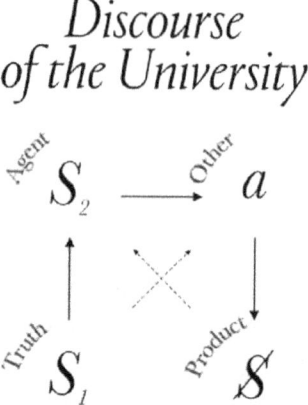
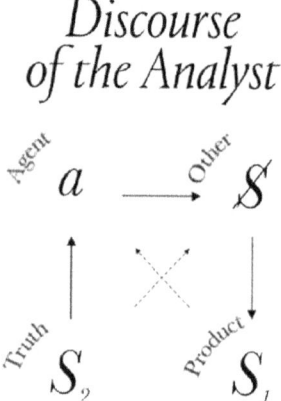
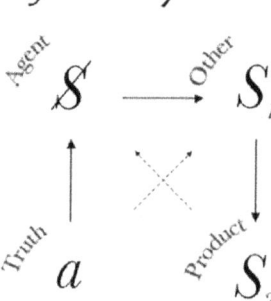

Figure 7.1 Lacan's four discourses.

the evolution of a method to dialecticise hysteria. In the therapeutic situation, the analyst situates themselves as the cause of the subject's desire. This enigmatic point of fascination then addresses the subject in their lack and produces a new signifier, a master signifier capable of doing its job, and effectively anchoring the subject in the signifying chain. Out of this operation, the by-product is knowledge, this time positioned in the domain of truth but one that will always lie behind the mask of the object-cause of the subject's desire.

But at the point of crisis, the novel does not turn to the discourse of the analyst, but to the fourth of Lacan's discourses, that of the master. In Lacan's theory, the master's discourse is somewhat paradoxical, because what typifies it is the disappearance of speech. In the master's discourse the master signifier directly determines knowledge (i.e. the other signifiers), and externalises lack as its product. The split subject is the truth of this operation, but the subject hides its split behind the outward dictates of the master. In the novel, the key decision the group makes is "not" to tell the authorities about the murder of Victor by Gino. Had they pursued this conventional course of action, they would have taken the act out of their hands and placed it into the socialised matrix of legal processes and sanctions. The group would, as it were, take responsibility for their part in the act by deferring responsibility for its punishment (i.e. by handing over Gino to the law of the state). But instead of doing this, the group internalises the crime in a way that will permit no finalisation. The infernal quality of the burial of Victor's body in the frozen river in the dead of night is instructive in this regard. Like much that is evil, this action contains a perverse ethical impulse, which is to protect Gino from the consequences of his action. In this regard, at least, the group is taking on the responsibility for their part in the foundational violence of their symbolic order. This strikes directly against the denial of complicity (responsibility) that funds the hysterical structure, and their decision repudiates the ethics of ideal justice which had governed the group in its utopian phase. The group cannot both protect Gino "and" honour Victor by punishing his murderer. However, what emerges from their decision is not a new sense of responsible agency – an ethics of the act – but a fatalistic ethics of the "deed":

> Having no burden of consistency in their experimental community, they now slipped into a genre, into driven action, not reflection. They cancelled disquiet for deed; they wanted a procedure, a decisiveness that would take Victor away. In the future there would be no consoling explanation – in the disgrace of the event they were simply cowardly and passive … but for now an irrevocable plot had taken over, now they were compromised, and submissive, and must pretend they knew what they were doing. (209)

What this passage displays unambiguously is the emergence of a new master. The new master is no longer "Nabokov", but "genre". Once the group "slipped into a genre", their actions could be decided for them by the master. "Genre" exemplifies the being of the master insofar as it converts arbitrary arrangements (a grammar of actions) into a poetics. It is a notably metafictive moment in the novel in the sense that it signals not only a new discursive structure (master discourse replaces university discourse), but a genre-shift in the text itself, which becomes a crime novel for the duration of this episode. Nabokov, famous bender and breaker of genres, dissolves and is replaced by the basest pulp fiction, with its "driven action" and "procedure".

This chapter has sought to show that the achievement of *A Guide to Berlin* lies in its ingenious exposé of utopian impulses. It continues a longstanding interest that Jones has had in the dynamics of difference and desire. The achievements of the novel have not been particularly well recognised by critics of *A Guide to Berlin*, and while reviews in Australia have generally been approving, overseas reviewers have been less kind.[17] Nor, in a scholarly sense, has the novel yet attracted substantial critical attention, although this has been rectified with the publication of Tanya Dalziell's monograph on Jones' fiction.[18] *A Guide to Berlin* ends with no real resolution, and that may well explain some of the befuddlement expressed in the public views of readers. But it is simply the case that this novel is one that diagrams a very particular moment in the vicissitudes of discursive life. The masterstroke of the novel is to carefully ensconce its characters in the illusion of their university discourse, only to send them tumbling out of it and into the bare life of the master's discourse. And because it does not rotate once more, to the configuration that Lacan calls the discourse of the analyst, the experience is of a chord that has not been resolved. The characters, and the reader as well, remain suspended between the two *chains* of signification: the (*imaginary*) chain of linguistic utopia which "links" together "bodies and words" in an ideal speech, and the grim *reality* of the (real) father's body grotesquely enchained beneath a frozen river. The third chain – the one that is properly symbolic, with an efficient master signifier (symbolic father) – is the one that is yet to materialise.

References

Boyle, Danny, dir. *The Beach*. 2000.
Crispin, Jessa. "*A Guide to Berlin* by Gail Jones – A Shallow Tale of Nabokov-reading Expats." *The Guardian*, 23 January 2016.
    https://www.theguardian.com/books/2016/jan/23/a-guide-to-berlin-gail-jones-review-novel
Dalziell, Tanya. *Gail Jones: Word, Image, Ethics*. Sydney: Sydney University Press, 2020.

---

17 Australian reviews include: Susan Lever, "Innocent Abroad", *Inside Story*, 31 August 2015; Brenda Walker, "*A Guide to Berlin* by Gail Jones", *The Monthly*, September 2015; Gillian Dooley, "*A Guide to Berlin* by Gail Jones", *Australian Book Review* 374, September 2015. Overseas reviews include: Jessa Crispin, "*A Guide to Berlin* by Gail Jones – A Shallow Tale of Nabokov-reading Expats", *The Guardian*, 23 January 2016; and Sam Kitchener, "*A Guide to Berlin* by Gail Jones, Book Review: Heavy-handed Take on Nabokov", *The Independent*, 14 January 2016.
18 Tanya Dalziell, *Gail Jones: Word, Image, Ethics* (Sydney: Sydney University Press, 2020). Dalziell has also provided the most substantial review of the novel in "The Flurry of Letters: *A Guide to Berlin* by Gail Jones", *Sydney Review of Books*, 6 November 2015.

––. "The Flurry of Letters: *A Guide to Berlin* by Gail Jones." *Sydney Review of Books*, 6 November 2015. https://sydneyreviewofbooks.com/a-guide-to-berlin-gail-jones
Dooley, Gillian. "*A Guide to Berlin* by Gail Jones." *Australian Book Review* 374, September 2015. https://www.australianbookreview.com.au/abr-online/archive/2015/160-september-2015-no-374/2681-gillian-dooley-reviews-a-guide-to-berlin-by-gail-jones
Duras, Marguerite. *The Lover*. Translated by Barbara Brey. (1984) London: Harper Perennial, 2006.
Freud, Sigmund. *Totem and Taboo: Some Points of Agreement Between the Mental Lives of Savages and Neurotics*. (1913) London: Routledge, 1950.
––. *Moses and Monotheism*. New York: Knopf, 1939.
Gherovici, Patricia. "Where Have the Hysterics Gone? Lacan's Reinvention of Hysteria." *English Studies in Canada* 40, no. 1 (March 2014): 47–70.
Jones, Gail. *A Guide to Berlin*. North Sydney: Penguin Random House Australia, 2015.
Kitchener, Sam. "*A Guide to Berlin* by Gail Jones, Book Review: Heavy-handed Take on Nabokov." *The Independent*, 14 January 2016. https://bit.ly/3EZCtYs
Lacan, Jacques. *Le Séminaire: Livre V, Les formations de l'inconscient* (1957–1958). Edited by Jacques-Alain Miller. Paris: Seuil, 1998.
––. *The Seminar of Jacques Lacan, Book XVII, 1969-70: The Other Side of Psychoanalysis*. Translated by Russell Grigg. (1991) New York: Norton, 2007.
Lever, Susan. "Innocent Abroad." *Inside Story*, 31 August 2015. https://insidestory.org.au/innocent-abroad
Morrison, Toni. *Sula*. (1973) New York: Vintage International, 2004.
Nabokov, Vladimir. *Speak, Memory: An Autobiography Revisited*. London: Weidenfeld and Nicolson, 1967.
Palomera, Vicente. "The Ethics of Hysteria and of Psychoanalysis." In *Reading Seminars I and II: Lacan's Return to Freud*, edited by Richard Feldstein, Bruce Fink and Maire Jaanus, 287–96. Albany, NY: State University of New York Press, 1996.
Wajcman, Gérard. "The Hysteric's Discourse." *The Symptom: Online Journal for Lacan.com* 4 (Spring 2003), n.p. https://www.lacan.com/hystericdisc.htm
Walker, Brenda. "*A Guide to Berlin* by Gail Jones." *The Monthly*, September 2015. https://www.themonthly.com.au/issue/2015/september/1441029600/brenda-walker/guide-berlin-gail-jones
Williams, Megan. "Father Love: From Oedipus Complex to Paternal Metaphor." In *Studying Lacan's Seminars IV and V: From Lack to Desire*, edited by Carol Owens and Nadeshda Almqvist, 165–75. Routledge: London, 2019.
Winterson, Jeanette. *The Passion*. (1987) London: Vintage, 1996.

8

Silent Propinquities: Literary Selfhood and Modernity in *A Guide to Berlin*

Brigid Rooney

A Guide to Berlin (2015) opens in darkness with Marco Gianelli, orchestrator of literary community, speaking to a circle of listeners about the inadequacy of writing to any human death: "The death of any human was incomparable. It was not a writerly event. It was not contained within sentences".[1] As if both illustrating and confounding this thought, the next sentence concludes with a series of images of apparently unrelated things: an icicle, a governess' wrinkled forehead, a swimming body, a parking meter, a fluffy cloud, a tiny pair of boots with felt spats. This gathering of random images into one sentence underscores their mute discontinuity and fragmentation. In stringing them together, however, the sentence tempts the reader to guess at what connective narrative logic might be at work, even as such logic remains elusive. In both the particularity and the adjacency of their detail, these images and objects seem to hint at presences and absences, prompting speculation and narrative imagining. The time, the place and the nature of the event that has brought this circle together in the darkness to listen to Marco's words are at first withheld from the reader. But the scene's oscillation between muffled obscurity and sharply registered detail sustains a note of unease through the narrative, inciting and unsettling imagination. The unease produced by the oscillation between enigma and detail, between silences and haunting contingencies, is central to Gail Jones' meditation on storytelling. While, as Jones herself suggests, *A Guide to Berlin* explores the risks of artificially accelerated friendships among strangers in the modern city,[2] there is something

Brigid Rooney, Silent Propinquities: Literary Selfhood and Modernity in *A Guide to Berlin*. In *Inner and Outer Worlds: Gail Jones' Fiction*, edited by Anthony Uhlmann. Sydney: Sydney University Press, 2022. DOI: 10.30722/sup.9781743327791

---

1   Gail Jones, *A Guide to Berlin* (North Sydney: Vintage/Random House, 2015), 1. All subsequent references are to this edition and appear in parentheses in the text.

more at stake in her novel's dialogue with writings by Vladimir Nabokov and Walter Benjamin. What I propose to elucidate is this novel's palpable, if oblique, engagement with questions about the vitality, durability, significance and indeed value for human community of storytelling, literary endeavour and literature. These are recurring questions with contemporary local, national and international ramifications in a world in which literary endeavour and its associated communities are at once captive to the global-capitalist market and offer modes of resistance to the market's commodifying forces.

My reading of *A Guide to Berlin* will unearth its address to both the promise and the problem of the literary as a vehicle for community in the space-time of the contemporary metropolis. Drawing in particular on Benjamin's work for key understandings of storytelling, modern selfhood and community, I propose that *A Guide to Berlin* engages ambiguities embedded deep within the novel as a form that has evolved across successive stages of modernity. Once a privileged mode of storytelling, the novel is now, arguably, reduced in status, taking its place alongside other narrative technologies. Jones both revives and contemplates the novel's longstanding function as place-making device, investing meaning, memory and significance in the haunted chronotope of today's globalised Berlin. As such, her novel, like many other novels, presents itself as a mode of contemporary belonging, providing an imagined hearth around which otherwise estranged individuals can come together in community. But how adequate is the novel – any novel – to this task? As we will see, Jones is dedicated to realising the novel's storytelling, place-making, community-gathering promise and yet her narrative simultaneously asks us to dwell in a complex, difficult awareness that while the novel may figure desire for communal belonging, it lacks capacity to resolve, even formally, the contradictions engendered by globalised urban modernity.

Beyond its opening scene, Jones' narrative shifts back in time, introducing characters and unfolding interactions and events that ultimately test its fledgling literary community. But throughout *A Guide to Berlin*, the logic of causality – conveyed in the metonymic and hypotactic drive of its storytelling arc – exerts productive tension with the paratactic configuration of its scenes and images, and of things in their mute contingency. Jones' narrative itself and her characters alike are licensed by Nabokov's example, and they revel in the linguistic riches of his literary ecosystem, delighting in the sensory qualities of words and images, in

---

2 Gail Jones, quoted by Susan Wyndham: "What came to me early was what it might mean if you entered a narrative contract to accelerate friendship by using speak-memory as a sort of parlour game or a pretext for relationships ... How reliable is it as a means of knowing people? And I guess the point is that it's only ever partial" – Susan Wyndham, "*A Guide to Berlin* by Gail Jones Links Six Foreigners With the City's Dark Past", *Sydney Morning Herald*, 8 August 2015. https://bit.ly/3mbiUoG

their capacity to seduce and entrance the reader, and to carry the fragile promise of virtual connection, of pleasurable communion among writers and readers across time, space and difference. The promise of community, of communion with those who share such a literary passion, is perhaps most fully realised in Jones' explicit and intricate engagement with Nabokov's writings, not least through the title her book shares with one of his short stories, as more fully discussed below. Marco describes his avid first reading of Nabokov's works and his recording of Nabokov's images so that his words and the writer's "lay side by side": "I look at my notebooks now and think: this is what reading is, no? A silent propinquity made of words. And this is what attention is, seeing and notating with care" (115). The practice, indeed ethics, of reading depends on careful "attention" to words in their silent propinquity, their side-by-side muteness, their otherness. Words are themselves metaphorised here as silent community, taking shape as individuals that are mutely adjacent, set in a paratactical configuration that invites yet delays access to their interconnecting meaning. It is of course the role of the attentive reader to elicit such meaning. Yet in engaging with words on a page, the reader of novels is also (typically) silent. The silence of words and reader may intimate secrecy, hesitancy or even vulnerability – vulnerability, that is, to misprision. The gap between inner selves and stories told, between stories told and words on the printed page, remains to be bridged.

"Silent propinquity", a repeated phrase in Jones' novel, generates a spatial figure on which my reading dwells. The phrase not only registers the way the novel works as a long-form narrative in print but gestures to both reading and writing practices, and to correlated forms of modern subjectivity. The interior self of the individual reading subject is something that the novel, in its function as a modern technology, specifically requires, cultivates and affords. Here I turn to Benjamin who provides generative resources for thinking about the valencies of "silent propinquity" as central to the themes and preoccupations of *A Guide to Berlin*, notably his work on storytelling, the novel, and the bourgeois interior. In Benjamin's writings these themes become cognate by virtue of their relation to each other in the context of modernity. Benjamin pits the communal role and art of oral storytelling against the disjointed information delivered by print media such as newspapers. He further implicates the novel in the demise of storytelling, the former being both the inheritor of and substitute for the latter. *A Guide to Berlin*'s thematisation of "silent propinquity" needs to be understood by way of Benjamin's meditation on the novel as modernity's print-mediated avenue for storytelling. I construe "silent propinquity", moreover, as pointing to both the experience of novel reading (or writing for that matter) and the experience of inhabiting urban modernity. Reading novels and inhabiting cities may seem wildly unrelated activities, but they share, indeed habitually require, a silent propinquity in turn constitutive of the kind of modern selfhood compatible with living in contemporary Berlin or in globalised urban modernity at large. If silent propinquity expresses and perpetuates modern selfhood, how does the novel – storytelling in print form – contribute to the experience and shaping of modern community, including literary community?

Though the novel's genealogy is both ancient and cross-cultural, its contemporary form and conventions developed in the West in concert and collusion with industrial modernity and its emergent middle class. Though Benjamin's observations about the novel, notably in his 1936 essay "The Storyteller", are oblique and fragmentary, they are explicitly informed by the work of Georg Lukács and parallel the writings of Mikhail Bakhtin. This early twentieth-century work on novelistic form was a formative base for subsequent influential analyses and histories of the novel such as Ian Watt's *The Rise of the Novel* (1957). The theory and history of the novel have thus long been linked to the expansion of bourgeois forms of life and the cultivation of the private, interiorised worlds of modern individuals. It is important to note that beyond the novel's nineteenth-century heyday, to which Benjamin refers, the form has not been static but through its transnational circulations has trafficked in turn with colonialism, imperialism and postcolonialism, with modernism and postmodernism, and in adaptive response to emerging media technologies – whether photographic, cinematic or digital. For Benjamin in "The Storyteller", the emergence of the print-mediated novel accompanied a secularised production process that hastened the decline of the oral storytelling tradition. Consequently, the "novelist has isolated himself":

> The birthplace of the novel is the solitary individual, who is no longer able to express himself by giving examples of his most important concerns, is himself uncounselled, and cannot counsel others. ... In the midst of life's fullness, and through the representation of this fullness, the novel gives evidence of the profound perplexity of the living.[3]

If the novel as a form encodes the perplexity of the living rather than the wisdom of the collective, it nonetheless carries the trace of desire for those archaic forms of sociality, expression and community that Benjamin attributes to the storyteller. As a print-based medium that sculpts the interior experience of isolated reading subjects, the novel, both then and arguably now, is a channel for imagined and imaginative communications among mutely separated, widely distanced selves.

---

3   Walter Benjamin, "The Storyteller: Reflections on the Works of Nikolai Leskov", in *Illuminations*, trans. Harry Zohn (New York: Schocken Books, 1968), 87.

8 Silent Propinquities: Literary Selfhood and Modernity in *A Guide to Berlin*

The mute adjacency, the silent propinquity, of words and selves that accompany the private, interiorised act of reading also orients subjects towards the hope of a virtual communion – a communion that can somehow remain compatible with the promised individual freedom, autonomy and mobility of modern life. Virtual isolation doubles paradoxically, then, as the dominant form of imagined social connection across large-scale groups, whether city, nation or globe, betokening the promise and limits of what Benedict Anderson famously termed the "horizontal comradeship" of imagined community. For Anderson, the newspaper is kin to the novel; both mark that "community in anonymity which is the hallmark of modern nations".[4]

Silent propinquity, then, mediated by the reading of novels, is a constitutive form of urban modernity. The built shape and social functioning of modern cities are in turn formative of mobile, individualised subjectivities in which individual privacy and freedom from surveillance by adjacent others necessarily entail the deprivation of community. The tendency towards self-isolating subjectivity has been implicated, notably by Georg Simmel, in modernity's metropolitan forms of life. For Simmel, the collective, rule-bound sociality of the smaller-scale village unit contrasts with the sociality of larger metropolitan systems which foster individual selves averse to and dissociated from proximate, contingent community.[5] Large-scale cities offer freedom from localised oversight and restriction, enlarging the horizons of individuals and promoting freedom of inner life as well as freedom of movement – both characteristic of cosmopolitan style and values. The practical coupling of individual privacy with mobility finds expression in the most mundane of the city's spatial configurations: commuters and tourists, anonymous subjects, their private worlds intact, travel separately yet together in silent propinquity. The digital age with its screen-saturated mobile devices and addictive social media platforms has surely further accelerated and intensified this phenomenon. Privacy, anonymity and freedom are the delicious pleasures, even intoxications, of the contemporary era prized by many, not only city dwellers but all who join urban and suburban modernity. Global modernity's segmented, depersonalised systems, communication devices and algorithm-led networks disseminate the hegemonic ideology that sees us continually customising and performing our apparently uniquely individualised styles of self-expression for the benefit of chosen (and niche) virtual audiences. These

---

4   Benedict Anderson, *Imagined Communities: Reflections on the Origin and Spread of Nationalism* (London: Verso, 1983), 7 and 36.
5   Georg Simmel, "The Metropolis and Mental Life" (1903), in *The Blackwell City Reader*, eds Gary Bridge and Sophie Watson (Oxford and Malden, MA: Wiley Blackwell, 2002), 15.

self-same conditions arguably militate against, if not thwart, the prospect of socially entwined, mutually responsible, fully accountable community.

As I read it, Jones' *A Guide to Berlin* both expresses and meditates upon a highly cultivated and cosmopolitan form of modern selfhood that might be named the literary self. By "the literary self" I mean to implicate the type of habitus that embodies erudition about and passionate devotion to literature, literary works and the principles of literary art. The practices of the literary self also, in many cases, involve conscious commitment to the aesthetic, ethical and humanist value of literary endeavours. I would contend that the literary self or habitus, certainly as figured in Jones' fiction, is both the product of and in significant tension with capitalist modernity. Named after Nabokov's story "A Guide to Berlin" (written in 1925 but not published until 1976), Jones' novel dramatises what turns out to be the inherently unsettled, even conflicted, relation of literary selfhood to its yearned-for ideal: an elective community of like-minded selves wishing to share their love of literature.[6] The narrator of Nabokov's story, structured to resemble a tourist guide, tells us he is discoursing with his friend over a beer inside a cosy Berlin pub. Evocative vignettes about the wintry city are arranged under seemingly random headings, less touristic than mundane – "The Pipes", "The Streetcar", "Work", "Eden" and "The Pub". Both the content and silent propinquity of Nabokov's vignettes hint at wider narrative meanings that surface in response to the friend's sceptical interjections in the concluding section, "The Pub". These wider meanings are crystallised in the narrator's closing gesture, one that involves a crossing of gazes and times. In a key episode in Jones' novel, a conversation between characters about this 1925 story bears witness to Marco's aforementioned emphasis on attentive reading, framing "reading" not only as an ethical demand but also as a gauge of the acumen commensurate with an ideal literary self. The failure of Jones' protagonist on her first reading of Nabokov's story to register an especially crucial detail shocks her, precipitating anxious self-questioning and introducing an unsettling self-doubt. As we will see, the novel's culminating events amplify self-doubt, afflicting the literary self and unravelling community. Yet in my view this equally signals the indispensable role of self-doubt, sensitivity and attunement as integral to literary selfhood and to its optimal modes of reading and writing. Openness to self-doubt, in other words, is allied to ethical openness to others and hence to the possibility of community. In this way, Jones' narrative adheres to the ethical and aesthetic promise of the

---

6   Vladimir Nabokov, "A Guide to Berlin" (1925), translated by Dimitri Nabokov in collaboration with the author, *The New Yorker*, 1 March 1976, 27–28. http://dighist.fas.harvard.edu/projects/eurasia/exhibits/show/a-guide-to-nabokov-s--a-guide-/item/824

8 Silent Propinquities: Literary Selfhood and Modernity in *A Guide to Berlin*

literary, of storytelling, despite and because of its registration of melancholy, fragility and uncertainty.

Jones' novel engages not only with the 1925 story but with a full range of Nabokov's works, including, among others, *Lolita* (1955), *Pale Fire* (1962) and *Ada* (1969), along with several of his short stories. In particular, the novel draws for its central action from Nabokov's autobiographical work, *Speak, Memory* (1951). Jones' third-person narrative primarily relays the perspective of protagonist Cass Turner, a young Australian visiting Berlin for the first time. In many ways a typical Jonesian protagonist, Cass is a would-be writer, a devotee of literature, sensitive and a little melancholy. Soon after arriving in Berlin, she finds her way to the Nabokovs' former residence at Nestorstrasse 22, in that part of Berlin where Russian émigrés gathered in the 1920s. All the novel's events occur in this zone, encompassing several key locations detailed in the Nabokov story, notably the Aquarium and the Zoo. Outside Nestorstrasse 22, Cass comes into contact with Marco who recruits her to his newly formed circle of Nabokov aficionados. Across the ensuing weeks, in the depths of Berlin's freezing winter, six tourist-outsiders hailing variously from Australia, the United States, Italy and Japan gather in empty apartments to recount in turn, and in homage to Nabokov's autobiography, their "speak-memories". Each tells the group a story drawn from his or her most significant or formative childhood experience; each story recalls its teller's cultural context and intergenerational history in richly remembered detail. Traumatic histories mark at least three of the six tales: ebullient Polish-American Victor tells of his New York childhood with elderly parents who remained immovably silent about their experiences in Auschwitz; the Italian Gino tells of a childhood scarred by his father's untimely death in Bologna Centrale Station's terrorist bombing of 1980; and Japanese Yukio tells of withdrawing from the world after the 1995 Tokyo subway Sarin gas attack. The remaining three stories, by Mitsuko, Marco and Cass herself, are less locked in violent trauma, telling of ordinary life and circumstances with its difficulties and losses; yet all the stories withhold as well as disclose aspects of self, time and place. Cass' antipodean (Western) Australian perspective folds itself in and around these other voices and tales; in between gatherings we follow her as she transits through the city, visiting its sites alone or in company with other characters. At its successive meetings, this globally diverse group feels its way towards trust, friendship and community premised on their shared love of Nabokov. As well as enacting Nabokov's *Speak, Memory*, Jones' embedding of separate stories within the novel, through the device of its framing circle of tellers and listeners, reactivates the formal conventions of the story cycle associated with the pilgrimage narrative tradition that extends from the Arabic tales, *One Thousand and One Nights*, Boccaccio's *Decameron* and Chaucer's *Canterbury Tales* to Christina Stead's *The Salzburg Tales* (1934). Invoking this longer tradition,

A Guide to Berlin's speak-memory device resonates with Benjamin's model of storytelling as an embodied practice integral to communal life. In Jones' novel, the speak-memory ritual, however, conceals as well as reveals. The mix of personalities and things hidden from view make group dynamics increasingly murky and difficult. When events take a sudden, violent turn, there is genre confusion. Jones' narrative subsequently pivots to violent misadventure, disenchanting and fracturing its storytelling circle. Community unravels and things are left inconclusive. Closure, for the protagonist at least, is denied, making this novel's ending perhaps the most sombre of all Jones' fiction to date.

A quality of inconclusiveness attaches both to the narrative itself and to its portrait of wintry Berlin, a city still haunted by its past, making narrative and city analogous to each other. The volatile and unstable Gino characterises Berlin as an unconcluded city: "'all open systems, broken circles, damaged stars, ravaged 'scapes'" (69). Gino is writing a book about Berlin called "The Book of Conclusions". He intends to critique the touristic pleasures associated with Nazi kitsch which he sees as implicated in such sites as Berlin's Topography of Terror Museum. Cass is repelled by the morbidly self-aggrandising quality of Gino's take on Berlin. But his word "unconcluded" stays with her nonetheless, as it also does with those narrative elements that not only disrupt the pleasures of tourism but also unsettle the idyll of community. Cass' movements through the city reveal a Berlin in which grim historical sites stand in silent propinquity with altogether other sites, such as the gasometer, relic of an older industrial time, or those sleekly captivating networks of contemporary modernity, its U-Bahn and S-Bahn lines. Tourist sites, furthermore, stand in mute proximity to zones temporarily occupied by the homeless, by refugees from war-torn, famine-ravaged parts of the world. We are implicitly invited to connect, compare, and most concertedly contrast the plight of 1920s exiles like Nabokov who fled revolutionary Russia with the plight of contemporary refugees, and to consider the qualified hospitality of even as cosmopolitan a city as Berlin. The volatile Gino appears to Cass in a different light when he takes her into the refugee shantytown to meet his friend Ahmed. That Ahmed is from Eritrea, having journeyed by way of Lampedusa, places him as a survivor of the 2013 Lampedusa refugee boat tragedy. This detail, collocated with other atrocities past and present that haunt the narrative, in turn refers us, if obliquely, to Australia's notorious, obdurately cruel border protection regime targeted against refugees arriving by boat. Gino's personal warmth and generosity towards this refugee community challenges Cass' unspoken misgivings about him personally. Her feelings for Gino, however, oscillate between attraction and wariness, and remain "snarled" (153). She cannot quite distil her sense of Gino into clarity or resolve it into conclusiveness.

8 Silent Propinquities: Literary Selfhood and Modernity in *A Guide to Berlin*

The narrative's sense of the city as "unconcluded" makes the latter inherently ambiguous, so that its image always hovers between hope and fear. This ambiguity attends the narrative's depiction of its elemental and built spaces, and the dynamic relation the characters have to these spaces. The very next novel after Jones' *Five Bells* (2011), *A Guide to Berlin* recalls the former's psycho-geographic mode in which multiple characters – visitors, migrants, sojourners, residents – navigate urban space. Through shared titles each novel forges an explicit join with a precursor text – respectively Kenneth Slessor's poem "Five Bells" (1939) and Nabokov's "A Guide to Berlin". These pairings are silently propinquitous, ushering in dialogue across time, and constituting a virtual communion that amplifies the literary significance of urban Sydney and Berlin. The suturing and interweaving of multiple literary works with urban space invites contemplation of what Joseph Hillis Miller calls the metaleptic exchange of literature and place in mutual processes of meaning-making.[7] Walking, riding, reading and conversing, Jones' characters respond to the iconic sites and elemental, natural features that constitute each city. The movement of Jones' characters through external, physical space, in these and her other novels, is accompanied by inward marks of personal, historic or intergenerational trauma. Inner life and external environment, mutely propinquitous, are situated in reversed, mirroring relations. The chiasmus of interior self and outer physical movement, the mirrored pairing of backward flowing memory with forward moving narrative, is characteristic of Jones' method. Through its chiasmatic configurations Jones' fiction visualises self and other relations as at once interdependent and marked by difference: yearning for communion is qualified by the observable gap between self and other. In short, the fiction of Gail Jones engages a poetics of silent propinquity that figures both the inner isolation and the tentative striving of modern individuals towards community.

In *A Guide to Berlin* the mirroring reversals of chiasmus appear in the way speak-memory stories resonate with each other, most obviously in the complementary stories told by the Japanese lovers, Mitsuko and Yukio. Goth-costumed "Lolita Girl" Mitsuko rescues Yukio who, having survived Tokyo subway's 1995 Sarin gas attack, becomes *hikikomori*, withdrawing into his silent "room-world" (49, 60). The way Mitsuko and Yukio's consecutive speak-memories about this situation are "entwined" with each other (57) echoes the infinity symbol, "infinity" being the one English word Yukio has learned from Mitsuko. This prompts Cass' subsequent recollection of Nabokov's "lemniscate", the term for the infinity symbol turned sideways, "the figure of eight lying on its belly" (70). Later still, the coupling of Cass and Marco in her room evokes for her the

---

7   J. Hillis Miller, *Topographies* (Stanford, CA: Stanford University Press, 1995), 16.

correlated symbol of the ampersand: "This was the shape of her desire and its relentless wish for connection" (110). The infinity symbol, figuring the ceaseless flow of desire and potential connectivity, can be read as a positive if fragile counter to the chaos threatened by Gino's image of the "unconcluded" city. The novel holds these opposites in silent, chiasmatic propinquity.

Chiasmus can be glimpsed not only in each novel's imagery, in the adjacency of selves/others and in interior/exterior patterns and flows, but also in the relation that *Five Bells* and *A Guide to Berlin* bear both to their precursor texts and to each other. Jones has described how, in writing *A Guide to Berlin*, she recognised that it might be considered a companion piece to *Five Bells*.[8] This licenses a reading of both texts as reciprocal, bearing complementary elements and patterns (humid, watery Sydney; wintry, snowy Berlin). This pairing – indeed the serial patterning across much of Jones' fiction – thickens the virtual dialogic space, projecting imagined community. Despite this complementarity, which warrants consideration by her readers, it is striking that *A Guide to Berlin* is yet to receive the level and depth of critical attention paid to the more obviously Australian novel, the Sydney-based *Five Bells*. Not only were there fewer and more mixed reviews than for *Five Bells* but also, to date, no extended critical studies of *A Guide to Berlin* have appeared. In contrast, several substantial critical essays on *Five Bells* were published within two years of its publication. An important exception is Tanya Dalziell's illuminating extended review for *Sydney Review of Books* in which she observes *A Guide to Berlin*'s intertextual dialogue not only with Nabokov's and Benjamin's writings but with the writings of W.G. Sebald.[9] Both here and in an expanded reading in her subsequent critical monograph *Gail Jones: Word, Image, Ethics* (2020), Dalziell writes about *A Guide to Berlin*'s images of umbrellas, butterflies and especially snow, its Nabokovian flurries of such words as lemniscate, conchometrist, kibitzer or fritillary (71). Tracing the webbed metaphorics and ethics of "weather" in this novel, Dalziell elaborates on Jones' implied recourse to Benjamin's favourite image of the snow globe, a child's toy world under glass, a miniaturised landscape that for Benjamin figures historical relations as frozen time. To shake the globe is to shatter the stillness.[10] Dalziell persuasively suggests that "qualities of suspension and shattering" accumulate significance in

---

8 Jones has observed that *A Guide to Berlin* "is a kind of companion piece to *Five Bells* ... The difference with this is it's vocalised through the Australian, Cass, but with a kind of cosmopolitan complexity". Jones cited in an untitled interview, *The West Australian* (*West Weekend*), 22 August 2015, 14 (no author attributed).
9 Tanya Dalziell, "The Flurry of Letters: *A Guide to Berlin*", *Sydney Review of Books*, 6 November 2015. https://sydneyreviewofbooks.com/a-guide-to-berlin-gail-jones/
10 Tanya Dalziell, *Gail Jones: Word, Image, Ethics* (Sydney: Sydney University Press, 2020), Kindle, especially Loc 723–1270.

A Guide to Berlin.[11] The alignments ventured in the novel, the tentative yet warm friendships formed, the circle of storytellers and listeners assembled – all are ultimately exposed to shock.

Reactivating his thought and putting it to the test, *A Guide to Berlin* resonates in several key ways with Benjamin's work on the storyteller. By reading its dialogue with Benjamin's essay we can discern how Jones' novel probes the possibility and limits, the internal contradictions, of literary community. As mentioned earlier, Benjamin's essay sets the storyteller in living community against modernity's print media and its isolated novelist, as well as, by implication, its readers. Reflecting on the works of Nikolai Leskov, an influential nineteenth-century Russian novelist and journalist, Benjamin writes of the storyteller's location within community, his role in providing counsel, and the mantle of authority given him by the experience of death as something encountered in life's midst rather than, as in modernity, banished or hidden away. "Death", says Benjamin, "is the sanction of everything the storyteller can tell".[12] The storyteller's tale told to his circle of listeners is archaic, organic and never concluded: the oral tale is unfinished; mouth-to-mouth transmission only enriches and burnishes the tale over time through its repeated telling by others. The tale, therefore, is not individual but communal, both source and repository of collective wisdom. By contrast, the novel tends to require the isolation of individual readers; it depends, in other words, on conditions of silent propinquity. For Benjamin, following Lukács, the novel's constitutively formative struggle with time is conditioned by modernity's banishment of death and consequent loss of the transcendental home. The novel is thus a function of placelessness, homelessness and, by extension, modernity. The novel ushers in the demise of the storyteller yet bears the latter's bequest. Though divorced from living community, unable to bring counsel, the novel has at its core a quest for the meaning of life. The suspense with which we, its readers, follow the fictive stranger's fate provides the consuming "flame" that "yields us the warmth which we never draw from our own fate".[13] Benjamin's meditation, in short, implicates the novel in the historical conditions of modernity. Its form is imprinted by the loss of communal wisdom, and its quest for meaning by the necessarily vicarious experience of the isolated reader who reads of the death of the stranger – that is, the death of the character, or else the figurative death of narrative endings, brought by a novel's conclusion.

Needless to say, Benjamin's meditation on the storyteller comes to us in writing. He therefore, no doubt knowingly, bears witness to the contradictions

---

11 See Dalziell, "The Flurry of Letters", n.p.; and Dalziell, *Gail Jones*, Loc 1109.
12 Benjamin, "The Storyteller", 93.
13 Benjamin, "The Storyteller", 98–100.

that mediate modern novelistic form: the anonymity of urban modernity, the isolation of the bourgeois individual, and the loss of communal belonging. Jones' *A Guide to Berlin* is attuned to the interplay in Benjamin's vision of pre-modern storytelling between nostalgic longing and acutely self-aware reflection. Where Benjamin associates the vanishing of the storyteller with the loss of community, and the novel with isolated modern individualism, *A Guide to Berlin* reactivates these seeming polarities by embedding its circle of storytellers and listeners within the form of the novel, by layering the pre-modern within the modern. The result, in sympathy with Benjamin's essay, is a nested structure in which the storytelling circle (of tellers and listeners) mirrors the implied circle of the novel's writer and readers. This imagines and rehearses the idea of community at several levels. Jones' storytellers try to emulate the model of community associated (by both Simmel and Benjamin) with small-scale, pre-modern societies. But as a nested structure this scene also conjures more attenuated visions of community – of modern literary community – which attempt, despite the anonymising scale of urban worlds, to bring readers and/or writers together, virtually or in person, via book clubs, festivals or through online and social media platforms. Jones' novel is predicated on both an allegiance to the possibility of literary community shared across time and space and an abiding attachment to the novel. Yet her vision is far from naïve or simple. Aware of social, ethical and aesthetic contradictions, in active dialogue with Benjamin's meditation, *A Guide to Berlin*'s speak-memory circle rehearses not only the difference but also the entanglements between archaic modes of storytelling and the novel, modernity's quintessential form. Jones' novel invites us to behold the gap that marks modernity's homelessness while at the same time tracing the longing for home. The mode of belonging, of literary community, most likely to persist and endure, the one in which *A Guide to Berlin* may be most invested, is that yielded in the transmission and reciprocity of story between one text and another – through the dialogue, in other words, between Jones' novel and the writings of Nabokov.

The sensitivity and self-doubt of protagonist Cass are crucial to this reciprocity of story, as well as to the tonal complexity of the narrative which is both aware of and drawn to what might be called the literary Scylla and Charybdis of romanticism and nihilism. Both attitudes or tendencies, channelled significantly through Cass, arguably map onto and exercise classic twin modalities of the novel as a genre: both its affective-melodramatic and naturalist-realist pulses. Cass' guardedness, springing in part from a vulnerability connected with a long-unspoken, private shame, contends with her longing for connection, her desire to take herself into the world, to make herself provisionally at home in wintry, impersonal Berlin. The vivid orange and crimson tulips Cass buys on first arrival prefigure the warmth generated by her attraction to Marco and their episodes of lovemaking that warm, soften and temporarily hold at bay the cold anonymity of the apartment she rents. This tonal and affective complexity characterises both Jones' *A Guide to Berlin* and Benjamin's essay, particularly with respect to the problem of dwelling. Before identifying how this problem is figured in *A Guide to Berlin*, I therefore turn briefly once more to Benjamin, whose interest in dwelling is palpable not only in "The Storyteller" but also in *The Arcades Project*. In a section of the latter called "The Interior, the Trace", Benjamin thinks about the spatial forms of the nineteenth-century bourgeois interior as these relate to the problem of "dwelling", of place and placelessness, in modernity. In an oft-quoted passage citing Adorno's early work on Kierkegaard, Benjamin meditates on the interior as a space in two interdependent senses: space in the built, material, architectural sense and psychic space, the space of inner bourgeois subjectivity:

> The nineteenth century, like no other century, was addicted to dwelling. It conceived the residence as a receptacle for the person, and it encased him with all his appurtenances so deeply in the dwelling's interior that one might be reminded of the inside of a compass case, where the instrument with all its accessories lies embedded in deep, usually violet folds of velvet. What didn't the nineteenth century invent some sort of casing for! Pocket watches, slippers, egg cups, thermometers, playing cards – and in lieu of cases, there were jackets, carpets, wrappers, and covers.[14]

This bourgeois interior channels the primal human need for dwelling into an exaggerated habit of self-enclosure, enabling an illusion of retreat from the capitalist marketplace by way of the market's own multitude of protective, talismanic commodities. Indeed, Benjamin's meditation on the bourgeois interior includes mention of the novel, hinting that both house the self or subject, and both enact the interiorising mode. That the novel can be deemed an interior space is suggested by a fragment, found adjacent to the above passage, from French literary critic Paulin Limayrac: "A novel is not a place one passes through; it is a place one inhabits".[15] Both the bourgeois interior and the novel, in other words, are sites of belonging for transiting modern subjects, bespeaking the condition of a world in which place suffers attrition, in which the transcendental home is lost. Benjamin goes on to suggest that the nineteenth-century interior was in turn abolished by *Jugendstil*, the twentieth century's porous and glassy modernist

---

14 Walter Benjamin, *The Arcades Project*, trans. Howard Eiland and Kevin McLaughlin (Cambridge, MA and London: The Belknap Press of Harvard University Press, 1999), 220–21 [14, 4].
15 Benjamin, *Arcades Project*, 221 [14a, 2].

architecture: "dwelling", he wrote of his own time, "has diminished: for the living, through hotel rooms; for the dead, through crematoriums".[16]

In *A Guide to Berlin*, the interiors of three different apartments, ranging in homeliness, serve as locations for its speak-memory scenes in terms that dramatically recall and embody Benjamin's thought. The three spaces on the one hand enact Jones' poetics of silent propinquity: each space is self-contained, mutely set apart from other spaces, yet each holds and hints at its hidden history. On the other hand, the mute self-containment and isolation of each of these spaces contends with the narrative drive which prompts consideration of their cumulative, sequential significance. For these propinquitous spaces work progressively in the novel, propelling us from an initially ambiguous promise or vacancy, through to the illusory warmth of cosy enclosure and thence to shock, shattering and disillusion. I will come last to Cass' own studio apartment, the space in which the illusion of bourgeois shelter is most comprehensively ruptured. The other two apartments, still bearing the Benjaminian compass case imprint of their absent or former owners, provide transient settings for the group's speak-memory rituals. With his day job as high-end realtor, Marco is able to accommodate the group's collective desire for:

> the old, incrusted place, somewhere which, even empty, would seem to carry embedded secrets and a hidden history. Creaking stairs, figures in the carpet, the allure of relic architecture and gentrified remains: this was the antiquarian aesthetic they all silently coveted. (111)

Enacting the ritual of storytelling inside these vacated spaces, the novel dramatises Benjamin's bourgeois interior as signifier of dwelling and community in the modern era. All the while, given that these vacant apartments house her transient modern tellers and listeners, Jones' scenarios play with the anachronism that clings both to archaic storytelling as envisaged by Benjamin, and to the novel itself as the once dominant bourgeois form with now residual cultural status in a globalised, multimedia-saturated contemporary world.

The first apartment is said to have belonged to an art dealer named Oblomov. What strikes Cass about the Oblomov apartment is its "empty walls and the pale squares and rectangles where once had rested paintings":

> Oblomov's disappeared images were now secretive shapes. There was a black leather lounge and two matching leather armchairs, but no coffee table, so that the drinks were served on the floor. There were two vintage standing lamps, of

---

16 Benjamin, *Arcades Project*, 221 [14, 4].

enamelled green metal, Venn-diagrammatically arranged to pour rings of light where a coffee table might have been. (18)

Though Oblomov is an art collector, his "egglike literary name" (5) distinctly invokes the slothful fictional nobleman created by nineteenth-century Russian novelist Ivan Goncharov. The word "oblomovism" was subsequently adopted to describe an attitude of passivity, a tendency to avoid problems. The negative spaces on the wall where paintings once hung are ambiguous. Is this a space for something new, for experimental storytelling, or is it amnesic? The group gathers in the crossed beams of the two lamps, explicitly figuring Benjamin's "storyteller against death" (53). Here four of the six stories, told by Victor, Mitsuko and Yukio, and then Gino, relay memories of exile and loss; loneliness, healing and love; disaster, trauma and violence. Each story is also a performance of the self before community, an act of trust but also an attempt at self-authentication. In this sense, a barely spoken but palpable rivalry enters the scene as pressure builds for each new teller to equal the sincerity and authenticity of previous stories. The last speak-memory at Oblomov's is Gino's and his account of the aggravated wound brought by the failure of officials to record his father's death in the Bologna bombing is both ominous and unconcluded, like his vision of a still-unconcluded Berlin. Foreboding intensifies when Marco observes the thousands of still buried, still unexploded bombs in Berlin, prompting the characters' silent contemplation of "a newly exploded Berlin" (86).

They next gather in an apartment called Kępiński's. Arriving at the building's entrance, Cass sees three stumble stones shining through the icy pavement, laid in memory of its former inhabitants, a Jewish family sent to Auschwitz. The interior of Kępiński's is a nineteenth-century bourgeois museum piece. To paraphrase, it is lavishly appointed with brocaded curtains, frilly standing lamps, commodious settees, plush armchairs, gold-framed mirrors and paintings, giant chandelier, writing desk and tulip reading lamp, but tellingly neither bookcases nor books. Cass registers the embellishment and faded glory, and the vapidity of the apartment's opulence (113). In Kępiński's, ease becomes suffocation, and through its overly luxurious comforts nihilism emerges. Benjamin writes:

> Such nihilism is the innermost core of bourgeois coziness – a mood that in hashish intoxication concentrates to satanic contentment, satanic knowing, satanic calm, indicating precisely to what extent the nineteenth-century interior is itself a stimulus to intoxication and dream ... To live in these interiors was to have woven a dense fabric about oneself within a spider's web, in whose toils world events hang loosely suspended like so many insect bodies sucked dry. From this cavern, one does not like to stir.[17]

At the end of the last scene in this second apartment, the endearingly inept Victor jokingly asks: "So who was this Kępiński anyway?" (195). The question is never answered. As noted above, all the novel's settings are in the specific zone of Nabokov's Berlin with its tourist haunts. Considered in this light, the Kępiński apartment may allude to Hotel Kempinski – the latter's full name being the Hotel Adlon Kempinski. Indeed *Speak, Memory* offers in passing the detail that the young Nabokov and family stayed briefly at the Adlon in the years before the Revolution. But given the specific association harnessed by the "Oblomov" of the first apartment, and the diacritical precision of "Kępiński", it is salient that this second apartment conjures the life and circumstances, and arguably the theories, of World War Two Polish concentration camp internee Antoni Kępiński.

Working with former Auschwitz prisoner Stanislaw Kodziński to interview hundreds of concentration camp survivors, Antoni Kępiński identified symptoms of suffering that he termed "the Auschwitz syndrome"; he is consequently regarded as a pioneer in the field of post-traumatic stress disorder.[18] These details resonate with the stumble stones that Cass notices by the apartment's entrance, mute memorials to its previous inhabitants. We can also construe a connection with Victor whose parents were Auschwitz survivors, and whose boisterous question – who was this Kępiński anyway? – echoes his lifelong frustration at never knowing anything of their experience of the camp. In addition, intriguingly, Antoni Kępiński developed an information theory about the metabolic relation of self and environment, their mutually shaping properties, their creative plasticity.[19] This theory – prefiguring neuroscientific understandings of "the brain's 'autopoiesis' or poetic self-creation"[20] – meshes with *A Guide to Berlin*'s network of images of modern Berlin that invoke the mutual circuitries of self and environment. The frequency of mention of the electrified transit system ridden by Cass, its U-Bahn and S-Bahn lines, highlights a metaphorics of connection between inner life and urban energy

---

17 Benjamin, *Arcades Project*, 216 [12, 6].
18 See Maximilian Schochow and Florian Steger, "Antoni Kępiński (1918–1972), Pioneer of Post-Traumatic Stress Disorder", *The British Journal of Psychiatry* 208, no. 6 (2016): 590.
19 For analyses of the theories, see, for example, Jan Ceklarz, "Revision of Antoni Kępiński's Concept of Information Metabolism", *Psychiatria Polska* 52, no. 1 (2018): 165–73; and Andrzej Kapusta, "Life Circle, Time and the Self in Antoni Kępiński's Conception of Information Metabolism", *Filosofija Sociologija* 18, no. 1 (2007): 46–51.
20 This quotation is from Eva Hoffman, *Time* (London: Profile Books, 2009), Kindle, Loc 889. In the interview with Wyndham (2015), Gail Jones refers to Hoffman's book and its account of autopoiesis, and is quoted as follows: "There is some aspect of remaking the self through books that fascinates me too. Eva Hoffman ... talks about autopoiesis, the idea that we have the capacity for self-fashioning partly through rigorous thinking and attentiveness to being in the world. I'm a very hopeful, optimistic person and I find these ideas hopeful, that we don't have to be oppressed by our pasts, and people who are can be doomed to melancholic self-destruction."

systems, between biochemistry and electrical currents. These currents prove uncanny when they take the form of electrical charges inside the human brain. For Marco is subject to epilepsy: Cass witnesses one of his convulsions, an event that precedes his speak-memory account of his childhood experience of epilepsy. As I argue elsewhere, electrical circuitry functions as a literary trope in fictions in which individual selves in domestic interiors are plugged into modernity's invisible circuits, binding interior domestic selves to shaping external conditions and forces.[21] Electrical flows, with their capacity to shock, are at once potentially fatal and potentially illuminating. *A Guide to Berlin*'s metaphorics of internal electrical convulsion and smoothly transiting flows – its autopoietic energies – suggest the dynamic interactions of inner and outer worlds. These energies, however, gather together and culminate in a very precise Benjaminian moment of shock, one that shatters the frozen time of relations.

Around the last two speak-memories – by Marco and, after an interval, by Cass – foreboding intensifies. Both memories are told at Kępiński's in an increasingly compromised atmosphere: Gino is on a chemical high, his descent into addiction recalling Benjamin's "hashish intoxication". Marco's speak-memory which, as mentioned above, concerns the mark epilepsy made on his childhood, falters in its conclusion. He finishes on a recollection of the strange moment in *Speak, Memory* that tells of Mademoiselle, Nabokov's beloved but histrionic governess, and that includes its author's seemingly random, disturbing memory of an ungainly old swan hopelessly struggling to get into a moored boat (88). The "misery of Nabokov's ending", says Marco, is "a true surprise" (123). The capricious and the confusing muddy, mar and thwart the ideal realm, the rosy memory of childhood or the vision of perfect community. Similarly, Cass' subsequently told speak-memory does not go as planned. In her otherwise vivid account, she conceals from her listeners the traumatic memory of her brother's death in a freak accident during a cyclone, and of her own abiding guilt over her unbidden feelings at the time, as she later tells Marco when they are alone. After Cass' speak-memory, the group indulges in drink and carouses late into the night.

After an agreed interval, the group gathers once more outside Kępiński's but the apartment is no longer accessible – and so they detour to Cass' apartment. It's in this third space that the dream of a sheltered literary community is most shockingly tested. Cass' studio apartment has no name. It is strikingly bare, verging on inhospitable, relieved only by the glowing pink tulips she has bought and the warmth of her lovemaking with Marco. Cass' apartment makes visible the problem of dwelling: the possibility of leaving an impression is thwarted by

---

21 See Brigid Rooney, *Suburban Space, the Novel and Australian Modernity* (London: Anthem, 2018), especially chapter 5, 101–19.

the apartment's obdurate impersonality, its vacancy and transience. Cass prizes its long view of Berlin's gasometer in the distance, its opening to the limitless sky, its orientation to park and cemetery just across the way, all suggesting recourse to the Romanticist sublime of which she is otherwise sceptical. Cass herself, a lonely and sensitive figure, is an ethical questioner. We identify with her, we are involved with her perspective, yet her judgement is not absolutely privileged. Her namesake, the seer, Cassandra of Troy, was a lonely figure too, cursed with the power to see the future but powerless to intervene. Jones' Cass is simultaneously perceptive and blind. She prides herself on her reading acuity yet, as previously mentioned, fails to register the chief revelatory detail concerning the narrator of Nabokov's "A Guide to Berlin". His reflection in the mirror – a reflection relayed through a child's future anterior gaze, and that reaches from public room into private quarters across thresholds of time and space – reveals to us that the narrator is an amputee, a veteran disfigured by war. This detail retrospectively infuses Nabokov's "A Guide to Berlin" with that kind of vertiginously unfolding narrative meaning that is otherwise absent, according to Benjamin, from newspaper reports about war.

Disaster befalls the group in Cass' apartment. It is an unforeseen, crudely violent event. In accord with Benjamin's snow globe, it shatters the frozen time of idealised, historical and communal relations. More significant still is the ethical challenge this shattering event brings. As a fledgling, experimental community, the group has "no burden of consistency", and they all slip "into another genre, into driven action, not reflection" (209). The group can neither reason through nor respond to the crisis. They flounder in the midst and through the immediate aftermath with all Benjamin's "perplexity of the living". They are without counsel. Their stunned drift into passivity and complicity, their all-too-human response, more than the event itself, inexorably fractures the charmed circle. Returning later, Cass registers the state of her apartment in the wake of the event: the glass doors to the balcony had been left open as they all fled. Now,

> weather had entered; the outside had swept in. Snow ... had been blown in streaks across the floor and the edges of her little world had been made indistinct ... no geometry of flakes but a chaos of elements, no poetic impulse but disgust and ruination ... (217)

Resonating with crises past, present and to come, the ramifications of this collapse of the putative divide between cosy private interior and brutal historic forces, between past and present violence, particularly given the narrative's setting in Berlin, need no further parsing.

8 Silent Propinquities: Literary Selfhood and Modernity in *A Guide to Berlin*

Cass makes attempts at reparation but emotional closure is denied. It is denied to both Cass and to the reader. For the novel comes to rest on an image of loneliness and desolation, figuring that which conditions its very form: the evaporation of meaning and an abiding condition of transcendental homelessness: "And there was she, meaninglessly riding on a train through the night. Her mournful self, second-hand, carrying other people's images. Her self lovelorn, and sorry, and now simply sliding away" (260). Jones' narrative inconclusiveness confounds the distinction Benjamin makes between the continuity of oral storytelling and the conclusiveness of the novel. It is possible, after all, for a contemporary novel such as this to diverge from the more bounded forms of its nineteenth-century realist precursors. Through the inconclusiveness of its ending, *A Guide to Berlin* signals its formally rigorous recognition of the problem of the literary as a vehicle for community in modernity, even while its dedication to literary art is abundantly apparent.

Art, including literary art, may be that most transient of shelters amid history's mounting storm, its pile of debris growing ever higher.[22] Amid the desolation, what wisdom might be drawn from silent propinquity, from the reading, writing and imagining of that virtual community, that "vast population of others also trying to make sense"? What faith in the novel, and in its forms of enchantment, its "philosophical learning, impossible to unlearn", as Marco puts it? It may only be through this narrative's gesture of negative capability, its dwelling with the pain of radical uncertainty – its inconclusiveness – that the final hollowing out of that beautiful, lost world conjured in Nabokov's *Speak, Memory* is forestalled. In the exercise of negative capability may lie the best hope of community, even modern literary community – enacted through the unflinching recognition of lived contradiction, human complexity, communal failure and radical uncertainty. The preparedness to dwell with inconclusiveness might here be understood at the levels of both formal aesthetics and ethical comportment. It might be, too, that Jones' novel ventures its own counter claim in response to Benjamin's weighing of storyteller against novelist, his sense of the novel as merely vestigial, as remnant of richer communal modes of storying. Perhaps Jones' novel, with its intertwining of oral storytelling and novelistic form, and its dialogue with precursor writers and future readers alike, demonstrates the hopes and vulnerabilities of human communities across times and spaces. We might then agree, even if only provisionally and wistfully, with Victor about the value of the literary and its associated reading and writing practices, "this sense of solitude and observation, this longing for a pure and concentrated reality. The

---

22 As per Benjamin's essay, "Theses on the Philosophy of History", in *Illuminations*, 249.

way stray words knit with specific moments. The intuition that this, more than anything, is our truest experience" (27–8).

Acknowledgements

I thank both Elizabeth McMahon and Monique Rooney for their excellent feedback on working drafts of this chapter.

References

Anderson, Benedict. *Imagined Communities: Reflections on the Origin and Spread of Nationalism.* London: Verso, 1983.
Benjamin, Walter. *The Arcades Project.* Translated by Howard Eiland and Kevin McLaughlin. Cambridge, Mass., and London: The Belknap Press of Harvard University Press, 1999.
Benjamin, Walter. *Illuminations.* Translated by Harry Zohn. New York: Schocken Books, 1968.
Ceklarz, Jan. "Revision of Antoni Kępiński's Concept of Information Metabolism." *Psychiatria Polska* vol. 52, no. 1 (2018): 165–73.
Dalziell, Tanya. *Gail Jones: Word, Image, Ethics.* Sydney: Sydney University Press, 2020. Kindle Edition 1.0.
—. "The Flurry of Letters: A Guide to Berlin." *Sydney Review of Books,* 6 November 2015. https://sydneyreviewofbooks.com/a-guide-to-berlin-gail-jones/
Hoffman, Eva. *Time.* London: Profile Books, 2009. Kindle edition.
Jones, Gail. *Five Bells.* North Sydney: Vintage/Random House, 2011.
Jones, Gail. *A Guide to Berlin.* North Sydney: Vintage/Random House, 2015.
Kapusta, Andrzej. "Life Circle, Time and the Self in Antoni Kępiński's Conception of Information Metabolism." *Filosofija Sociologija* vol. 18, no. 1 (2007): 46–51.
Miller, J. Hillis. *Topographies.* Stanford, California: Stanford University Press, 1995.
Nabokov, Vladimir. "A Guide to Berlin" (1925). Translated by Dimitri Nabokov in collaboration with Vladimir Nabokov. *The New Yorker,* 1 March 1976, 27–28. http://dighist.fas.harvard.edu/projects/eurasia/exhibits/show/a-guide-to-nabokov-s--a-guide-/item/824
Rooney, Brigid. *Suburban Space, the Novel and Australian Modernity.* London: Anthem, 2018.
Schochow, Maximilian and Florian Steger, "Antoni Kępiński (1918–1972), Pioneer of Post-Traumatic Stress Disorder." *The British Journal of Psychiatry* 208, no. 6 (2016): 590.
Simmel, Georg. "The Metropolis and Mental Life" (1903). In *The Blackwell City Reader,* edited by Gary Bridge and Sophie Watson, 11–19. Oxford and Malden, MA: Wiley Blackwell, 2002.
Watt, Ian. *The Rise of the Novel: Studies in Defoe, Richardson and Fielding.* (1957) London: Pimlico, 2000.
The West Australian (*West Weekend*), Interview with Gail Jones, 22 August 2015, 14. Factiva Database. Document TWAU000020150821eb8m0002x.
Wyndham, Susan. "*A Guide to Berlin* by Gail Jones Links Six Foreigners with the City's Dark Past." *Sydney Morning Herald,* 8 August 2015. https://bit.ly/3mbiUoG

9
Figures in Geometry: *The Death of Noah Glass*

Robert Dixon

In Gail Jones' 2018 novel about the life and death of Noah Glass, his "vocation" as an art historian begins when, as a small boy growing up in the remote north of Western Australia, he opens a book about the *Great Art Museums of the World*. It translates him miraculously from the Mars-orange landscape of the outback to the rarefied, Prussian-blue world of Piero della Francesca: it was a "window to elsewhere" and "other worlds and times blazed as portents from the pages".[1] The significance of this moment is confirmed twenty years later when, as a student in London, Noah discovers Piero's *The Nativity* (c. 1470–75) hanging in the National Gallery: "Noah walked around the National Gallery, taking meticulous notes, registering line by line his self-improvement" (69). These are instances of what Peter Wagner calls intermediality: the intertextual use of one medium, such as painting, in another medium, such as prose fiction.[2]

What we have entered here is a *mise-en-abyme* of ekphrasis: the text and images of one book, and the description of a painting in a notebook, all contained within another book, call up a cascade of images for the reader of this novel about art. Its cover, in turn, carries a Photoshopped image of Piero's *The Dream of Constantine*, a panel from the Arezzo frescoes or *The Story of the True Cross* (c. 1466).

Robert Dixon, Figures in Geometry: *The Death of Noah Glass*. In *Inner and Outer Worlds: Gail Jones' Fiction*, edited by Anthony Uhlmann. Sydney: Sydney University Press, 2022. DOI: 10.30722/sup.9781743327791

---

1. Gail Jones, *The Death of Noah Glass* (Melbourne: Text, 2018), 70, 45. All subsequent references are to this edition and appear in parentheses in the text.
2. Peter Wagner, ed., *Icons – Texts – Iconotexts: Essays on Ekphrasis and Intermediality* (Berlin and Boston: De Gruyter, 2012), 17.

Figure 9.1 Piero della Francesca, *Saint Jerome and a supplicant*.

But there is nothing new in any of this. A similar *mise-en-abyme* of intermediality appears, for example, in Piero's *Girolamo Amadi Kneeling Before Saint Jerome* (c. 1451), (Fig. 9.1), an oil painting in which the saint opens one of several books in front of his disciple, in this case the Holy Scriptures, as a source of commentary on an image of the crucified Christ, which the student "sees", as it were, through a process of textual elucidation. A textual scholar and translator, Jerome is Noah's "favourite" (63), and he owns a small icon of the saint behind which he conceals a coded message about the location of a stolen artwork. We are reminded that art history itself is a fundamentally ekphrastic discipline in the sense that it seeks to master images by words: Noah Glass describes it as "the poncy, embarrassing business of writing about paintings" (49). These examples suggest that at the heart of *The Death of Noah Glass* lies what W.J.T. Mitchell calls the problematic of the image/text.

In a series of influential books, including *Iconology* (1986) and *Picture Theory* (1994), Tom Mitchell, who is Gaylord Donnelley Distinguished Service Professor in the Department of English Language and Literature and the Department of Art at the University of Chicago – notice the cross-disciplinary affiliation – established the discipline of iconology as the study of images across the media, or images that move, as it were, between media. Picture theory is a form of "applied iconology" concerned with the way pictures themselves are "self-analytical" or "metapictures", becoming forms of theorising in their own right, and not just inanimate objects that have to be explained by language.[3] *The Death of Noah Glass* has similar qualities as a work of fiction that is concerned with the image-text dialectic, but in such a way that the novel form itself – its narrative structure, its characters and settings, its intermedial allusions and its complex temporality – becomes a device for actively staging such theorisations. "Novels", as Jones puts it, "are machines for thinking as well as feeling".[4]

Mitchell's formulation of the image/text problematic in *Picture Theory* was a response to the provocation of one of the classic documents in the late twentieth-century culture wars, the 1988 report of the National Endowment for the Humanities, *Humanities in America*, and especially the section on "Word and Image", which attributes an alleged decline of "western civilization" to the contemporary promotion of a culture of the image above the culture of the book. A novelist and Professor of Writing, Gail Jones has always been interested in the history of visuality: "I began as a painter", she reminds us, "not as a literary person. So I'm very interested in the visual arts … [and] the history of cinema. In everything I've written, there are images and words in contention".[5] "Modernity", the first short story in Jones' first book, *The House of Breathing* (1992), is about the impact of early cinema on its first audiences. Among Jones' earlier novels, the protagonist of *Black Mirror* (2002) is an Australian art historian researching the biography of a surrealist painter who flourished in Paris in the 1930s, while *Sixty Lights* (2004) is an example of neo-Victorian historical fiction that draws upon the history of nineteenth-century visual ephemera, photography and early cinema, and the rich modern tradition of writing about photography.

Citing Raymond Williams, Tom Mitchell denies that there is or has ever been an opposition between words and images, and that in both literary and visual media, words and images "'flow' into one another".[6] His largest claim in *Picture*

---

3   W.J.T. Mitchell, *Picture Theory: Essays on Verbal and Visual Representation* (Chicago, IL: Chicago University Press, 1994), 36.
4   Gail Jones, in Caroline Baum, "Gail Jones: Novels Are Machines for Thinking as Well as Feeling", *Sydney Morning Herald*, 6 April 2018. https://bit.ly/3yvCkcB
5   Gail Jones, in Martin McKenzie-Murray, "Gail Jones and the Art of Words", *The Saturday Paper*, 10 March 2018, 3. https://bit.ly/30yZEKa

Theory is that "the interaction of pictures and texts is constitutive of representation as such: all media are mixed media, and all representations are heterogeneous; there are no 'purely' visual or verbal arts".[7]

Yet the theorist in Mitchell is also impatient with the centuries-old humanistic traditions of *ut pictura poesis* and "the sister arts", which too readily assume a principle of homology or equivalence between words and images that can be subsumed under such rubrics as "the timeless classics" or a "period style". He proposes instead a threefold typography that registers "the whole ensemble of *relations* between media", including "antagonism, dissonance and division" as much as "similarity, resemblance and analogy".[8] While the term "imagetext" designates "composite, synthetic works (or concepts) that combine image and text", and "image-text" with a hyphen designates the active field of relations between the visual and the verbal, the backslash in "image/text" signifies a problematic gap, the cleavage or rupture in representation that is a potential site of play, difference and creative possibility: "the key thing ... is not to foreclose the inquiry into the image/text problem with presuppositions that it is one kind of thing".[9] The point is not simply to compare or connect image and text as two separate systems of representation, but to develop "the concept of the medium (visual or verbal) as a heterogeneous field of representational practice". The figure of the image/text is "a wedge to pry open the heterogeneity of media and of specific representations".[10]

The Death of Noah Glass is a virtuosic staging of this rich field or "problematic". The idea of a productive gap or rupture in representation is repeatedly invoked by the novel's explicit allusions to and staged, ekphrastic descriptions of paintings, films and other visual texts. These include quattrocento paintings, such as Piero's *The Baptism of Christ* and the Arezzo frescoes; ottocento sculpture, such as Vincenzo Ragusa's *Japanese Woman* (c. 1881); the precious icons and cheap religious artefacts of Roman Catholic worship; the double helix of intermediality represented by the Italian *giallo* novels and film adaptations of the 1950s and 1960s; and the proliferating screen culture of the internet. As each of these media and genres re-crosses time and space, from the Renaissance to the contemporary era, from Italy to Australia and back via Japan, Jones demonstrates not a quaint equivalence between the sister arts, but an unruly dynamic of disjunction, rupture, play and appropriation that sets off a force field of narrative and semiotic energies.

---

6   Mitchell, *Picture Theory*, 4.
7   Mitchell, *Picture Theory*, 5.
8   Mitchell, *Picture Theory*, 89.
9   Mitchell, *Picture Theory*, 89–90.
10 Mitchell, *Picture Theory*, 100.

This staging of the "hyphenation" of words and images can be seen in the relation between Piero's *The Story of the True Cross* and the cover of *The Death of Noah Glass* itself. What we "see" is not Piero's fresco, as if that were even possible. Instead, the cover is described very carefully as comprising "figures derived from Piero della Francesca's *The Dream of Constantine*". In her acknowledgements, Jones thanks the designer Chong Weng Ho for his "sympathetic artistry" (315). The phrase "derived from" belies both the presence of the originary artwork and its homology with the novel, signifying instead the "problematic" of the image/text and its multiple sutures across time, space and format. It is in this hyphenated space, this zone of intermediality, that the complexity and ambiguity of Jones' novel, her own "sympathetic artistry", erupts.

In the broad conception of her novel, Jones exploits the ekphrastic relation between words and images to create multiple links between her plot and various traditions in the history of visual culture. The conventions of the heist genre provide an envelope for her plot in the same way that those of Cold War-era Hollywood monster movies, such as *Creature from the Black Lagoon* (1954), frame reflections on contemporary issues in Guillermo del Toro's 2017 film *The Shape of Water*.

The Death of Noah Glass opens with the discovery of Noah's body floating in his swimming pool, an allusion to both high art – the sprawling historical narrative of Piero's *The Legend of the True Cross* commences with the death of Noah – and mid-twentieth century popular culture: Billy Wilder's film *Sunset Boulevard* (1950) opens with the corpse of Hollywood script writer Joe Gillis floating face-down in a swimming pool, and his voice over, "Let's go back six months to where it all started". After the funeral, Noah's son Martin and daughter Evie are interviewed by the friendless Detective Frank Malone, who informs them that Italy's Carabinieri Cultural Heritage Agency is investigating their father's involvement in the theft of a stolen artwork, a nineteenth-century sculpture by Vincenzo Ragusa.

The events in which Martin and Evie are subsequently caught up resemble the plot of a *giallo* novel or film. The word *giallo* is Italian for yellow, deriving from the yellow covers of Mondadori's series of cheap paperback mystery novels, often translated from English-language American and British originals, which were then made into Italian films, such as Mario Bravo's *The Girl Who Knew Too Much* (*La ragazza che speva troppo*, 1963). In Jones' novel, the *giallo* genre is a double helix of cross-cultural linguistic translation and intermedial adaptation that echoes Ragusa's ottocento project of a hybridised Italo-Japanese style. "Noah's concluded life" is like a B-grade crime novel or film, "a story running backwards" (16). The intermedial comparison is sustained by a pattern of references to *giallo* films and their Hollywood equivalents, including John Huston's *The Maltese*

Falcon (1941), Alfred Hitchcock's *The Man Who Knew Too Much* (1956) and Francis Ford Coppola's *The Godfather* (1971). Like Jimmy Stewart in *The Man Who Knew Too Much*, Martin Glass arrives in Palermo as a naïve "tourist" (84) who finds himself in the classic position of a good man in the wrong place at the wrong time. Entangled in a web of deceit while pursuing his inquiries into the alleged heist, he lodges with the ironically named Tommaso Salvo, who ultimately betrays him to the mafia: "Martin saw how outside the community he was, and how worthlessly foreign ... All around was the spatter of threatening motorbikes and imminent danger" (118). With its deconsecrated, dilapidated churches and stinking laneways, Palermo is an epitome of contemporary Europe in ruins, a stage set of "remembered images from old movies" (89).

The ekphrastic relationship between the plot of Jones' novel and the many artworks and films to which it alludes is inscribed thematically in Evie Glass' job as an assistant to the blind movie buff Benjamin, a former barrister suffering from *retinitis pigmentosa*. His interest in Derek Jarman's films *Caravaggio* (1986) and *Blue* (1993) reiterates Jones' own engagement with Renaissance imagery. Evie's job is to provide a *"descriptive audio"* (120) to Benjamin's movie viewing, which includes "action and thrillers" (123). Where Evie's work is ekphrastic in "connecting sound and image" (145) in cinema, Noah's as an art historian is to master images by words. His books, his "scholar's library", are his "word-and-image paraphernalia" (146). The point perhaps is that Evie's work describing movies to the blind oddly resembles Jones' use of words to describe the characters, settings and events of the novel inside which Evie's own "narration" (150) to Benjamin is contained. This hall of mirrors is like M.C. Escher's famous "metapicture" of an artist's hand drawing the artist's hand. Jones' exposure of her novel's mechanism is like Hitchcock's signature appearance in *Marnie* (1964), in which he "glances at the camera and disappears" (150). Benjamin sees this with his "unseeing eyes" (151), just as Saint Jerome's pupil, Girolamo Amadi, "sees" the image of Christ, or the mind's eye of a contemporary novel reader "sees" the events of Jones' narrative.

Structurally, the spaces between the novel's plot and its high art and cinematic references are reflected in the alternation of the core chapters between Martin's present visit to Sicily and his father's in the past, and Martin's engulfment by the toxic legacy of his father's crime. Martin's following in the footsteps of his father, and his interviews with the people who knew him in Palermo, including his colleague Antonio Dotti and his lover, the Caravaggio expert Dora Caselli, recalls the posthumous interviews in Orson Welles' *Citizen Kane* (1941), which also fail to penetrate the mystery of personal identity. In Palermo, in the square near the cathedral, Noah witnesses an Indian hawker bashed by a bus driver who is protecting another tourist. The eruption of public violence and Noah's powerless witnessing of the event echoes the plot of *The Man Who Knew Too Much*.

When Noah is drawn into the heist by Dora Caselli and her uncle Vito, Vito's plan for the theft is pitched to him like a film script, and its narrative has a classic "twist" in the redirection of the stolen statue from Tokyo to Sydney, and its mysterious disappearance. Vito acknowledges, "this will sound to you like the movies" (173). Noah and Martin are caught up in the same heist story but at different times, the rapidly alternating chapters making their experiences seem to be synchronous. Noah senses "that all his life was gathering in to this point, rucking in folds as though pulled up by a drawstring" (190). His trip to the temple of Diana at Cefalu with Dora, where the heist begins, is repeated in Martin's later pilgrimage to Monte Pellegrino in the narrative present, where the violent climax of the vendetta plot takes place, an echo of the earlier bashing witnessed by Noah in Palermo. In the end, Evie and Martin return to their father's theories about the cyclical temporality of Piero's paintings, discussing *The Legend of the True Cross* as a kind of time machine, a "co-presence of the finite and the infinite", "a piece of wood appearing and disappearing throughout history" like the Ragusa bust (292).

This theory of "temporal folds" (157) is expressed in the novel in Noah Glass' major contribution to art historical scholarship, his argument that Piero's paintings exhibit a mastery not only of space but also of time:

> Noah developed his ideas on Piero della Francesca and time. Piero was known for his mathematical mania in the development of perspective ... Most scholars wrote on Piero and space. ... But gazing at the familiar reproductions, Noah thought that the images might be more about the mystery of time. ... the famous panels on *The Legend of the True Cross* declared the loops of time – repetition. (156–7)

A case in point is Jones' use throughout *The Death of Noah Glass* of a figure caught in the act of undressing, their clothes awkwardly enveloping the arms and head. The figure is introduced by Noah's ekphrastic description of Piero's *The Baptism of Christ* (Fig. 9.2), whose serene and hieratic image of Christ is juxtaposed with the more realistic figure of a man undressing behind him in the middle distance. In "The Spiritual World of Piero's Art", the art historian and Roman Catholic priest Monsignor Timothy Verdon explains that this is a man disrobing in preparation for his own baptism, an image exemplifying the ideal of *imitatio Christi*.[11]

---

11 Timothy Verdon, "The Spiritual World of Piero's Art", in *The Cambridge Companion to Piero della Francesca*, ed. Jeryldene M. Wood (Cambridge: Cambridge University Press, 2002), 30–50, 43.

Figure 9.2 Piero della Francesca, *The Baptism of Christ*.

Yet Jones' interest in these folds in time is not about strict homologies, still less about timeless theological or aesthetic values that link the Italian Renaissance with twenty-first century Australia; it is instead about play, ambiguity and contemporary appropriation – about the usefulness of high art in negotiating everyday life. Jones uses the figure not as an index of timeless spirituality but as a way of evoking human vulnerability. Examples include Evie Glass as a child bathing in the sea at Glenelg, or as an adult undressing in her lover's bedroom on the cusp of a new sexual relationship, "pulling her clinging dress over her head" (175); Noah's removal of his shirt in a panic after experiencing public violence in Palermo, and the image of his lover, Dora Caselli, bathing in the sea at Mondello.

As Derrida points out, even famous works of art like *The Baptism of Christ* are "already talkative, full of virtual discourses":

> The fact that a spatial work of art doesn't speak can be interpreted in two ways. On the one hand, there is the idea of its absolute mutism, the idea that it is completely foreign or heterogeneous to words. ... But on the other hand ... we can always receive them, read them, or interpret them as potential discourse. That is to say, these silent works are in fact already talkative, full of virtual discourses.[12]

In reading Jones' novel, it is therefore salutary to recall that the figure of the image/text "is not a template to reduce ... things to the same form, but a lever to pry them open".[13]

Folds in Time: The Legend of the True Cross

Martin's pilgrimage to Monte Pellegrino, where he is beaten in revenge for his father's theft of the statue, parallels Noah's earlier pilgrimage to the Temple of Diana on Cefalu with Dora Caselli, when the heist is first conceived, and is an effect of the folding of time caused by the mechanism of the revenge plot. These are the patterns of everyday life that are inscribed in the formal properties of artworks, like the flight paths of aeroplanes through space, "the calculated alignment, the inexorable route to a destination" (262); the "arc" of the route (263).

A similar sense of "figures in geometry" (8), of crossings in time and space, is underwritten by the novel's principal intermedial relationship with Piero's *The Legend of the True Cross*, which can be seen as a "machine" for producing different spatial and temporal relations between the constitutive elements of its Biblical narrative:

> Through the fug of hospital potions, [Martin] heard Evie speak of pleated matter and folds in the soul. He heard 'multiplicity, not unity'; he heard 'co-presence of the finite and the infinite'; he heard her say something about serial time giving way to curves and bending motions. He could understand nothing. Was it the medication? When she began speaking of the fresco sequence called *The Legend of the True Cross*, he had at least a few images to pin to her words. A

---

12 Jacques Derrida quoted in Peter Brunette and David Wills (eds), *Deconstruction and the Visual Arts: Art, Media, Architecture* (Cambridge and New York: Cambridge University Press, 1994), 12–13.
13 Mitchell, *Picture Theory*, 106.

piece of wood appearing and disappearing throughout history, and its afterlife in millions of icons around the world, substance remade as an image, continuing in time. (292)

Commissioned for the Cappella Maggiore of San Francesco at Arezzo, *The Legend of the True Cross* was completed in 1466 and comprises a series of frescoes that trace the history of the cross from its origin as a tree in the Garden of Eden, through King Solomon's disposal of the wood, to St Helena's rediscovery of the Cross on Golgotha and its theft and return to Jerusalem in the seventh century. As we have seen, the cover of *The Death of Noah Glass* is derived from *The Vision of Constantine*, in which an angel holding the cross informs the sleeping Constantine that he will become the first Christian Emperor. Two aspects of the cycle are relevant to Jones' meditation on the problematic of the image/text. The first is that Piero's cycle is itself intermedial in being already a visual rendering of textual sources: the Bible, of course, but more immediately of Jacopo da Voragine, Bishop of Genoa's thirteenth-century devotional tract, *The Golden Legend*. Art historian Jeryldene M. Wood explains that Piero's "translation of Jacopo's literary imagery into visual form presupposes a knowledge of this kaleidoscopic narrative", which is not sequential but "meanders back and forth in time", interspersing its principal characters and events.[14] This "kaleidoscopic" quality is enhanced by Piero's "zigzag composition".[15] Piero's departure from Biblical and historical chronology is facilitated not only by the devices of allegory and typology, but also by the *trompe l'oeil* architecture of the chapel:

> The cast of characters in the paintings propels the story across the centuries, while the signifying objects – first the wood and then the Cross itself – communicate the timeless message of humanity's redemption. Piero emphasizes these symbols throughout the cycle by foreshortening them, placing them diagonally across the pictorial surface, or situating them before penetrations into depths that break with the mostly horizontal arrangement of figures and spatial planes in his compositions. The division of the walls into three distinct registers by fictive architecture encourages a more or less vertical reading that follows the chronology of the legend; nevertheless, parallel themes … and corresponding visual motifs (repetition of color and consistent figure types) prompt typological comparisons between the facing scenes at each level

---

14 Jeryldene M. Wood, "Piero's Legend of the True Cross and the Friars of San Francesco", in *The Cambridge Companion to Piero della Francesca*, ed. Jeryldene M. Wood (Cambridge: Cambridge University Press, 2002), 56, 59.
15 Wood, "Piero's Legend", 59.

of the chapel so that the allegorical components of the myth ultimately prevail over strict temporal sequence.[16]

This is a remarkably suggestive passage for thinking about the structure and temporality, and the settings, colours and imagery of Jones' novel. It points to the fundamental elements of narrative as a "machine" for thinking and feeling, including the foundational distinction between plot and story, as well as the energising relations between image and story, and space and time, that are fundamental to the image/text problematic.

Imposed upon an uneven architectural space, Piero's Biblical chronology is both temporally disrupted and spatially displaced. As a "kaleidoscopic" machine for generating stories, it resembles Michel Serres' account of historical eras as "disparate aggregates", and his metaphor of the temporal pleat or fold. In her 2004 novel *Sixty Lights*, Jones acknowledged Lynda Nead's account of this theory of modern time in *Victorian Babylon* (2000). Serres argues that:

> historical eras themselves are always simultaneously an amalgam of the past, the contemporary and the future: "every historical era is likewise multi-temporal, simultaneously drawing from the obsolete and the futuristic. An object, a circumstance, is thus polychronic, multi-temporal, and reveals a time that is gathered together with multiple pleats".[17]

Pleated time is visualised by Serres' metaphor of the handkerchief. Spread out and ironed, the handkerchief represents a metrical, geometric concept of time, in which distance and proximity are stable and clearly defined; but crumpled in the pocket, the handkerchief evokes a "topological" concept of time, in which previously distant points "become close, or even superimposed". Moreover, if the fabric is torn, previously adjacent points may be rendered distant and unrelated: "Our experience of time resembles the crumpled version of the handkerchief rather than the flat, ironed one".[18]

As Marilyn Aronberg Lavin's analysis of "Piero the Storyteller" reveals (Fig. 9.3), the superimposition of Biblical chronology onto the uneven surfaces of the Arezzo interior produces pleats, folds and juxtapositions across linear space and time in Piero's paintings, the "eternal" presence of Christ being the principal example.[19] Jones' novel has a similar structure. Her characters are mobile in space and time, the circumstances of their lives apparently repeated like Biblical

---

16 Wood, "Piero's Legend", 58.
17 Lynda Nead, *Victorian Babylon: People, Streets and Images in Nineteenth-Century London* (New Haven, CT and London: Yale University Press, 2000), 8.
18 Nead, *Victorian Babylon*, 8.

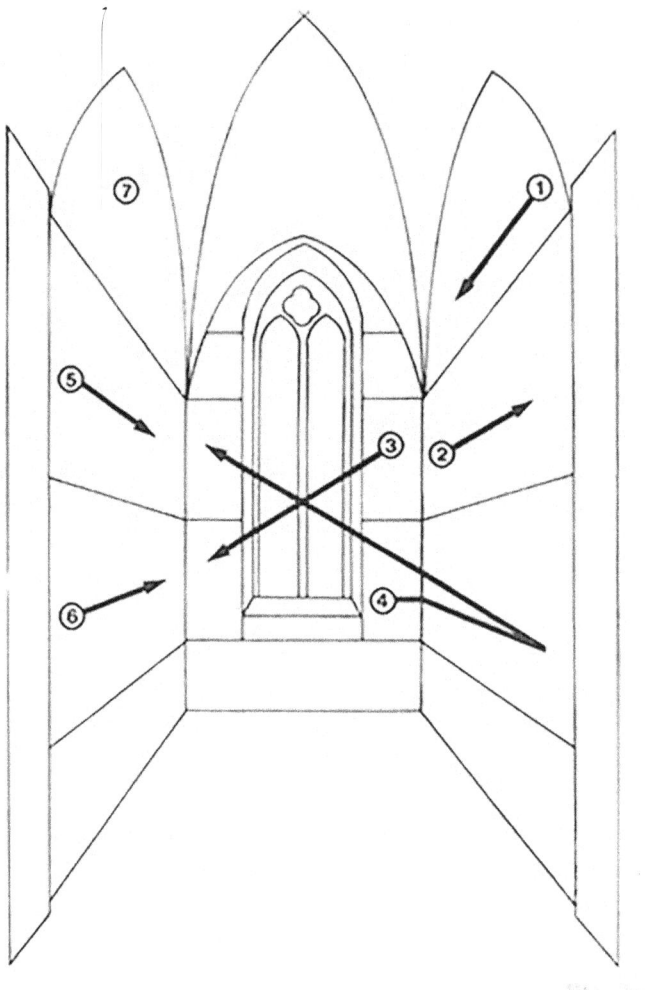

Figure 9.3 Disposition of the narrative in Piero della Francesca's *Legend of the True Cross*. Source: Lavin, 2001.

typology as the legacies of the fathers, Vincenzo, Joshua and Noah, reach out across the generations. The zigzag lives of Eleonora Ragusa and Noah Glass between Sicily and Japan, and Sicily and Australia, are imprinted across the "parts" and chapters into which Jones' novel is formally divided, like the panels of the Arezzo frescoes or the mosaics of Palermo's Monreale Cathedral.

---

19 Marilyn Aronberg Lavin, "Piero the Storyteller: Tradition and Innovation in the 'Legend of the True Cross'", in *Piero della Francesca: The Legend of the True Cross in the Church of San Francesco in Arezzo*, ed. Maetzke and Bertelli (Milan: Skira, 2001), 27–38.

Modern Perspective as Symbolic Form

In formulating the problematic of the image/text, Tom Mitchell's intention was that it be used neither as a method of purely formal description nor of reductively historical analysis, but both at once: it is, he suggests, "like an aperture or cleavage in representation, a place where history might slip through the cracks".[20] For all the formal and stylistic perfection for which she is now renowned as a novelist, Gail Jones' interest in what she calls the "contention" of words and images is also rigorously historical. Inevitably, the Mars-orange landscape of outback Western Australia, where Noah Glass has his formative encounter with European art, is just such a place where history slips through the cracks.

In his introduction to *Studies in Iconology* (1962), Irwin Panofsky famously describes the primal scene of the modern science of iconology by contrasting the acquired visual knowledge of modern Europeans with the "primitive" visuality of Australian Aborigines. In our native, untutored inability to understand a painting, Panofsky suggests, "all of us are Australian bushmen".[21] As Mitchell points out, central to Panofsky's understanding of modern visuality is the Renaissance invention of perspective, which is the subject of his 1924 essay, "Perspective as Symbolic Form". This model of vision and subjectivity remained the core narrative of art history, with the shift from the Renaissance, perspectival, or normative model of vision signalled by the arrival of artistic modernism in the 1870s and 1880s. This is to grasp Panofsky's concept of perspective not as neutral or natural, but as ideological, a form of totalising world view inherited by the settler society into which Noah Glass is born in mid twentieth-century Australia, and from which he seeks to escape through the discipline of art history.

Noah's own primal scene as an art historian also involves an encounter between European culture and the Australian Aborigines, and as such it is overdetermined by the traumatic legacy of settler colonial history in Australia. His father Joshua Glass was a mission doctor who "had given his life to the poor Aborigines of Western Australia. He brought them the light, when they were lost in leprous darkness" (130). Having grown up on a mission station surrounded by lepers and tormented by his dread of infection, Noah has a life-transforming experience when he discovers the book about European art. The foundational role of Renaissance perspective in the formation of the Western subject is confirmed when Noah's son Martin recognises the continuity between his daughter's Barbie house, an artefact of contemporary mass consumer culture, and the architectural

---

20   Mitchell, *Picture Theory*, 104.
21   Panofsky, quoted in Mitchell, *Picture Theory*, 27.

Figure 9.4 Anonymous, *The Ideal City*.

studies of idealised urban space, such as *The Ideal City* (Fig. 9.4) once attributed to Piero della Francesca:[22]

> Martin bent his face to the level of the tiny house, and then lowered his whole body. He stayed like that, curled on the floor, looking into the Barbie rooms as one might seek a saint's face in the galleried spaces of a quattrocento painting. There was a chessboard floor, and he thought of those early works that situated figures in geometry – Piero's *Flagellation*. (7–8)

If, as Panofsky suggests, the invention of perspective plays a constitutive role in the formation of the modern Western subject, then Noah's career allows him to put his originary proximity to Aboriginal Australia "in perspective", as it were, potentially opening up a life-affirming distance between himself and the Australian outback in space and time. In London's National Gallery in 1971, Noah understands that the Australia of his childhood is "more or less barbaric", and he attempts to "refashion" a "tainted" self, his head full of "old-world imagery" (68). Confronted by the power of Piero's canvas, "Noah walked around the National Gallery, taking meticulous notes, registering line by line his self-improvement, missing almost nothing" (69). In London and Cambridge, Noah and his future wife Katherine study European art and English literature, those two transformative projects for expatriate colonials in the mid-twentieth century, but they are neither British nor European. Later, returned to Katherine's home town of Adelaide, itself a transplanted European grid, Noah finds himself "stranded in the wrong air" (76).

---

22 Philip Jacks, "The Renaissance *Prospettiva*: Perspectives of the Ideal City", in *The Cambridge Companion to Piero della Francesca*, ed. Jeryldene M. Wood (Cambridge: Cambridge University Press, 2002), 115.

But when Martin visits Sicily on a quest to discover the secret of his father's life, these carefully constructed relations in time and space collapse, as the pre-modern aspects of contemporary European life re-emerge. During a pilgrimage to the Catholic shrine on Monte Pellegrino, which is embellished with devotional imagery that pre-dates Renaissance art, Martin is called out and identified as an *"Australiano"*, an echo of Panofsky's encounter between the modern European and the primitive bushman, and then attacked by Sicilian peasants intent on kicking him to death in revenge for his father's crime. Curled up for self-protection in another loop in time, Martin reverts to childhood, repeating his posture when inspecting the Barbie house. The attack constitutes a return of the repressed, a collapse of the modern European epistemology enshrined in the concept of Albertian space, with its implicit separation of subject and object. Jones is here interrogating the culturally specific assumptions embedded in art history about the primacy of (modern) European vision and civility; about the taken-for-granted models of visual culture and its history which are themselves embedded in and answerable to questions of politics and power from a postcolonial perspective.

Jones' staging of the problematic of the image/text in *The Death of Noah Glass* is therefore deeply aware of its own production in a settler society with an ambivalent relation to both Indigenous and European cultures. The cleavage caused by the death of Noah Glass opens up this leakage of history into a narrative about his life in images. With its suggestive typological relation to Biblical narrative, the genesis of that life is located in the Australian desert, where Noah opens a book that inducts him into a life of art. But these are images from another culture, images that screen him, in a psychoanalytic sense, from exposure to the traumas of Australia's settler culture, to the spectacle of Indigenous disadvantage, and Australia's proximity to Asia, to which Joshua Glass' experience as a prisoner of the Japanese bears witness.

With his "word-and-image paraphernalia" (146), Noah Glass becomes a mimic European, a master of its visual culture. But this is a rearguard action against Australia's own legacy as a settler society. European art in Australia is always already displaced in space and time. We might recall A.D. Hope's infamous description of white Australia as "a vast parasite robber-state / Where second-hand Europeans pullulate / Timidly on the edge of alien shores".[23] All of Jones' Australians are second-hand Europeans and damaged people: Joshua's experience as a prisoner of the Japanese, Noah's fear of infection from the Aborigines, Katherine's illness and premature death, Martin's heroin addiction,

---

23 A.D. Hope, "Australia". Australian Poetry Library. https://www.poetrylibrary.edu.au/poets/hope-a-d/poems/australia-0146006

Evie's obsessive-compulsive disorder, Benjamin's blindness, Nina's deafness. Irene Dunstan, Noah's neighbour at Elizabeth Bay, fears contamination of the swimming pool by his dead body, and all his life Noah suffers from a nervous rash like the plaques symptomatic of contagion by leprosy. These are the marks of settler "shame" (48).

Ekphrasis and the Other

Tom Mitchell defines the goal of ekphrastic hope as "the overcoming of otherness".[24] The qualities of otherness might, in formal or aesthetic terms, include such oppositions as word and image, or space and time, but these aesthetic properties are also embedded in larger social and political relations of otherness:

> Insofar as art history is a verbal representation of visual representation, it is an elevation of ekphrasis to a disciplinary principle. Like the masses, the colonized, the powerless and voiceless everywhere, visual representation cannot represent itself; it must be represented by discourse.[25]

As an art historian, Noah's act of ekphrastic hope is to master Italy and its art as a way of screening settler Australia's proximity to Aboriginal Australia and Asia, and its dislocation in time and space from Europe. And yet, when Noah and Martin arrive in Italy, its visual and physical immediacy produces moments of ekphrastic fear, when the self would wish that the other "not" become manifest, where its manifestation "as" otherness – as random acts of violence or the rituals of religious superstition – threatens the disciplinary achievement of the self. "The ambivalence about ekphrasis", Mitchell explains, "is grounded in our ambivalence about other people, regarded as subjects and objects in the field of verbal and visual representation. Ekphrasitic hope and fear express our anxieties about merging with others".[26] Mitchell's example of this return of the repressed is the figure of the Medusa in Shelley's poem "On the Medusa of Leonardo da Vinci in the Florentine Gallery":

> Medusa is the perfect prototype for the image as dangerous female other who threatens to silence the poet's voice and fixate his observing eye. Both the utopian desire of ekphrasis (that the beautiful image be present to the observer) and its

---

24 Mitchell, *Picture Theory*, 156.
25 Mitchell, *Picture Theory*, 157.
26 Mitchell, *Picture Theory*, 163.

counter desire or resistance (the fear of paralysis and muteness in the face of the powerful image) are expressed here.[27]

The Medusa in Jones' novel is Vincenzo Ragusa's sculpture *Japanese Woman* (1881), (Fig. 9.5), a portrait of his wife Eleonora, whose personal transformation is a chiastic or mirror image of Noah Glass' act of colonial self-fashioning. Where Noah had deliberately "hauled himself to another country" (98) by becoming an art historian, Eleonora is "split between countries" (94) through her "transnational marriage" (213), and as the exotic subject of her European husband's practice of representation. In the 1870s, Meiji Japan had sought to acquire the cultural legitimacy of Europe, bringing to Tokyo the young Sicilian sculptor Vincenzo Ragusa to introduce Italian artistic traditions to the Japanese. He there married a Japanese woman, Kiyohara Tama, who changed her name to Eleonora when she returned with Vincenzo to Palermo.

It is Vincenzo's portrait of Eleonora that Noah helps Dora Caselli to steal for the Sicilian mafia. As the statue of a Japanese woman made by an Italian artist in the neoclassical style of the late ottocento, it is an epitome of the subaltern woman, or of woman as subaltern. But as a work of art mastered by the ekphrastic discipline of art history, *Japanese Woman* is also the Medusa that turns her gaze back onto the European self. Even the customs man at Narita airport testifies to its remarkable beauty, and when Noah Glass finally sees it, he is sapped of health and wellbeing. Noah returns to Sydney dazed and exhausted, deciding to hide the statue in a locker, a kind of psychological screening or encryption, its concealment protected by a code written on the back of his icon of St Jerome, and meant for the eyes of his daughter Evie, who is destined never to see the statue. Noah's paralysis before the object culminates in his death by a massive heart attack, which causes him to fall into his swimming pool.

"Beauty", Mitchell writes of the Medusa, "the very thing which aestheticians like Edmund Burke thought could be viewed from a safe position of superior strength, turns out to be itself a dangerous force".[28] And as postcolonial scholars like Sara Suleri have shown, even Burke's ekphrastic text on the sublime and the beautiful is embedded in the historically specific practice of colonial power through its relations to empire and colonialism, which it shares with Noah Glass' relation to Indigenous Australia, Europe and the orient.[29] In this sense the bust of Eleonora Ragusa plays a similar role in the novel to the eponymous fetishistic

---

27 Mitchell, *Picture Theory*, 172.
28 Mitchell, *Picture Theory*, 172.
29 Sara Suleri, *The Rhetoric of English India* (Chicago: University of Chicago Press, 1992).

Figure 9.5 Vincenzo Ragusa, *Japanese Woman*, 1881.

objects in films about the return of the postcolonial repressed, such as *The Maltese Falcon* (1941) and *The Mummy's Curse* (1944).

Noah and Martin Glass' situation as settler Australians "pullulating timidly on the edge of alien shores" personifies a legacy of postmodern, postcolonial displacement. At Narita airport, in the midst of a long-haul flight while smuggling the Ragusa bust from Sicily to Australia via Tokyo, Noah watches a Japanese woman dressed in a crimson kimono employed to promote sake. In another of those loops in time she becomes Eleonora returned from the nineteenth century to the present: "Eleonora Ragusa – Kiyohara Tama – had returned and was serving sake at Narita airport. She had punctured time, risen from the dead, and come to offer him a drink" (224). Noah's thoughts move from the woman to a memory of his pregnant wife in her dressing gown, and then to Piero's Madonna del Porto: "He stared at the Japanese woman, grasping the way images slide into and onto each other, the unpredictable metonymies of seeing, the unexpected association" (226). This "vortex of a blended modernity" (229) is the world that Jean-Francois Lyotard famously dubbed "the postmodern condition".[30]

But what power do classic images like Piero's and Ragusa's still have to challenge that world in the age of Skype and the internet? Ironically, Noah Glass shares his name with the American founder of Twitter,[31] and Jones describes Skype as "a machine for invigoration" (128), recalling her own definition of the novel as a machine for thinking and feeling. In the sake woman at Narita airport, Piero's Madonna seems reduced to the commercial banality of global capitalism rather than providing it with an alternative context of value: she "continued her task, administering to barely awake men in transit. She moved with ceremonial slowness, disguising commerce as ritual" (226). This reduction of sacred "ritual" to advertising is a textbook example of what Fredric Jameson calls "the cultural logic of late capitalism".[32] Under the ubiquitous impact of market forces and market values, elements from the past no longer provide any challenge to our assumptions, and are effortlessly accommodated into the self-regulating system of mass consumer culture, their value entirely defined by their current market price. It is what Martin Glass perceives as a desacralised and dilapidated world. However, Jameson elsewhere acknowledges the energy that can still render a work of art – a painting, a sculpture, a musical composition or a novel – "modern" in the sense of having a powerful impact upon us now no matter how archaic its form or content might seem. In *A Singular Modernity*, Jameson compares this meaning of the "modernity" of the image or artwork to an electrical charge: "to isolate this or that Renaissance painter as the sign of some first or nascent modernity is ... always to awaken a feeling of intensity and energy that is greatly in excess of the attention we generally bring to interesting events or monuments in the past".[33] Bakhtin attributes a similar energy, a capacity to incite "rethinking" and "revaluation", to the "modernity" of the novel: the "modernity of the novel is indestructible":

> thanks to the intentional potential embedded in them, such works have proved capable of uncovering in each era and against ever new dialogizing backgrounds

---

30 Jean-François Lyotard, *The Postmodern Condition: A Report on Knowledge*, trans. Geoffrey Bennington and Brian Massumi (1979; Minneapolis: University of Minnesota Press, 1984).
31 See Nicholas Carlson, "An Interview with Twitter's Forgotten Founder, Noah Glass", 14 April 2011, *Tech Insider*. https://www.businessinsider.com.au/twitter-cofounder-noah-glass-2011-4.
32 Fredric Jameson, *A Singular Modernity: Essays on the Ontology of the Present* (London and New York: Verso, 2002).
33 Jameson, *Singular Modernity*, 35.

ever new aspects of meaning; their semantic content literally continues to grow, to further create out of itself.[34]

For all her apparent engagement with postmodern culture, Gail Jones therefore seems committed to "art" and to "the novel" in Jameson's and Bakhtin's sense, to their power and energy, their "modernity" or "contemporaneity". Her willingness to explore the rupture of the image/text is perhaps explicable in terms of that release of creative energy. Yet her acknowledgement of the power of images across time is always underwritten, as we have seen, by an historically informed awareness of art's location in the history of colonialism and its cultures.

I began with the moment of Noah's vocation, his ekphrastic self-transformation through the power of art. Yet this is also an act of colonial mimicry by a "second-hand European", and therefore of the appropriation and displacement of another culture. Its immediate purpose is to distance Noah from his childhood friend, the poignantly named Aboriginal boy Francis. Art's shameful politics is revealed in Noah's encounter with Sister Perpetua years later in Adelaide. Sister Perpetua was his teacher at the mission for lepers. It was she who had seated him next to Francis and "encouraged their friendship" (45). But it was also through her that he had found the art book that allowed him to change his life, translating himself by a sustained act of ekphrastic hope to another time and place. Noah's account to his former teacher about the power of art is at once a tribute to the "modernity" of the image and a confession of settler "shame":

> To Sister Perpetua ... he described how the leper colony had deformed him ... Noah described the *Nativity* in the National Gallery ... here he was describing it to a nun. He was revealing that moment when, like a panicked saint, he'd come alive with inception and changed the direction of his life. He was speaking with passion of an image, and the timeless call of images. He might have had flames coming from his body, or a blaze of blood in his eyes. In this moment of disclosure, heart to heart with his past, he understood how art had made his loneliness endurable. (78)

That is to say that Noah Glass' life-transforming encounter with Piero della Francesca is achieved at the expense of the Aboriginal boy Francis, just as Eleonora Ragusa is created through the suppression of Kiyohara Tama.

---

34 M.M. Bakhtin, *The Dialogic Imagination: Four Essays*, ed. Michael Holquist (Austin: University of Texas Press, 1981), 421.

References

Bakhtin, M.M. *The Dialogic Imagination: Four Essays*. Edited by Michael Holquist. Austin: University of Texas Press, 1981.

Baum, Caroline. "Gail Jones: Novels Are Machines for Thinking as Well as Feeling." *Sydney Morning Herald*, 6 April 2018, https://www.smh.com.au/entertainment/books/gail-jones-novels-are-machines-for-thinking-as-well-as-feeling-20180328-h0y2hu.html

Brunette, Peter and David Wills, eds. *Deconstruction and the Visual Arts: Art, Media, Architecture*. Cambridge and New York: Cambridge University Press, 1994.

Carlson, Nicholas. "An Interview with Twitter's Forgotten Founder, Noah Glass." *Tech Insider*, 14 April 2011. https://www.businessinsider.com.au/twitter-cofounder-noah-glass-2011-4

Dow, Steve. "Gail Jones and the Art of Words." *The Saturday Paper*, 10 March 2018.

Jacks, Philip. "The Renaissance *Prospettiva*: Perspectives of the Ideal City." In *The Cambridge Companion to Piero della Francesca*, edited by Jeryldene M. Wood, 115–33. Cambridge: Cambridge University Press, 2002.

Jameson, Fredric. *A Singular Modernity: Essays on the Ontology of the Present*. London and New York: Verso, 2002.

Jones, Gail. *The Death of Noah Glass*. Melbourne: Text, 2018.

Lavin, Marilyn Aronberg. "Piero the Storyteller: Tradition and Innovation in the 'Legend of the True Cross.'" In *Piero della Francesca, The Legend of the True Cross in the Church of San Francesco in Arezzo*, edited by Anna Maria Maetzke and Carolo Bertelli, 27–38. Milan: Skira, 2013.

Lyotard, Jean-Francoise. *The Postmodern Condition: A Report on Knowledge*. Translated by Geoffrey Bennington and Brian Massumi (1979). Minneapolis: University of Minnesota Press, 1984.

Mitchell, W.J.T. *Picture Theory: Essays on Verbal and Visual Representation*. Chicago, IL: Chicago University Press, 1994.

--. *Iconology: Image, Text, Ideology*. Chicago, IL: Chicago University Press, 1986.

Nead, Lynda. *Victorian Babylon: People, Streets and Images in Nineteenth-Century London*. New Haven and London: Yale University Press, 2000.

Panofsky, Erwin. *Studies in Iconology: Humanistic Themes in the Art of the Renaissance*. New York: Harper & Row, 1962.

Suleri, Sara. *The Rhetoric of English India*. Chicago, IL: University of Chicago Press, 1992,

Verdon, Timothy. "The Spiritual World of Piero's Art." In *The Cambridge Companion to Piero della Francesca*, edited by Jeryldene M. Wood, 30–50. Cambridge: Cambridge University Press, 2002.

Wagner, Peter, editor. *Icons – Texts – Iconotexts: Essays on Ekphrasis and Intermediality*. Berlin and Boston: De Gruyter, 2012.

Wood, Jeryldene M. "Piero's Legend of the True Cross and the Friars of San Francesco." In *The Cambridge Companion to Piero della Francesca*, edited by Jeryldene M. Wood, 51–65. Cambridge: Cambridge University Press, 2002.

10
Blueness and Light in the Art of Gail Jones

Meg Samuelson

> "Ah, prisms! … Whiteness shattered! The spectrum revealed!"
> – Jones, *Sixty Lights*

> "Blue … I need to think about blue"
> – Jones, *The Death of Noah Glass*

Gail Jones' oeuvre is pervaded by light. Her second novel, *Sixty Lights* (2004), most notably takes illumination as thematic focus, formal device and – through its interest in photography – representational medium. The lens of the focal character, Lucy Isaac Newton (née Strange), enacts the "writing of light" referred to in its epigraph from Eduardo Cadava, and her name provokes the exclamation "Whiteness shattered! The spectrum revealed!"[1] Jones' most recent novel, *The Death of Noah Glass* (2018), returns to this conceit as Noah and his two children, Martin and Evie, together comprise a triangle of glass through which the light referred to in its opening sentence is refracted. While continuing to revel in the prismatic spectrum, *Noah Glass* isolates the colour to which the name of its titular character alludes in its reference to a flooded world, and which he partly realises and partly deflects when his body is found floating in a turquoise pool.[2]

Meg Samuelson, Blueness and Light in the Art of Gail Jones. In *Inner and Outer Worlds: Gail Jones' Fiction*, edited by Anthony Uhlmann. Sydney: Sydney University Press, 2022.
DOI: 10.30722/sup.9781743327791

---

1   Gail Jones, *Sixty Lights* (2004; London: Vintage, 2005), 196. All subsequent references are to this edition and appear in parentheses in the text.
2   I refer of course to his first name, "Noah", but his surname also drifts suggestively between illumination and blue manifestations of watery expanses: the English "glass" comes from the Germanic "*glas*", which means "to shine, shimmer, glow" and thus references Jones' persistent preoccupation with light; but it is tinted by the Celtic word "*glas*" that originally described

A discerning review by Carolyn Baum notes that "Noah Glass is bathed in various shades of blue, referencing artists from Piero della Francesca to Derek Jarman".[3] Thus inviting attention to the question of how writing might be said to be coloured, and how it responds to the visual arts and film, the novel draws readers to the word-image interface. Jones emphasises that her art as a writer is informed by her initial training as a painter, along with a sustained interest in film. In all her writing, as she points out, "there are images and words in contention", and through which she explores "what images can do that words can't, and what words can do that images can't".[4] This enquiry is heightened through colour, which both eludes language and discloses its allusive potential.[5]

Ekphrasis is identified by Jones as a "significant category" in her art "because it is precisely about how you can put in words the details of a visual image as though it is another reality" – and thus cuts to the quick of the question of how worlds are drawn in fiction as well as how words might intimate that which withdraws from view.[6] It is, for instance, pivotal to her first novel, *Black Mirror* (2002), which revolves around a surrealist painter and her biographer, while her second, *Sixty Lights*, plays further with the presence/absence dialectic of word-and-image through Lucy's "light writing" and her "diary [of] Photographs Not Taken" (1, 178.). Characterisation similarly serves the ekphrastic enquiry of *Noah Glass*: Noah is an art historian, Martin a painter, and Evie a philosopher who takes a job providing "[d]escriptive audio" to a "blind movie viewer".[7] The visual is translated into language as they variously recount a plethora of images ranging from Caravaggio's *Burial of St Lucy* to Hitchcock's *Marnie* and including, most significantly, one of the quattrocento "painters of light", Piero della Francesca.

---

aquatic bodies and which names the spectrum from blue-green to blue-grey. See Philip Ball, *Bright Earth: Art and the Invention of Colour* (2001; London: Vintage, 2012), 15; Ball also notes: "One can hardly avoid the conclusion, in surveying the history of colourmaking, that blue has always been special" (Ball, *Bright Earth*, 262).

3 Carolyn Baum, "Gail Jones: Novels Are Machines for Thinking as Well as Feeling", *Sydney Morning Herald*, 6 April 2018. https://www.smh.com.au/entertainment/books/gail-jones-novels-are-machines-for-thinking-as-well-as-feeling-20180328-h0y2hu.html.
4 Jones in Steve Dox, "Gail Jones and the Art of Words", *The Saturday Paper*, 10–16 March 2018. https://www.thesaturdaypaper.com.au/2018/03/10/gail-jones-and-the-art-words/15206004005912.
5 Wassily Kandinsky puts it thus: "each tone will find some probable expression in words, but it will always be incomplete, and that part which the word fails to express will not be unimportant but rather the very kernel of its existence. For this reason words are, and will always remain, only hints, mere suggestions of colours"; Wassily Kandinsky, *Concerning the Spiritual in Art* (1914; New York: Dover Publications, 1977), 41.
6 Jones in Maria del Pilar Royo Grasa, "In Conversation with Gail Jones", *JASAL: Journal for the Study of Australian Literature* 12, no. 3 (2013). https://openjournals.library.sydney.edu.au/index.php/JASAL/article/view/9828/9716.
7 Gail Jones, *The Death of Noah Glass* (Melbourne: Text Publishing, 2018), 121. All subsequent references are to this edition and appear in parentheses in the text.

Piero's signature works are related by Noah in an inversion of Piero's own "transformation of words into images" in the Arezzo fresco cycle, *The Legend of the True Cross*, in which discrete episodes are integrated into narrative by a continuous blue sky.[8]

The word-image interface that Jones draws through Piero is what holds her Glass triangle together and casts a blue light over the narrative. Of his young family, we are told that Noah's "interest in Piero supplied images that became a language they shared" (75). Martin, in turn, composes the world into "relations of colour and space" (230), and gives this chapter its focus with a declaration dispatched across oceanic space and received through the high-energy visible light emitted by Evie's computer screen: "Blue … I need to think about blue" (129). Evie, finally, is portrayed as a creature of water: Noah is haunted by a memory of her "blue-coloured and almost drowned" as a baby (302); and, as a motherless child, she finds succour in the material body of blueness and is observed swimming in the sea at critical moments. In contrast to the visual perspective that Martin offers, Evie "[catches] at words flowing by" to reveal a "world … full of patterns and connections" (66) through a series of alphabetical lists (including one of fifteenth-century pigments and another of the world's oceans and seas). A veritable assemblage of reflections on blue, Evie herself evinces qualities ascribed to the colour through her "withdrawn" and "inward" nature (67).[9]

*

Blue, claims William Gass, is the "colour of interior life".[10] Yet the external world, too, appears predominantly blue. This paradox is not unique to blueness. Colour, in general, "veers between its location in the mind and being out there in the world".[11] But blue, surely, does so more particularly.[12] This is due to the peculiar properties of blue light.

Along with violet, blue light has the highest energy and shortest wavelengths of the bands comprising the colour spectrum. It is thus scattered rather than absorbed by molecules in the atmosphere and in water. When this scattered light

---

8   James R. Banker, *Piero della Francesca: Artist & Man* (Oxford: Oxford University Press, 2014), 53, 56.
9   Kandinsky, for instance, ascribes to blue a "concentric movement" that he likens to "a snail retreating into its shell", Kandinsky, *Concerning the Spiritual in Art*, 37.
10 William H. Gass, *On Being Blue: A Philosophical Enquiry* (1976; New York: NYRB Classics, 2014), n.p.
11 Natasha Eaton, *Colour, Art and Empire: Visual Culture and the Nomadism of Representation* (London: I.B. Taurus, 2013), 142.
12 On blue as "a particularly paradoxical colour", see also Carol Mavor, *Blue Mythologies: Reflections on a Colour* (London: Reaktion Books, 2013), 10.

beats against the human retina, the sea and the sky – and thus much of the outer world – manifest in blue. Paradoxically, these properties mean that inner worlds are also bathed in blue. This is alluded to in *Noah Glass* when Evie tells Benjamin – who suffers from retinitis pigmentosa and whose name cues readers to watch for "flashes" of illumination[13] – about Derek Jarman's last film, *Blue*, which was made as he was dying of AIDS and nearly completely blind. "There is just one image", she relates, "a blue screen": "Images come into being, as it were, from the hypnotic effect of contemplation alone … It's about losing sight, but not losing vision" (175).

Why does Jarman use blue to elicit inner vision? *Noah Glass* casts oblique light on this question when Evie tells Martin about the nineteenth-century Czech anatomist Jan Evangelista Purkyně's experiments with "entoptic images": "You close your eyes and there are images, but they are not images of the outside world" (163). He also observed the Purkinje effect, which Evie does not note but to which her suggestion to "google" Purkinje might direct readers to find on their own blue screens (168). This optical effect is evoked also in Julia Kristeva's reflections on Giotto's Padua frescoes. Discussing the remarkable use of blue, Kristeva cites "Purkinje's law", which "states that in dim light, short wavelengths prevail over long ones; thus, before sunrise, blue is the first colour to appear".[14] Blue, she concludes, materialises as unrepresentable excess, overflowing the didactic purpose of the frescoes to produce the non-linguistic *jouissance* that she calls "Giotto's Joy".[15]

*

Seeping into the fringe between perceptible and imperceptible things, blue makes manifest the ungraspable elements of water and air that together comprise the greater portion of the surrounding world while at the same time intimating the "unrepresentable" and "not quite visible".[16] Its paradoxical properties evidence Jones' preoccupation with "the *necessary failure* of language to contain everything".[17]

---

13   See Walter Benjamin's aphorism: "[K]nowledge comes only in lightning flashes. The text is the long roll of thunder that follows", the first sentence of which provides an epigraph in *Sixty Lights*; Walter Benjamin, *The Arcades Project*, trans. Howard Eiland and Kevin McLaughlin (Cambridge, MA: Belknap Press, 1999), 457. See also: Walter Benjamin, "Theses on the Philosophy of History", in *Illuminations: Essays and Reflections*, ed. Hannah Arendt, trans. Harry Zohn (1968; New York: Schocken Books, 2007), 253–65.
14   Julia Kristeva, "Giotto's Joy" (1972), in *Desire in Language: A Semiotic Approach to Literature and Art*, ed. Leon S. Roudiez, trans. Thomas Gora, Alice Jardine and Leon S. Roudiez (New York: Columbia University Press, 1980), 225.
15   Kristeva, "Giotto's Joy".
16   Jones in Grasa, "In Conversation".
17   Jones in Grasa, "In Conversation".

*

"For Blue", says Jarman, "there are no boundaries or solutions".[18] Drenched as it is in blue, *Noah Glass* ends on Evie's reiterated words – "I don't know" (308). The question to which she responds is itself an absent-presence that floods across the bounds of the narrative.

*

Seeking to perform a critical dive into Jones' art, rather than survey it from the outside, this chapter draws its form and method from the properties of blueness that saturate her fiction. It thus proceeds by way of scattered and drifting reflections on a colour that surfaces out of the deep, dissolves into distance, shades whiteness and portends the yet-to-come.[19] Thinking through blue presents an occasion to forgo coherence and abandon an aspiration to arrive at a conclusion. By licensing a certain critical failure, blue may in turn issue an invitation to open thought.

*

"What might it mean to take the fragment or the trace as a paradigm of knowledge and to assume that assemblage, not reconstitution, is our critical task?"[20] Jones, who poses this question, discloses that her "fictive and critical practice" might be "illuminate[d]" by a "recurring dream" she had as a child:

> I dreamt I was walking underwater on the ocean floor ... What I found here and there were drifting bones, which I gathered in the flimsy concave of my skirt. A thighbone here, an ulna there, the small white components of former hands. The dream of bones, as I now think of it, is an allegory of loss and incomplete recovery, of the aesthetic failure to *fully figure*.[21]

Rather than proffering "textual plenitude and recreated presence", Jones' art "favour[s] signifying absence" and "assume[s] ontological gaps and incompletion".[22]

---

18 Derek Jarman, *Blue: Text of a Film by Derek Jarman* (London: Channel 4 Television, 1993).
19 A survey of the literature on blueness reveals that the colour lends itself to reflection in fragmentary and associative forms; see, *inter alia*, William Gass, Derek Jarman, Carol Mavor, Ellen Meloy, Maggie Nelson and Rebecca Solnit, all of whom are cited in this chapter.
20 Gail Jones, "A Dreaming, A Sauntering: Re-imagining Critical Paradigms", *JASAL: Journal for the Study of Australian Literature* 5 (2006): 13.
21 Jones, "A Dreaming, A Sauntering", 12.

In *Noah Glass*, which is if anything a meditation on the "loss and incomplete recovery" experienced in filial grief, it finds expression in "a cathedral with no roof" in Palermo: "Not bombed, but splendidly, audaciously, unfinished. Gazing up at the blue sky, arched outlines blazing, Noah felt shyly grateful" (97). As it does in the firmament and in ocean basins, blue spills into "ontological gaps" and incomplete works without sealing or solidifying them. It is the medium of drifting things from which Jones assembles her art.[23] The chromatic quality of this reiterated motif is emphasised in the image of Noah's "drifting form" framed by a turquoise pool (57).

*

Evoking the perspective of the "floating ghost", Jones proposes that "both reading and writing" inhabit a position which is "[n]either subject nor object".[24] In "To Write: An Intransitive Verb?", Roland Barthes notes how the distance between these two positions dissolves into the "middle voice" in writing.[25] Mavor argues that blue behaves similarly: "the colour blue yields meaning, but paradoxically will also give way to opposite meanings, as if it were performing the intransitive form of the verb, *to blue*".[26] The drift of meaning that occurs in blueness characterises also the condition of the floating things through which Jones writes. Bronislaw Szerszynski demonstrates this in the essay "Drift as a Planetary Phenomenon", which takes up and extends the Situationist's concept of "*dérive*" that informs Jones' earlier novel *Five Bells*.[27] As he elaborates:

> In the middle voice the subject does not "do" or have something "done to" them; neither can they simply opt out from or reverse the action of which they are a part. They undergo change while engaged in interactive processes from which they cannot simply withdraw; they *are not* and *cannot* be exterior to the process.[28]

---

22   Jones, "A Dreaming, A Sauntering", 12.
23   For other instances of the trope of drifting in Jones' oeuvre, see *inter alia* the reimagined narrative of "The Flying Dutchman" in *Sixty Lights*; the plotting of *Five Bells* (2011; Sydney: Vintage Books, 2012; all subsequent references are to this edition and appear in parentheses in the text) according to the Situationist strategy of "*dérive*" in order to recast the city as a work of art; and, the jellyfish drifting in the "bluish radiance" of the aquarium in *A Guide to Berlin* (Sydney: Vintage Books, 2015; all subsequent references are to this edition and appear in parentheses in the text).
24   Jones, "A Dreaming, A Sauntering", 18.
25   Roland Barthes, "To Write: An Intransitive Verb?" (1966), in *The Rustle of Language*, trans. Richard Howard (Berkeley: University of California Press, 1989), 11–21.
26   Mavor, *Blue Mythologies*, 96.
27   See Robert Dixon, "Invitation to the Voyage: Reading Gail Jones' *Five Bells*", *Journal for the Study of Australian Literature* 12, no. 3 (2013). https://openjournals.library.sydney.edu.au/index.php/JASAL/article/view/9827/9715.
28   Bronislaw Szerszynski, "Drift as a Planetary Phenomenon", *Performance Research* 23, no. 7 (2018): 140.

Whereas locomotion "encourages us to make a division between the active animal and its passive environment", drift names a motion that "results from the immersion of the body in the medium, and is the conjoined achievement of all".[29]

*

The drifting fragments comprising this chapter result in turn from immersion in the medium of Jones' blue art. Modelling a form of criticism that is immanent to its object/subject, they follow the eddies and flows through which agency floats between text and reader rather than charting a course towards an established destination.

*

Szerszynski deduces "that things adrift can help us trace the lineaments of a planetary ethic: an ethic that extends beyond the human, the animal, and the living to the whole extended body of the Earth …; and that helps us to recognize our obligations of care towards all drifting things".[30]

Drift thus affords apprehension of the blue planet – "a planet that Spivak insists 'is in the species of alterity, belonging to another system … [inhabited] on loan'".[31] The concept of planetarity that Szerszynski invokes is sketched out by Spivak as alternative to the flattened, consumable globe of "world lit.": "imagin[ing] ourselves as planetary creatures rather than global entities" is what leads her to the understanding that "alterity remains underived from us; it is not our dialectical negation, it contains us as much as it flings us away".[32]

*

In an essay that had been lost before it "arrived by email, out of the blue",[33] Jones writes resonantly:

> We have gazed at the moon for millennia and its enchantment was in part its utter remoteness. We love what evades our grasp; we admire radical otherness, we adore the sublimity of nature phenomena that imply a completely separate scale of being. While art strives to register our forms of interconnection and

---

29 Szerszynski, "Drift as a Planetary Phenomenon", 140.
30 Szerszynski, "Drift as a Planetary Phenomenon", 136.
31 Szerszynski, "Drift as a Planetary Phenomenon", 136.
32 Gayatri Chakravorty Spivak, *Death of a Discipline* (New York: Columbia University Press, 2003), 72–73.
33 Gail Jones, "Five Meditations on a Moonlit Night (I.M. Veronica Brady)", *Le Simplegadi* 14, no. 16 (2016): 23.

correspondence, it also seeks, I think, to affirm this separateness – that humanity is not, after all, the measure of all things, but that we exist in local, planetary and cosmic contexts that require our humility and our awe.[34]

*

"The world is blue at its edges and in its depths", Rebecca Solnit observes in *A Field Guide to Getting Lost*.[35] This is due to the optical effect of aerial perspective, which cloaks all that is distant from the perceiver in shades of blue. (Jones registers this effect in *Black Mirror*, when two characters in remote Australia "catch sight of a pack of wild camels which buck away into the far blue distance", and which precedes a reflection on whether "*vanished things*" or "presence" are what compel and constitute art.)[36] Solnit notes that the quattrocento painters with which Noah Glass is preoccupied used the "blue of distance" as much as the "art of perspective" to grant depth and dimension to their work.[37]

Blue is thus vital to verisimilitude. We might describe it thus: because distant objects in the world appear blue to human eyes, art creates an illusion of depth by rendering them in blue pigment. But such a statement commits a category error. As Natasha Eaton points out, "colours create their own unique category of appearance which is not about illusions or deception".[38] Creating the sensation of space, blue is less an illusion of presence than the elusive stuff of world-making.

*

Blue is equally the medium through which the world withdraws from the perceiver. Goethe, whom Evie mentions alongside Purkyně, notes in his *Theory of Colour*, that,

> As the upper sky and distant mountains appear blue, so a blue surface seems to retire from us.
>
> But as we readily follow an agreeable object that flies from us, so we love to contemplate blue – not because it advances to us, but because it draws us after it.[39]

---

34   Jones, "Five Meditations on a Moonlit Night", 16.
35   Rebecca Solnit, *A Field Guide to Getting Lost* (New York: Viking, 2005), n.p.
36   Gail Jones, *Black Mirror* (Sydney: Picador, 2002), 32, 33.
37   Solnit, *Field Guide to Getting Lost*, n.p.
38   Eaton, *Colour, Art and Empire*, 12.
39   Johann Wolfgang von Goethe, *Theory of Colours* (1810), trans. Charles Lock Eastlake (Santa Cruz, CA: BLTC Press, 2008), 209.

The colour that, for Jarman, makes the invisible world tangible is also, to quote Solnit again, "the color of where you can never go. For the blue is not the place those miles away at the horizon, but in the atmospheric distance between you and the mountains".[40]

*

Blue is thus the colour of art that invites one to reach towards it while eluding one's grasp. Noah begins to articulate this in his response to Piero's *Nativity*, which features a "thin baby set apart on a field of blue, reaching" and which draws Noah after it: "He saw at last a painting whose singular majesty moved him and was reminded of why art history was worth pursuing" (71).

*

Blue also names the distance that Jones' Australian characters traverse in their multiple journeys to "the other side of the planet" (121) – whether through ocean and air travel or in the blue glow emitted from the screens on which they Skype. If it appears to measure an antipodean alterity, it also points to the plenitude of space that Noah finds himself missing on a crowded Sicilian beach. Blue is thus the colour through which Jones crafts her writerly location as simultaneously Australian and cosmopolitan.

*

In *The Anthropology of Turquoise*, Ellen Meloy concludes of blue that it is "the fugitive light", emitting as it does sufficient "energy to escape complete absorption by water, snow, and glacial ice".[41] It is thus an appropriate hue with which to colour a narrative plotted into an art-heist thriller while unleashing fugitive meanings that refuse resolution.

*

Returning to Sydney with the stolen sculpture, Noah drives towards the Blue Mountains but does not arrive at his destination. Blue, like the Southern Cross, "the bright heaven" to which he turns his gaze, names the unattainable (272). It is only weeks later, after a reverie that begins with his memory of the "hazy drive on the road heading away from the Blue Mountains" (302), that he falls

---

40   Solnit, *Field Guide to Getting Lost*, n.p.
41   Ellen Meloy, *The Anthropology of Turquoise: Reflections on Desert, Sea, Stone, and Sky* (New York: Vintage, 2002), n.p.

into the moon and stars blinking on the reflective surface of a deep blue pool when his heart stops. In this "end of time" (302) that is also eternity (the word "abide" arrives unbidden in Evie's mind such that "[s]he half-expects to see Noah, resurrected in light" [308]), Noah falls, as it were, into both blueness and art, and what he earlier described on the beach of Glenelg as the "co-presence of the finite and the infinite" (288).

*

During his last flight home, Noah is struck by the "unpredictable metonymies of seeing, the unexpected association" evoked by blue (224). Thus, in her own reflections on blue, Maggie Nelson concludes: "There are no instruments for measuring color; there are no 'color thermometers'. How could there be, as 'color knowledge' always remains contingent upon an individual perceiver?"[42]

*

That may be so. But there is in fact an instrument for measuring blue, and to which Martin refers: this is the cyanometer that was formulated by the geologist Horace-Benedict de Saussure in 1760. (As Evie indicates, de Saussure is better known for being a "Neptunist" [241], with reference to his belief that the Alps had been formed by the waters of Noah's flood, and from which theory he developed an early contribution to contemporary understandings of deep time.) Martin describes the cyanometer thus:

> a little pie chart to estimate the shade of blue in the sky. In a circle he had painted graded slices of blue, all derived from carefully diluted tinctures of Prussian, so that the sky itself submitted to the calculations of science. How blue is the sky? Today it is *this* blue. (23)

De Saussure's computation of blueness is dismissed by the narrative as "false … European knowledge", the cyanometer's Prussian tints rendering it inexpressive of a "*cerulean* … southern sky" (42).

*

But Jones' art doubles back on the distinction that it draws in blue between north and south when Noah falls "into the stars" blinking on the surface of a "Prussian" tinted pool that reflects the night sky in which he had earlier sought

---

42 Maggie Nelson, *Bluets* (Seattle, WA: Wave Books, 2009), 39.

the Southern Cross (302). The south is indeed the more vividly blue of the two hemispheres,[43] and Jones does often contrast a "cobalt" or "indigo" southern sky with the ashen hues of the north. At the same time, as Robert Dixon notes, *Noah Glass* uses the setting of the Sicilian city of Palermo to "collapse" the dichotomy that a callow Noah posits between an enlightened north and the "more or less barbaric" southern continent of Australia (69).[44] Blending the "Prussian blue" of the "European sky chart" with "turquoise" and "a tint of Verdigris", Palermo's skies are after all received as similar to those that frame Sydney (102–3), and Jones invites readers to track blueness across the Mediterranean city's melancholic state of dilapidation, its surrounding seas, and the drifting things that compose it ("Africa was here, and the Arabs, and the energy of ages intermingling" [96]).

*

Noah Glass shades another distinction into gradation when implicitly contrasting two different de Saussures ("Linguist or Neptunist?" Evie asks in response to Martin's query, "Who's de Saussure?" [18]). One points to the arbitrariness of the sign and thus to the instability of meaning; the other to the physical substance of the earth and to deep histories that are written in rock.

Michael Taussig notes that, "[f]ar from being symbols, distinct from their referents … colours *are* those referents in a deeply organic sense".[45] Somewhat like the "photo-graphy" that elsewhere fascinates Jones, "colour cannot easily be separated from substance".[46] Colour may not be arbitrary, but the association that Jones draws through the word "de Saussure" surely is. If word and image seem to pull apart here, *Noah Glass* also foregrounds the materiality of language by lingering over terms that intimate blueness while at the same time destabilising and decentring meaning.

Martin thus follows up on Purkyně rather than Ritter because he claims to "like the name", while a trace of Ritter's experiments "in the instability of vision" remains in the novel as an unsettling alternative to de Saussure's efforts "to calculate the blue tint of the sky" (121). Evie's alphabetical lists are another case in point, as is the word "dilapidation" that is bestrewn across the narrative: Evie recalls "how excited she'd been to learn that words could work in this way, could have objects inside them, and archaeological histories" when Noah tells

---

43 See Meg Samuelson, "Toward the Blue Southern Hemisphere" (unpublished presentation, 2018); and Meg Samuelson and Charne Lavery, "The Oceanic South", *English Language Notes* 57, no. 1 (2019): 37–50.
44 Robert Dixon, "Figures in Geometry: *The Death of Noah Glass* by Gail Jones", *Sydney Review of Books*, 7 September 2018. https://sydneyreviewofbooks.com/review/death-noah-glass-jones/.
45 Michael Taussig, *What Color is the Sacred?* (Chicago, IL: University of Chicago Press, 2009), 8.
46 Taussig, *What Color is the Sacred?*, 145.

her and her brother how it came "from the Latin for stone, *lapis*. It meant a scattering of stones" (106, 146). Word and image drift together again when Noah follows a trail of sliding signifiers through the folds of time to the appearance of his long-deceased wife, pregnant with Evie and wrapped in a dressing gown of "lapis blue" (224).

*

The expressive tonal range of blue is both substantial and conventional. The Virgin Mary is cloaked in ultramarine by decree of the twelfth-century church because this rich and vivid blue was the most precious pigment – alongside or even exceeding gold – being sourced only from lapis lazuli before it was synthetically reproduced after 1828: blue is not an earth colour and its first stable form was ground from this semi-precious stone mined in Afghanistan (hence its naming as "ultramarine" or "beyond the seas").[47] And yet, as Nelson notes, "if blue is anything on this earth, it is *abundant*".[48]

*

Simultaneously ubiquitous and exceptional, blue drifts between the mundane and the transcendent. It is this conjunction that first draws Noah to Piero's art when he is struck by *The Nativity*:

> Images local and from afar enigmatically coincided. The mundane and the divine, he told himself, in seamless coalition. Afterwards, saner with his decision, he realised that it was the singing magpie he loved most of all, and the touch of the commonplace, and the thin baby set apart on a field of blue, reaching. (71)

Marilyn Lavin argues of "Piero's meditation on the nativity" that "this paradoxical approach … makes the high spiritual value of nature's lowliest forms into his overt subject" thus "showing the sanctity of his native land".[49] As in *The Baptism of Christ*, "his purpose … is to define, with great precision, the scene's locale".[50]

---

47 Natalie Angier, "Blue Through the Centuries: Sacred and Sought After", *The New York Times*, 23 October 2012. https://www.nytimes.com/2012/10/23/science/blue-through-the-centuries-sacred-and-sought-after.html; Electric Light Company, "Pigment: The Blue from Over the Sea", *The Electric Light Company*, 11 May 2018. https://eclecticlight.co/2018/05/11/pigment-the-blue-from-over-the-sea-ultramarine/.
48 Nelson, *Bluets*, 95.
49 Marilyn Aronberg Lavin, "Piero's Meditation on the Nativity", in *Piero della Francesca and His Legacy*, ed. Lavin (Washington: National Gallery of Art, 1995), 128.
50 Lavin, "Piero's Meditation on the Nativity", 128.

*

The Baptism of Christ is the work in which Noah starts to perceive Piero's treatment of time: a "radiant" Jesus is "consecrated for eternity by a single drop of water" – while another quotidian figure behind him might be "any man", or "Christ himself, just after or before the baptism" (156). The "audacity of the painting" is seen to lie "in imagining a man exceeding time" (156). As Evie later explains, Noah "was attracted not to Piero's mathematical virtuosity – as many scholars are – but to something more mysterious about his arrangement of figures, certain anomalies in time and space. Eternity implied, that sort of thing" (197). Thus, noting the portraits of two grieving fathers in the foreground of Piero's *Flagellation of Christ*, Noah observes in this most geometric work a "temporal fold" in which "human and divine were radically continuous" (156), while the panels of *The Legend of the True Cross* that are knitted together in blue "declared the loops of time – repetition" (156).

Jones resituates this theory of time into a southern locale when Noah tries to impart it to Martin on Glenelg beach in Adelaide as they settle into a triangular configuration watching Evie swim, "united by looking not at each other, but in her direction":

> There were her churning arms and her small head, cresting and falling; there was her slight form asserting its shape in the dappled wavelets and foam. Every now and then she dived under, disappearing, flicking her feet upwards, and then returned, as in an ancient enactment. (156)

Emerging from the depths of his own loss, Martin will later return this scene to the narrative present before it loops back to that of Noah's death. Glenelg beach – a littoral setting with a palindrome name – itself articulates something of "the idea of time as water" that Jones explored in *Five Bells*,[51] and which Dixon describes resonantly as a novel that explores "the tidal effects of memory and mourning in relation to chronological time".[52]

*

The Death of Noah Glass begins with Martin recalling a report about "[t]wo brothers in their late seventies attend[ing] the funeral of their father, aged

---

51 Jones in Catherine Keenan, "Novelist Gail Jones Explores Tacky Tourist Traps", *Sydney Morning Herald*, 5 February 2011. https://www.smh.com.au/entertainment/novelist-gail-jones-explores-tacky-tourist-traps-20110204-1agdg.html.
52 Dixon, "Invitation to the Voyage", 3.

forty-two" (4). The father had been buried beneath ice while skiing in the Chamonix, only for his frozen remains to be "exposed" years later "in an unseasonable thaw" (4). While around him Sydney "hum[s] with irrepressible life", Martin gazes at his sleeping sister, remarking on her "cyan blue" eyelids and envisioning the two brothers looking on their father in the same manner, perceiving "this combination of the meagre and the indestructible" (12).

*

"Ice has a memory and the colour of this memory is blue", Robert MacFarlane finds in *Underland: A Deep Time Journey*. Coloured by "the blue of time", "deep ice" acts as a "recording and storage medium" in that it "collects and keeps data for millennia", but it also functions "as a 'medium' in the supernatural sense: a presence permitting communication with the dead and buried, across gulfs of deep time".[53] Because this storage medium is blue – that is, "because it continues to flow" – "it distorts its record, its layers folding and sliding, such that sequence can be almost impossible to discern".[54] So too for Noah's reframing of Piero's art as one of "serial time giving way to curves and bending motions" (288): as with *Noah Glass* itself, it may be said to emulate the structure of deep blue ice.

*

The dreadful untimeliness of the "unseasonable thaw" that exposes the revenant[55] is thrown into further relief by the "coral light of a summer dawn" in which Martin recalls it: the fecund potential of daybreak is belied by the chromatic adjective that directs attention to submarine ecosystems which are proving to be as vulnerable to global warming as the retreating glaciers. MacFarlane begins his journey into the "radiant blue" of the "underland" with a reflection on what it means to be living in the Anthropocene: "Time is profoundly out of joint – and so is place. Things that should have stayed buried are rising up unbidden".[56]

*

The "collapse of time" that occurs in this "unseasonable thaw" manifests also the "hauntology" of a settler nation. Jones makes pointed reference to Jacques Derrida's *Spectres of Marx* in various essays on Australia and in reflections on

---

53 Robert MacFarlane, *Underland: A Deep Time Journey* (New York: W.W. Norton, 2019), n.p.
54 MacFarlane, *Underland*, n.p.
55 Noah's name might also allude to the American frontiersman Hugh Glass, who was portrayed in the film *The Revenant* (2015).
56 MacFarlane, *Underland*, n.p.

her own art. The "ghost", she concludes, "requires us not to forget the wrongs of history and to work for reparation in the future, for the *arrivants*, the not-yet-born or arrived".[57]

Noah, the father who is no longer alive in the narrative present, recognised this claim on the future in the swelling belly of his wife, Katherine, who materialises before him, clothed in "lapis blue", "as Piero's pregnant Madonna, in which Mary stands with her gown slightly agape over her swelling belly" (224). This figure reappears during his last flight home as he observes a woman in a kimono (224). "It was the strangest connection", he reflects, ruminating on "the way images" – like ice – "slide into and onto each other" (224). As, indeed, they do in Jones' blue art.

*

Appearing in *Noah Glass* as the colour of the *revenant* and the *arrivant*, blue also recurs in haunting patterns across Jones' oeuvre, heavy with the weight of the "not-yet-born".

*

Secreted into blue – the shade emitted from that which has absorbed red – are the "*remorseless* crime[s]" that disturb the present, reminding that it is "not all sparkles and sunshine" (*Five Bells*, 183). Thus, in *A Guide to Berlin*, Cass finds herself unsettled by the dreamy blue light flooding the aquarium when she returns after Victor, the child of Holocaust survivors, is killed and disposed of in a river: "What was consoling here, she realised, was this eradication of history, this facile escape" (220). The "*remorseless* crime" of settler colonialism and the Stolen Generations to which Jones returns iteratively across her art is figured through lost and bereft children.[58] Tellingly, in *Five Bells*, the novel in which the words "*remorseless* crime" (183) are written, a photograph of a lost child taken at Circular Quay picks out in red rings the surrounding adults, of whom the Australian and Irish characters are clothed in blue. Surfacing histories of colonial violence, Jones' art evokes "an unquiet feeling" through the "juxtaposition" or "union" of blue and red.[59] Thus, *Sixty Lights* returns twice to the image of Lucy, pregnant in a blue sari,

---

57 Jones, "A Dreaming, A Sauntering", 16.
58 Dixon's analysis of *Five Bells* makes helpful reference to Peter Pierce's argument in *The Country of Lost Children* "that the lost child is one of the central, recurring motifs of Australian literature": "it reveals a foundational guilt at the heart of white Australia as a settler culture that is never quite comfortable with its right to belong, with its relation to place, a place that has been stolen by an act of violent invasion and is therefore a haunted space"; and, it expresses the shameful history of the Stolen Generations (Dixon, "Invitation to the Voyage").

"spattered bright red" with the "blood" of an Indian man impaled on shards of mirror when falling from a colonial building (4, see 156). *Sorry* (2007), similarly, twice presents an image of the Indigenous woman, Mary, in a hydrangea-blue dress, stained purple with the blood of her rapist, Perdita's father.

*

Another haunting pattern is traced out in blue and white. In *Sixty Lights*, a blue fan both partitions and unfolds across time: "Duck-egg blue, [Lucy] will recall as an adult. My mother's chrysanthemum fan was duck-egg blue" (7). And then, again, now in the past tense, she "remembered her mother lying very still on a long wicker chair, her pregnant belly huge", fanning herself "just before her death": "The wave of a duck-egg blue fan, patterned with chrysanthemums: this small detail retained, held close, held in mournful embrace, so that her ever-fading mother would not completely disappear" (132, 133). In *Dreams of Speaking* (2006), Stephen similarly holds on to the image of his mother leaving in "a blue dress with a print of tiny white flowers",[60] while in *Five Bells*, the memory that returns to Ellie of her and James making love at fourteen as he, haunted by the loss of his mother and the drowning of another child, slips into the blue waters of Sydney Harbour is of a "thin blue dress, covered in sprigs of tiny white blossom (how these details remain)" (98).

*

Folded into the memory of that "thin blue dress, covered in sprigs of tiny white blossom" is another: "[t]hat year, their fourteenth, 1988, had been the year of Australia's bicentennial commemorations ... Into this very harbour, in 1788, Captain Arthur Phillip had sailed his first fleet of convicts. Bosomy sails against the blue" (*Five Bells*, 135). James, who will later succumb to that blue, teaches Ellie that "Aborigines had called Australia Day 'Invasion Day', and the year one of 'mourning'" (137).

*

The recurrent detail of small white print across an expanse of blue becomes the figure of what Jones presents elsewhere as "sorry-in-the-sky":

---

59   Goethe, *Theory of Colours*, 210, 215.
60   Gail Jones, *Dreams of Speaking* (Sydney: Vintage, 2006), 51.

10 Blueness and Light in the Art of Gail Jones

In my study at home I have a small photograph … of the word *sorry* written in the sky by a sky-writing plane. The image is wobbly and the skywriting touchingly awkward; moreover the word is clearly dissolving even as it appears. There is a magnificently blue sky, with the enamelled and glittering qualities of a high-summer day, and there, faint, contingent, blurred by invisible wind, is the suspended word "sorry" … In its simplicity, its double reference, its slow fading to nothingness, the sorry-in-the-sky is emblematic of the speech act which it betokens. Apology and mourning are here interlaced, time is here suspended, space is deterritorialized, and there is no opportunity at all for rhetorical enshrouding.[61]

*

Drifting between apology and mourning, "sorry-in-the-sky", like the "ghostly tremble" of the father revenant in *The Death of Noah Glass*,[62] eludes the dream of forgetful whiteness that Perdita draws over herself at the end of *Sorry*. Anticipating her failure to apologise after her voice and memory return to her out of "a glass dome containing a multi-petalled flower of startling turquoise",[63] the conclusion obliterates the opening to the yet-to-arrive that is promised by this brilliant blue:

> Afraid of slumbery agitation, or ghostly visits, I willed myself to think instead of Stella's snow dream: a field of flakes descending, the slow transformation of the shapes of the world, the slow, inconclusive, obliteration, all forgetful white, reversing its presences. I saw Mary, and Billy, covered by snowflakes … Everything was disappearing under the gradual snow. Calmed, I look at the sky and saw only a blank. Soft curtains coming down, a whiteness, a peace. (214)

*

"*Snow shadows are blue*. This principle she had learnt years ago in her painting class", Cass recalls just before she is handed a note inscribed with the "simple word

---

61 Gail Jones, "Sorry-in-the-sky: Empathetic Unsettlement, Mourning, and the Stolen Generations", in *Imagining Australia: Literature and Culture in the New New World*, ed. Judith Ryan and Chris Wallace-Crabbe (Cambridge, MA: Harvard University Press, 2004), 168–69.
62 "Irrationally, she sensed her father still there, drifting as a breeze might, in a ghostly tremble" (Jones, *The Death of Noah Glass*, 197).
63 Gail Jones, *Sorry* (Sydney: Vintage, 2007), 159. All subsequent references are to this edition and appear in parentheses in the text.

'sorry'" (*Guide to Berlin*, 226, 227). Snow may suggest a "rhetorical enshrouding" – it may be a "symbol" of "white-washing", a "consolation", a "lush erasure of signs" (225) – but, like ice, it too is fundamentally blue.[64] Thus, Cass – herself also "sorry" in conclusion rather than "lost" like Perdita – draws under this sign "the mass drowning of African refugees … off the island of Lampedusa" and the Australian "policy of hard hearts" to cast a light over it that would reveal its blue shadow and its propensity to drift: "There were refugees everywhere, forming drifts of miserable humanity, moving in tired, desperate clusters all over the globe" (256).

*

As Szerszynski points out: "we need to ask what acts of solidarity drift should draw from us. Some can only drift safely because of the resources and networks that they happen to have – and others are forced to drift, often very precariously, for exactly the opposite reason".[65]

*

"Blue", Jones' art reveals, is what "protects white from innocence".[66]

References

Angier, Natalie. "Blue Through the Centuries: Sacred and Sought After." *The New York Times*, 23 October 2012. https://www.nytimes.com/2012/10/23/science/blue-through-the-centuries-sacred-and-sought-after.html

Ball, Philip. *Bright Earth: Art and the Invention of Colour*. (2001) London: Vintage, 2012.

Banker, James R. *Piero della Francesca: Artist & Man*. Oxford: Oxford University Press, 2014.

Barthes, Roland. "To Write: An Intransitive Verb?" (1966). In *The Rustle of Language*. Translated by Richard Howard, 11–21. Berkeley: University of California Press, 1989.

Baum, Carolyn. "Gail Jones: Novels Are Machines for Thinking as Well as Feeling." *Sydney Morning Herald*, 6 April 2018. https://www.smh.com.au/entertainment/books/gail-jones-novels-are-machines-for-thinking-as-well-as-feeling-20180328-h0y2hu.html

Benjamin, Walter. *The Arcades Project*. Translated by Howard Eiland and Kevin McLaughlin. Cambridge, MA: Belknap Press, 1999.

--. "Theses on the Philosophy of History." In *Illuminations: Essays and Reflections*, edited by Hannah Arendt and translated Harry Zohn (1968), 253–65. New York: Schocken Books, 2007.

Dixon, Robert. "Figures in Geometry: *The Death of Noah Glass* by Gail Jones." *Sydney Review of Books*, 7 September 2018. https://sydneyreviewofbooks.com/review/death-noah-glass-jones/

--. "Invitation to the Voyage: Reading Gail Jones' *Five Bells*." *Journal for the Study of Australian Literature* 12, no. 3 (2013). https://openjournals.library.sydney.edu.au/index.php/JASAL/article/view/9827/9715

---

64 Jones, "Sorry-in-the-sky", 169.
65 Szerszynski, "Drift as a Planetary Phenomenon", 143.
66 Jarman, *Blue*, n.p.

Dox, Steve. "Gail Jones and the Art of Words." *The Saturday Paper*, 10–16 March 2018. https://www.thesaturdaypaper.com.au/2018/03/10/gail-jones-and-the-art-words/15206004005912

Eaton, Natasha. *Colour, Art and Empire: Visual Culture and the Nomadism of Representation*. London: I.B. Taurus, 2013.

Eclectic Light Company. "Pigment: The Blue from Over the Sea." *The Eclectic Light Company*, 11 May 2018. https://eclecticlight.co/2018/05/11/pigment-the-blue-from-over-the-sea-ultramarine/

Gass, William H. *On Being Blue: A Philosophical Enquiry* (1976). New York: NYRB Classics, 2014.

Goethe, Johann Wolfgang von. *Theory of Colours* (1810). Translated by Charles Lock Eastlake. Santa Cruz, CA: BLTC Press, 2008.

Jarman, Derek. *Blue: Text of a Film by Derek Jarman*. London: Channel 4 Television, 1993.

Jones, Gail. *Black Mirror*. Sydney: Picador, 2002.

--. *The Death of Noah Glass*. Melbourne: Text Publications, 2018.

--. "A Dreaming, A Sauntering: Re-imagining Critical Paradigms." *JASAL: Journal for the Study of Australian Literature* 5 (2006): 11–24.

--. *Dreams of Speaking*. Sydney: Vintage, 2006.

--. *Five Bells* (2011). Sydney: Vintage, 2012.

--. "Five Meditations on a Moonlit Night (I.M. Veronica Brady)." *Le Simplegadi* 14 no. 16 (2016), 16–24.

--. *A Guide to Berlin*. Sydney: Vintage, 2015.

--. *Sixty Lights* (2004). London: Vintage, 2005.

--. *Sorry*. Sydney: Vintage, 2007.

--. "Sorry-in-the-sky: Empathetic Unsettlement, Mourning, and the Stolen Generations." *Imagining Australia: Literature and Culture in the New New World*, edited by Judith Ryan and Chris Wallace-Crabbe, 159–71. Cambridge, MA: Harvard University Press, 2004.

Kandinsky, Wassily. *Concerning the Spiritual in Art*. Translated by M.T.H. Sadler (1914). New York: Dover Publications, 1977.

Keenan, Catherine. "Novelist Gail Jones Explores Tacky Tourist Traps." *Sydney Morning Herald*, 5 February 2011. https://www.smh.com.au/entertainment/novelist-gail-jones-explores-tacky-tourist-traps-20110204-1agdg.html

Kristeva, Julia. "Giotto's Joy." (1972) In *Desire in Language: A Semiotic Approach to Literature and Art*, edited by Leon S. Roudiez, translated by Thomas Gora, Alice Jardine and Leon S. Roudiez, 210–36. New York: Columbia University Press, 1980.

Lavin, Marilyn Aronberg. "Piero's Meditation on the Nativity." In *Piero della Francesca and His Legacy*, edited by Marilyn Aronberg Lavin, 127–41. Washington: National Gallery of Art, 1995.

MacFarlane, Robert. *Underland: A Deep Time Journey*. New York: W.W. Norton, 2019.

Mavor, Carol. *Blue Mythologies: Reflections on a Colour*. London: Reaktion Books, 2013.

Meloy, Ellen. *The Anthropology of Turquoise: Reflections on Desert, Sea, Stone, and Sky*. New York: Vintage, 2002.

Nelson, Maggie. *Bluets*. Seattle, WA: Wave Books, 2009.

Pilar Royo Grasa, Maria del. "In Conversation with Gail Jones." *JASAL: Journal for the Study of Australian Literature* 12, no. 3 (2013). https://openjournals.library.sydney.edu.au/index.php/JASAL/article/view/9828/9716

Samuelson, Meg. "Toward the Blue Southern Hemisphere." Unpublished presentation, Further South Roundtable. Other Worlds ARC Discovery Project and Department of English and Creative Writing, University of Adelaide, 15 February 2018.

Samuelson, Meg and Charne Lavery. "The Oceanic South." *English Language Notes* 57, no. 1 (2019): 37–50.

Solnit, Rebecca. *A Field Guide to Getting Lost*. New York: Viking, 2005.

Spivak, Gayatri Chakravorty. *Death of a Discipline*. New York: Columbia University Press, 2003.

Szerszynski, Bronislaw. "Drift as a Planetary Phenomenon." *Performance Research* 23, no. 7 (2018): 136–44.

Taussig, Michael. *What Color Is the Sacred?* Chicago, IL: University of Chicago Press, 2009.

Contributors

Valérie-Anne Belleflamme works as an assistant teacher in Anglophone literatures at the University of Liège, Belgium, and is a member of Centre d'Enseignement et de Recherche en Etudes Postcoloniales (CEREP; www.cerep.uliege.be), the English Department's postcolonial research unit. Her research focuses on temporality and the craft of fiction in Gail Jones' literary oeuvre. She has published several articles on Jones and maintains a bibliography of her work as part of CEREP's project on online bibliographies of postcolonial writers. She has also co-edited *The Journal of the European Association for Studies of Australia* issue entitled "Australia–South Asia: Contestations and Remonstrances", which was published in 2017.

Tanya Dalziell is Discipline Chair of English and Literary Studies at the University of Western Australia. She is the author of *Gail Jones: Word, Image, Ethics* (Sydney University Press, 2020) and with Paul Genoni of *Half the Perfect World: Writers, Dreamers and Drifters on Hydra, 1955–1964* (Monash University Press, 2018), which won the 2019 Prime Minister's Literary Award for Non-Fiction.

Robert Dixon is Emeritus Professor of Australian Literature at the University of Sydney and General Editor of the Sydney Studies in Australian Literature series at Sydney University Press.

James Gourley is a Senior Lecturer in Literary Studies at Western Sydney University where he is a member of its Writing and Society Research Centre. His research addresses twentieth and twenty-first century literature and culture. His recent work has been published in *ISLE: Interdisciplinary Studies in Literature and Environment*, *Sydney Review of Books*, *English Studies*, *College Literature* and

Thomas Pynchon in Context (Cambridge University Press). James is currently researching the literature produced in Australia as a consequence of its historical medical epidemics.

Tony Hughes-d'Aeth is the Chair of Australian Literature at the University of Western Australia. His books include *Like Nothing on this Earth: A Literary History of the Wheatbelt* (UWA Publishing, 2017), which won the Walter McRae Russell Prize for Australian literary scholarship, and *Paper Nation: The Story of the Picturesque Atlas of Australasia* (Melbourne University Press, 2001), which won the Ernest Scott and WK Hancock prizes for Australian history. In 2019 he convened the annual Association for the Studies of Australian Literature (ASAL) Conference Perth. Tony is also the Director of the Westerly Centre, which publishes *Westerly Magazine*, a literary journal founded in 1956. Tony was co-editor of *Westerly* from 2010 to 2015.

Lou Jillett completed her doctorate at Western Sydney University (WSU) in 2018. Lou's thesis investigated the theme of wandering within the worlds of James Joyce's *Ulysses* and Cormac McCarthy's *Suttree*, incorporating both the notion of the wandering political subject (the "Wandering I") and scientific micro and macro applications of optics, parallax and astronomy (the "Wandering Eye"). Lou spent three months at the Cormac McCarthy Archive in San Marcos, Texas in 2013, publishing a paper on her experience of the archive in *They Rode On: Blood Meridian and the Tragedy of the American West*, Volume Two of Casebook Studies in Cormac McCarthy. Lou co-convened the three-day international McCarthy conference at WSU's Writing and Society Research Centre in July 2014, and was editor of the 2016 collection of essays that arose from conference proceedings, both of which shared the title: "Cormac McCarthy's Borders and Landscapes". Lou is currently writing and residing in Tasmania, where her research focus is on ecocritical approaches to the theme and representation of disappearance in Australian literature, and the function of walking within that literature: as record, as remembrance and as reclamation of space.

Elizabeth McMahon is a Professor of English at the University of New South Wales. She researches in the fields of Australian literature and island studies and her 2016 monograph *Islands, Identity and the Literary Imagination* won two national awards. She has edited Australian journals continuously for over nearly twenty-five years, including *Southerly*, Australia's oldest literary magazine since 2008. With Brigitta Olubas she has edited numerous collections on Australian literature and culture including *Antigone Kefala: New Australian Modernities* (UWA Publishing, 2021).

Contributors

Brigid Rooney taught Australian literature in the Department of English at the University of Sydney. She has published widely on twentieth-century and contemporary Australian literature and co-edited scholarly collections on such topics as Christina Stead and Australian literature as world literature. She is the author of *Literary Activists: Writer-Intellectuals and Australian Public Life* (University of Queensland Press, 2009) and *Suburban Space, the Novel and Australian Modernity* (Anthem Press, 2018).

Meg Samuelson is Associate Professor in the Department of English & Creative Writing at the University of Adelaide, and Associate Professor Extraordinary at Stellenbosch University. She has published widely in southern African and Indian Ocean studies. Her recent research includes enquiries into: "Coastal Form" and "Amphibian Aesthetics" in fiction from the African Indian Ocean littoral; "Coastal Thought"; "The Oceanic South" and the "blue southern hemisphere"; "The Oceans in World Literature"; "J.M. Coetzee and 'literatures of the South'"; "The African Anthropocene and Mia Couto's Poetics of the Planet"; "Thinking with sharks: racial terror, species extinction and other Anthropocene faultlines"; photography in Zanzibar; and "Indian Ocean Australia". She coedits the Palgrave series Maritime Literature and Culture.

Anthony Uhlmann is Professor of Literature in the Writing and Society Research Centre and Discipline Leader of English and Creative Writing at Western Sydney University. He is the author of four monographs, *Beckett and Poststructuralism* (Cambridge University Press, 1999), *Samuel Beckett and the Philosophical Image* (Cambridge University Press, 2006), *Thinking in Literature: Joyce, Woolf, Nabokov* (Bloomsbury, 2011) and *J.M. Coetzee, Truth, Meaning, Fiction* (Bloomsbury, 2020). He has edited a number of critical collections, including most recently *Gerald Murnane: Another World in This One* (Sydney University Press, 2020).

Index

affect *see* emotions
anachronism 6, 10, 20, 32, 44
apologia 77
art history 11, 153
assonance 2
astronomical metaphors 17, 22
Australian history 5

Barthes, Roland 61
belonging 120, 130, 131
bioluminescence 31, 37
Blake, William 35
Blanchot, Maurice 68
Burke, Edmund 36

Cadava, Eduardo 33
chiasmus 128
Chinese culture 11
Coleridge 33
colonialism 5, 46, 151, 154, 155
colour 11
communal reading 11, 105, 116, 120, 129
community 107, 121, 122, 137
connections 16, 88, 97, 101
consciousness 65, 73, 77, 91
consonance 2
constellations 15, 27

Deleuze, Gilles 20, 37, 38
Derrida, Jacques 30, 39
Darwin, Charles 32
difference 11, 103, 116
death 40, 49
dreams 60, 79

discourse analysis 113

Eagle, Christopher 8
ekphrasis 29, 69, 139, 140, 142–144, 162
Eliot, T.S. 4
emotions 85, 94
Enlightenment 33

families 21
feminism 53
fixation 85
forgiveness 86, 95
Forster, Georg 32
Francesca, Piero della 148
friendship 119

Global South 75
Great Expectations (novel) 46, 48, 54
grief 110
Guattari, Felix 20, 37, 38
guilt 86, 175

haecceity 38, 81–83
Harvey, E. Newton 32
history 92, 100, 175
Hopkins, Gerard Manley 38
hysteria 105, 107, 108

iconology 141, 151
imagery 3, 127, 128, 141, 166
image-text relations 140, 142, 162
injustice *see* justice and injustice
insomnia 66
intertextuality 4, 54, 69, 84, 96, 125, 127

Index

Jacobs, Lyn 29
Jane Eyre (novel) 46, 47, 53
Jones, Gail 7, 8
   Black Mirror 19, 60, 162, 168
   Death of Noah Glass, The 61, 69, 142–147, 161, 171
   Dreams of Speaking 17
   Fetish Lives 66
   Five Bells 25, 27, 68, 78–80, 84, 86, 92–95, 128
   Guide to Berlin, A 26, 67, 103, 104–107, 111–113, 119–120, 132–137, 175
   House of Breathing, The 24
   Sixty Lights 16, 29, 35–38, 43–46
   Sorry 27, 60, 65, 78–78, 89, 176
Joyce, James 4
justice and injustice 6, 105

Khorana, Sukhmani 34

Lacan, Jacques 11, 105, 113
Levinas, Emmanuel 64
light 163
literary community 130, 137; *see also* community
literary self 124
loneliness 137

materiality 97, 98
memory 26, 78, 80, 94, 106–107, 127
modernism 3, 6, 33, 43, 44, 52, 53, 120, 129, 158
moon 17, 167

Nabokov, Vladimir 4, 67, 108, 112, 125, 134
Neo-Victorian fiction 45, 141

past *see* history
place 5, 11, 84, 93, 99, 103, 120, 121, 126, 127, 131, 132, 173

postmodernism 44, 157
praxis 75
propinquity 123, 132
Proust, Marcel 66

rapprochement *see* reconciliation
reading 47, 51, 121, 124, 137
realism 130
reconciliation 84, 86, 92
relationality 77, 82, 135
Romanticism 36, 76

Shakespeare, William 65
sleep 10, 59, 61–64, 73
Slessor, Kenneth 4, 80
Smith, Bernard 32
space 15, 167; *see also* place
spatiality 10
Spinoza, Benedict 76, 82, 84, 87
storytelling 120, 122, 126, 129, 133
symbols and symbolism 23, 112, 127

textuality 1
time and temporality 6, 23, 34, 39, 44, 70, 80, 83, 103, 120, 127, 145, 149, 156, 173
trauma 6, 11, 86, 107, 109, 125, 127, 134

utopia 106

Victorian fiction 3, 5, 45, 50, 55

Watt, Ian 51
Whitehead, Alfred 36
Woolf, Virginia 66
world literature 75

www.ingramcontent.com/pod-product-compliance
Lightning Source LLC
Chambersburg PA
CBHW081826230426
43668CB00017B/2392